GLOBAL ENGLISH SLANG

Global English Slang brings together twenty key international experts and provides a timely and essential overview of English slang around the world today.

The book illustrates the application of a range of different methodologies to the study of slang and demonstrates the interconnection between the different sub-fields of linguistics.

A key argument throughout is that slang is a function played by specific words or phrases rather than a characteristic inherent in the words themselves – what is slang in one context is not slang in another. The volume also challenges received wisdom on the nature of slang: that it is short-lived and that slang is restricted to verbal language.

With an introduction by editor Julie Coleman, the topics covered range from inner-city New York slang and hip-hop slang to UK student slang and slang in Scotland. Authors also explore slang in Jamaica, Australia, New Zealand, India and Hong Kong and the influence of English slang on Norwegian, Italian and Japanese. A final section looks at slang and new media including online slang usage, and the possibilities offered by the internet to document verbal and gestural slang.

Global English Slang is an essential reference for advanced undergraduates, post-graduates and researchers working in the areas of lexicology, slang and World Englishes.

Contributors: Michael Adams, Dianne Bardsley, Julie Coleman, Tom Dalzell, Eli-Marie Drange, Connie Eble, Joseph T. Farquharson, Jonathon Green, Ingrid Kristine Hasund, Byron Jones, Madeline Kripke, James Lambert, Elisa Mattiello, Bruce Moore, Aaron Peckham, Maggie Scott, James Stanlaw, Tony Thorne, Terry Victor.

Julie Coleman is Head of the School of English at the University of Leicester, UK and Chair of the International Society for Historical Lexicography and Lexicology. She has published four volumes on the history of cant and slang dictionaries in addition to The Life of Slang (2012).

GLOBAL ENGLISH SLANG

Methodologies and Perspectives

Edited by Julie Coleman

Routledge
Taylor & Francis Group

LONDON AND NEW YORK

First published 2014
by Routledge
2 Park Square, Milton Park, Abingdon, Oxon OX14 4RN

and by Routledge
711 Third Avenue, New York, NY 10017

Routledge is an imprint of the Taylor & Francis Group, an informa business

British Library Cataloguing in Publication Data
A catalogue record for this book is available from the British Library

Library of Congress Cataloging in Publication Data
Global English slang : methodologies and perspectives /
edited by Julie Coleman.
pages cm
1. English language--Slang. 2. English language--Usage.
3. English language--Spoken English. I. Coleman, Julie.
PE3711.G56 2014
427--dc23
2013022317

ISBN: 978-0-415-84267-9 (hbk)
ISBN: 978-0-415-84268-6 (pbk)
ISBN: 978-1-315-85778-7 (ebk)

Typeset in Bembo
by Taylor & Francis Books

Printed and bound by CPI Group (UK) Ltd, Croydon, CR0 4YY

CONTENTS

LIST OF CONTRIBUTORS

Michael Adams teaches English language and literature, including courses on slang and lexicography, at Indiana University.

Dianne Bardsley is Director of the New Zealand Dictionary Centre at Victoria University of Wellington, where she also teaches New Zealand English in the School of Linguistics and Applied Language Studies.

Julie Coleman is a professor in the School of English at the University of Leicester, where she teaches and researches slang lexicography.

Tom Dalzell is an independent scholar and prolific lexicographer of slang who lives in Berkeley, California.

Eli-Marie Drange is an associate professor of linguistics at the Department of Foreign Languages and Translation at Agder University, where she researches Norwegian and Spanish teenage language.

Connie Eble is a professor in the Department of English and Comparative Literature at the University of North Carolina in Chapel Hill, where she has taught and collected the slang of her undergraduate students for more than thirty years. She is the author of *Slang and Sociability: In-Group Language among College Students* (1996).

Joseph T. Farquharson lectures in linguistics in the Department of Modern Languages and Linguistics at the St. Augustine campus of the University of the West Indies and is the founder and co-ordinator of the Jamaican Lexicography Project (Jamlex).

Jonathon Green is an independent scholar and a leading lexicographer of contemporary and historical Anglophone slang in the UK and around the world.

Ingrid Kristine Hasund is an associate professor of linguistics at the Department of Nordic and Media Studies at Agder University, and also a senior researcher at the Department of Children's and Adolescents' Mental Health at the Hospital of Southern Norway in Kristiansand.

Byron Jones is a tutor in linguistics in the Department of Modern Languages and Linguistics at the St. Augustine campus of the University of the West Indies, and is currently pursuing a doctorate researching the linguistics of Jamaican music.

Madeline Kripke, retired bookseller and editor, is a collector of antiquarian and rare dictionaries, with a special focus on slang. She is a long-time member of the Dictionary Society of North America.

James Lambert is an Australian lexicographer currently pursuing a doctorate in Indian English and lexicography at The City University of Hong Kong. He is the author of the *Macquarie Australian Slang Dictionary* (2004) and *Macquarie Best Aussie Slang* (2008).

Elisa Mattiello holds a PhD in English linguistics from the University of Pisa, where she carries out her research and teaches courses on English linguistics for undergraduate and postgraduate students.

Bruce Moore was Director of the Australian National Dictionary Centre at the Australian National University from 1994 to 2011, and is now a Visiting Fellow in the School of Languages at the Australian National University. His publications include *Speaking our Language: The Story of Australian English* (2008) and *What's Their Story: A History of Australian Words* (2010).

Aaron Peckham is the founder and sole owner of *Urban Dictionary*.

Maggie Scott is a lecturer in English at the University of Salford, having worked as a historical lexicographer on the *Historical Thesaurus of English*, the *Oxford English Dictionary* and for Scottish Languages Dictionaries in Edinburgh.

James Stanlaw is Professor of Anthropology at Illinois State University, where he has taught since 1990.

Tony Thorne is Language and Innovation Consultant at King's College London, where he was formerly Director of the Language Centre. He is the compiler of the *Bloomsbury Dictionary of Contemporary Slang* (forthcoming).

Terry Victor is an actor, director, story-teller and broadcaster, as well as being the co-editor of *The New Partridge Dictionary of Slang and Unconventional English* (with Tom Dalzell, 2006 and 2012).

LIST OF ABBREVIATIONS NOT IN GENERAL USE

adj.	adjective
adv.	adverb
ACOD	*The Australian Concise Oxford Dictionary*, first edition (Turner 1987), second edition (Ramson et al. 1992), third edition (Moore 1997)
AND	*The Australian National Dictionary* (Ramson 1988)
c.	*circa* 'about'
DJE	*The Dictionary of Jamaican English* (Cassidy and Le Page 1967, 1980)
DOSC	*The Dictionary of Street Communications* (O'Connor 2005, 2006, 2008)
DOST	*The Dictionary of the Older Scottish Tongue* (Craigie et al. 1931–2002)
et al.	et alia 'and others'
f.	feminine
interj.	interjection
JC	Jamaican Creole
JND	*The Jamaican National Dictionary* (Farquharson, forthcoming)
m.	masculine
MLE	Multicultural London English
MSP	Member of the Scottish Parliament
n.	noun
n.p.	no publication details (other than those given)
OED	*The Oxford English Dictionary* (Simpson and Weiner 2008–)
phr.	phrase
prep.	preposition
SND	*The Scottish National Dictionary* (Grant et al. 1931–76)
SNDS	the first Supplement to *The Scottish National Dictionary* (Grant et al. 1931–76)

SNDS2	the second Supplement to *The Scottish National Dictionary* (Macleod et al. 2005)
SSE	Scottish Standard English
s.v.	*sub verbo* 'under the word'
UNO	'Språkkontakt och Ungdomsspråk i Norden' research project
v.	verb

INTRODUCTION

Understanding slang in a global context

Julie Coleman

The workshop

Most of the contributors to this volume attended, either in person or virtually, a workshop on contemporary slang at the University of Leicester in September 2012. We presented draft versions of the chapters included here, and have provided each other with feedback verbally at the time and in writing since. Several sessions were put aside for discussion of more general issues, and these formed the basis of this chapter and of the other introductory sections.[1]

Defining *slang*

Traditional definitions of *slang*, such as those written for the first edition of the *Oxford English Dictionary* (hereafter OED: Simpson and Weiner 2008–) and currently unchanged in the online edition (as of 2 May 2013), suggest a hierarchy of users, status and value, with Standard English and its users at the top of a pyramid, and slang, along with other non-standard forms, at the bottom. As will become evident in the course of this volume, Standard English is not a well-defined concept in itself: its meaning varies according to geographical location and social context. Slang, of course, is even harder to define.

Although defining *slang* by what it is not is dangerously reductive, it might be useful to emphasize that in this volume we are not using *slang* to include the technical usage of particular professions or interest groups (jargon), usage that is geographically restricted on a sub-national level (dialect), usage that is geographically restricted on a national level (national Englishes), informal usage that enjoys a temporary high profile in the media (buzz words), informal usage that is widely distributed socially and geographically (colloquial language), informal language used within families (family language), informal language characteristic of particular social classes (sociolects or social dialects) or informal language used by a single individual (idiolect). We are also not using *slang* with any negative connotations.

In addition to its use in scholarship, *slang* is an everyday term that does encompass jargon, dialect, national Englishes, buzz words, colloquial language, family language, sociolects and idiolects. It is also frequently used with negative connotations. Describing *slang* as 'language of a highly colloquial type', as the OED's third definition does, implies that the difference between slang and colloquial language is a matter of degree rather than quality: that colloquial language is informal and slang is very informal, or that colloquial language is vulgar and slang is very vulgar. Any two-dimensional description of slang (as a pyramid or scale) necessarily simplifies the complexities of its use in social settings.

Slang is employed in conjunction with standard and other non-standard forms of the language: within a family setting, for example, we might hear examples of slang as well as standard, colloquial and family language; in a professional setting, we might hear professional and general slang used alongside jargon and the standard language. For example, a doctor might refer to *ashcash* 'the fee paid for signing a death certificate', which is professional slang; *bladdered* 'drunk', which is general slang; and *nephrology* 'the branch of medicine that deals with the kidneys', which is technical language or jargon. These terms will be deployed within sentences and clauses that conform to standard or colloquial grammar and syntax, such as 'Fancy getting bladdered on my nephrology ashcash?' Moreover, although a term might be slang in one person's usage, it can simultaneously be dialect or a media buzz word in other people's. For example, young people might use *chav* 'a working-class urban youth' as slang, but older people are more likely to have picked it up from the media, and these two groups of users will understand it with different connotations that might eventually lead to the development of separate senses. For example, I still picture a chav in Burberry check, but young people's prototypical chav is likely to have kept up with fashion trends.

One of the difficulties of talking about *slang* is that it is often used to encompass all types of non-standard language. In response to this instability of meaning, Dumas and Lighter (1978) famously asked whether *slang* was a word that linguists should be using at all. They concluded that it was and produced a set of criteria for determining whether or not a given term is slang, but the definition of *slang* remains unstable to the point that a dozen slang experts happily spent three days circling around this very issue during the workshop from which this book arose. This section is a summary of our discussion, which approached slang from a variety of disciplinary and geographical perspectives, and inevitably identified some differences of opinion that we were not able to resolve. This, we concluded, is intrinsic to the nature of slang: the meaning of *slang* and the meaning of individual examples of slang are entirely dependent on context. For this reason, the definitions provided for terms cited more than once in this volume will vary from chapter to chapter to reflect the way they are used in different contexts and parts of the world.

In his seminal paper on anti-languages, Halliday (1976) characterized an anti-language as one in which social values are foregrounded and which richly re-lexicalizes the areas of most concern to the anti-society it is associated with. By providing an alternative hierarchy and value-structure, Halliday argues, the anti-language re-socializes its users. He writes that:

> There is continuity between language and anti-language, just as there is between society and anti-society. But there is also tension between them, reflecting the fact that they are variants of one and the same underlying semiotic. They may express different social structures; but they are part and parcel of the same social system.
>
> *(Halliday 1976: 576)*

Although this provides a useful way to look at the functions of language in social settings, Halliday's discussion ranges across Elizabethan cant, literary language, Spike Milligan's verbal dexterity and African-American English. *Anti-language* is thus broader than *slang* and does not really help us to pin down its meaning.

Slang is informal and non-standard, that much is uncontentious. Slang can be used in formal contexts to lower or challenge that formality. Although this will sometimes have a disruptive effect, it need not. For example, at a formal press conference, a former chancellor of North Carolina University, who had been receiving treatment for cancer, responded to a query about his health by saying:

> Thank you for asking. I'm doing well, but let me tell you ladies and gentlemen, chemotherapy sucks.
>
> *(reported from memory, by Connie Eble)*

In this instance, slang was not used disruptively, but instead strategically to take the edge off a profoundly personal and serious subject that would not normally be discussed in such a public setting. This use of slang lightened the mood without lowering the tone.

Slang can also be used in informal settings, and in these situations the tone may already be fairly low. Whatever the setting, slang can be antagonistic or irreverent, but it can also create an implied agreement between the speaker and listener that may or may not include any other people who are present. Slang not only spreads through social networks, but also sustains them by creating and expressing bonds between people.

Although it is not necessarily the case that individual slang terms are substitutions for Standard English synonyms, there are relatively few slang terms that cannot be replaced with a more formal alternative. If this were not the case, slang lexicography would be impossible because we would not be able to define slang terms. However, Standard English often has to resort to paraphrase. For example, there is no Standard English equivalent to *melvin* 'the act of pulling up on the front waistband of (someone's) underwear; the resulting condition', but it is possible to express its meaning to some extent by using Standard English *sexual assault*, *bullying* or *horseplay* or by combining Standard English with a more familiar slang term, *a front wedgie*. What these terms do not convey are the connotations of *melvin*, which characterize the action as a normal, if unwelcome, part of social interaction between some young males. Crucially, it is the *melvined* person (also referred to as *the melvin*) who loses face rather than the person who *melvins* them.

The decision to use slang in a given context could be seen as an expression of dissatisfaction with the language that is otherwise available, but this need not necessarily be deliberate or conscious on the part of the speaker. If I say that I *melvined* someone it may be because the Standard English alternatives do not match my understanding of the action or the interpretation that I wish my listeners to put upon it. On the other hand, it may be because it is the only word I know for this action: if I do not see it as *sexual assault* or *bullying*, those terms would not apply for me.

Slang is often verdictive (Adams, Chapter 15), in the sense that it pronounces a judgement not only on the language, but also on the listener and the referent. For example, one female teenager might refer to another as a *ho*. By doing so she is not only expressing her own view of that individual, but also assuming that her hearers share that view. Like many apparently insulting terms, *ho* can be used in affectionate teasing between friends, so it is the context that determines whether and how far this is a negative judgement. The speaker may instead be passing judgement on the standard language for not providing a neutral term for a sexually active woman. Her use of *ho* might also function as an implicit criticism of people who use it to refer to women in general. The precise shades of meaning attached to *ho* in this context will be determined by the understanding of its users and hearers, which may be shared to some degree or not at all. The *ho* in question might be one of the hearers and her reaction to the label will depend as much on her judgement of the context as on how she feels about the term: if she feels affronted, she may use *ho* back to diffuse the perceived loss of face, and this may feed into the development of *ho* as a term of affectionate abuse within this group.

Slang can thus represent both a challenge to the listener and an assumption of complicity. These functions are not in opposition to one another. Similarly, there is no opposition between the use of slang both to stand out and to fit in. Few rebels are entirely original: rejecting one set of values often involves adopting another set. For example, the teenager who uses *yolo* 'you only live once' to justify the purchase of an expensive pair of shoes is rejecting adult values of caution and frugality, and simultaneously embracing youthful ideals of fashion and hedonistic consumerism.

Because serious slang lexicographers aim to be consistent, they sometimes decide to omit entire groups of words by meaning or use. For example, words used by drug users have been omitted from many general slang dictionaries on the grounds that they are specialized jargon or cant terms used in pursuing illegal activities. Partridge tended to label all terms for drugs as 'drug addicts' language' and considered them to belong to the language of the underworld (Partridge 1950) rather than to slang and unconventional English (Partridge 1937). Although these decisions are clearly sensible in practical terms, they obscure the shading between specialized and general usage in the language of the small number of people who are addicted to drugs and the much larger group of people who use them occasionally on a casual basis. A usage is not slang or jargon because of who it is used by or what it refers to, but because of how it is used in a particular context.

Slanginess is not a quality of words themselves. The word *awesome*, for example, is used in Standard English with the senses 'full of fear or reverence' and 'inspiring fear or reverence', and also in slang with the meaning 'excellent'. A colloquial usage 'overwhelming, remarkable' occupies the middle ground, and it is not always possible to determine from a written context which label would be relevant. Tone of voice and interpersonal knowledge would be necessary for the listener to be sure what a speaker meant by describing a church or a sporting achievement as *awesome*, and it is entirely possible for misinterpretations to occur and pass unnoticed: youths with low-slung jeans can have religious experiences and Christians can be trendy too. It would be inadequate and inaccurate to say that the word *awesome* is slang or that it is colloquial or Standard English. It can be any one of them and sometimes, punningly, more than one at a time.

Some slang, but by no means all (and it is not peculiar to slang), is linguistically playful or creative. Participants in an informal conversation do not tend to disrupt it by asking for definitions of unfamiliar terms. Context usually enables us to interpret the meanings and connotations of individual terms, particularly if we hear them often enough. However, it is possible that slang terms whose phonology is felt to be appropriate to their meaning are more likely to persist in use because they provide an additional clue to the uninitiated listener (see Nyikos 1994: 641–53). It is, unfortunately, difficult to prove that the success of a term like *bling* is connected to its phonology, and even if it were, individuals' interpretations of it would be inherently subjective. While it seems logical that slang terms that are linguistically unusual or pleasing should have a better chance of being adopted and passed on, it is also true that last month's novelty can quickly become this month's cliché: there is a thin line between linguistically striking and plain tiresome.

Novelty is often presented as a defining feature of slang: because of the constant need for renewal, slang terms are sometimes seen as characteristically short-lived. Although it is true that many slang terms are ephemeral, there are also plenty that are not, such as *cool* 'stylish' (cited in the OED since 1918) and *groovy* 'excellent' (since 1937). While not all slang words in use at a particular moment in time are new, they will often seem new to the people who are using them as slang. For example, *epic* 'excellent' is in current slang usage in Britain and the United States (and probably elsewhere too). To some users, the novelty might lie in the unusual application of a word they are familiar with in other contexts. To other users, it might be the word itself that is novel. Clearly, however, novelty is not enough in itself to distinguish slang from other words: many words have been used for the first time or changed in meaning without becoming slang. Similarly, the same slang words tend to be used with great frequency, particularly verdictive intensifiers and adjectives.

Slang often plays a role in defining group identity, which may operate on a very small or very large level: from a small group of friends to an entire nation. Moore and Bardsley (Chapters 7 and 8) show that the idea of *slang* is particularly problematic in Australia and New Zealand because there has been a historic tendency to identify all non-standard usage as *slang* in contrast with Standard (i.e. British) English. At the same time, these varieties tend to greater informality than British English, so that a word that sounds slangy to a speaker of British English might seem colloquial or unmarked to a native speaker. In these contexts, national identity is performed by using national forms and personal identity is performed by using a variety of standard and non-standard forms. Slang can play both of these functions. For example, Australian rappers Hilltop Hoods are unmistakably both Australian and rappers when they sing:

> I won't judge you tonight,
> Cos I'm paralytic [drunk], I ain't looking to lose a fight,
> So put your hands up if you're not too drunk to stand up,
> If you're bombing up [spraying graffiti on] the toilets put your man [name; tag] up,
> And put your can up spray it in the air mate,
> Check out my man, fuck it's all going pear-shaped [wrong].
>
> *(Hilltop Hoods 2006)*

As Green (Chapter 5) demonstrates, the language of ethnically diverse urban youths in Britain charts a similar path between global, national and local forms. This is a trend repeated in many other chapters in this book but generally overlooked in publications written from a more nationalistic perspective.

Clearly slang is not restricted to the United States, the United Kingdom and the English-speaking Commonwealth countries, which is why this volume samples slang used in English around the world. The original intention was to structure the book around Kachru's concentric-circle model of World Englishes (1985: 11–30), but it has not proved particularly useful for this purpose because it does not recognize the historical and sociolinguistic factors that continue to operate upon (for example) the English of England and the English of Scotland to produce different patterns of status and solidarity. The four diasporas model of Kachru and Nelson (2009) emphasizes historical sequence in categorizing World Englishes, but again assumes that differences between English English and Scottish English are historical rather than dynamic. Schneider's model (2007: 21–70) is more helpful in identifying five stages in the evolution of World Englishes. The chapters in the second section span Schneider's second to fifth stages: exonormative stabilization, nativization, endonormative stabilization and differentiation. Even within this analysis, however, Scottish slang serves as a useful reminder that sociopolitical developments can trump historical sequence by challenging established linguistic norms.

In Scotland and Jamaica, slang operates upon a continuum between Standard English and an unstandardized local form. Scots can fulfil some of the functions of slang in Scottish or Standard English and other terms function as slang in Scots (Scott, Chapter 9). Similar trends are observed in the continuum between Jamaican creole and Standard English (Farquharson and Jones, Chapter 10). Terms that might be slang in other English-speaking contexts can operate as part of the standard in Indian English (Lambert, Chapter 11), while other global slang terms join loanwords and indigenous neologisms to fulfil the functions of slang in an Indian context. Even where English is not spoken as a first language (Kachru's outer circle), we find its influence in the slang of Norway and Italy (Hasund and Drange, Chapter 12; Mattiello, Chapter 13). In these cases, it is often Standard English forms and meanings that are employed as slang in substitution for standard terms in the local language. In Japan the influence of English is found in the spoken language but also, much more fully, in writing (Stanlaw, Chapter 14).

After such a lengthy discussion, it is time to offer our collective definition of *slang*, which attempts to encompass the various ways in which the term is used in this volume: slang is informal, non-technical language that often seems novel to the user and/or listener, and that challenges a social or linguistic norm. It can also imply complicity in value judgements and thus play a performative role in defining personal or group identity.

Methodologies for studying slang

We move now to the subject of methodology in relation to slang. Under the influence of structuralism, the twentieth century saw philological approaches to the study of the lexis re-categorized as marginal or even irrelevant to the real business of linguistics. Lamenting the declining status of linguistic methodology in American linguistics, Labov wrote that:

> [Methodology] has fallen so fast and so far that it now lies in that outer, extra-linguistic darkness where we have cast speculation on the origin of language and articles about slang.
>
> *(Labov 1972: 97)*

Labov sees the extra-linguistic status of slang as uncontroversial: it is methodology that has been undervalued. Tensions between the citation-based practice of lexicographers and the fieldwork of proto-sociolinguistics were thrashed out in a heated exchange between Partridge and Maurer in the pages of *American Speech* (see Coleman 2011b). Despite the methodological and theoretical differences between lexicography and other branches of linguistics, the papers in this volume demonstrate that although practitioners in these fields adopt different approaches in their research, they also repeatedly refer to and learn from one another. This was replicated by our discussions during the workshop. Our different approaches complement rather than undermine one another.

Scholarly lexicography, whatever its focus, is evidence based. Evidence is collected in the form of citations, which were traditionally culled from literary sources, but now include newspapers, magazines, song lyrics, television, film and online materials. Some dictionaries rely wholly on a corpus designed to represent the language in use in its various written and spoken forms, others use corpora to supplement their citation evidence. Designing and building a corpus and collecting a useful number of citations are both expensive and labour-intensive tasks, requiring highly trained specialists and/or teams of enthusiastic and diligent volunteers. However, slang dictionaries have typically had one or two editors who have usually relied upon other sources of income. For this reason, and because written evidence of slang from earlier periods and from social sub-groups is in short supply, historical slang lex-icography has sometimes leant rather more heavily upon earlier dictionaries and glossaries than have other branches of historical lexicography (Scott, Chapter 9).

Reliable written sources provide evidence about when and with what meaning specific slang words have been used, but consideration of the broader social context provides a more nuanced understanding (Dalzell, Chapter 1; Green, Chapter 5). Sociolinguistic approaches can tell us more about the social functions of slang in specific contexts. Their results often challenge conventional wisdom about language use: for example, that males use slang more than females (de Klerk 1992). Theoretical approaches based on networks (Eckert 1988) and communities of practice (Bucholtz 1999) enable us to explore ways in which the use or avoidance of slang contributes to the creation and maintenance of personal and group identity. A variety of sociolinguistic methodologies are represented in the papers in this volume, and the advantages and limitations of each are considered in turn: ques-tionnaires (Hasund and Drange, Chapter 12; Mattiello, Chapter 13), interviews (Thorne, Chapter 6), participant observation (Eble, Chapter 3; Coleman, Chapter 4; Peckham and Coleman, Chapter 16) and recorded conversations (Hasund and Drange, Chapter 12).

Although the frequency of occurrence of individual slang words in a corpus is likely to be low, corpus linguistics offers an additional route into the study of slang (Hasund and Drange, Chapter 12), making it possible to quantify slang use and to explore its contextual functions. Judicial use of online resources can also enable the slang researcher to identify those contexts in which slang is likely to be best represented, and it introduces the possibility of a diachronic approach to real-life data (Adams, Chapter 15; Coleman, Chapter 18).

This volume closes by considering the possibilities that the internet offers for the documentation of slang in the future. Peckham and Coleman (Chapter 16) describe the origins of *Urban Dictionary* and analyse the various ways in which it is used by those who refer to it, contribute to it and review others' contributions. Unlike *Wiktionary*, which provides collectively written entries based on consensus, or *Wordnik*, which allows users only to comment on pre-written definitions imported from a variety of sources, *Urban Dictionary* enables users to define words for themselves. It embraces diversity of opinion and thus offers unparalleled access to slang users' descriptions of their own usage: the only difference in status between definitions is provided by other users' ratings. Victor (Chapter 17) also explores the possibilities offered by the internet for recording gestural slang: gestures used by social sub-groups as a non-verbal equivalent to or representation of slang. For example, contempt can be expressed non-verbally by extending a flat palm (*talk to the hand*), by forming a

<w> with the thumbs and forefingers (*whatever*) or an <L> with the thumb and forefinger of one hand (*loser*), by miming a talking mouth with the thumb as the lower jaw (*blah blah blah*) or by moving a loosely clenched fist from the wrist (*wanker*). The distribution and use of these gestures are likely to follow similar patterns as the distribution and use of slang, and this looks set to be a fruitful area for future research.

Note

1 The participants have also provided detailed feedback on my own contributions to this volume. Any errors that remain are entirely my own responsibility.

PART I

Contemporary slang in the United States and England

Julie Coleman

The first part of this book deals with slang used in the two varieties of English that have exerted the most international influence: the English of England and America (note that Scott discusses Scottish slang separately in Part II). These varieties have well-defined standard forms and a wealth of authoritative dictionaries and grammars to settle any disagreements between them. Learners and speakers of both varieties use terms such as 'British slang' and 'American slang' as if the slang of all speakers of British and American English is the same. A parallel assumption is that 'British slang' and 'American slang' are entirely separate entities. In order to explore continuities and differences between the slang of what can seem to be distinct but homogeneous varieties of English, there are six chapters in this section, covering the slang of hip hop, the slang of inner-city youths in London and New York, the slang of English and American students, and the slang of British criminals.

It used to seem possible to draw a clear distinction between British and American slang. Among the list of people to whom his dictionary might be useful, Partridge (1937: ix) distinguished between 'the foreigner and the American', but included in his wordlist only 'such Americanisms as have been naturalized' (title page). This finely tuned policy became increasingly difficult to observe in editions published after the Second World War (see Coleman 2010: 29). When Partridge's dictionary was revised for the twenty-first century, it aimed to include 'slang used anywhere in the English-speaking world' (Dalzell and Victor 2006: ix) and, instead of aiming to indicate regions of usage, gave the country of origin as 'UK' or 'US' (from among a range of options). This is a departure from normal dictionary labelling, in which 'US' generally implies 'but not UK'.

For almost a century now, American films, television programmes and music have been transmitting disparate varieties of American English to audiences around the world. American English is the language of global popular youth culture, and familiarity with current American slang is emblematic of familiarity with that culture. Combined with the political and economic power of the United States, these cultural exports have naturally led to changes in the varieties of English spoken in the United Kingdom. Nevertheless (or therefore) 'the influence of American English breeds a special resentment' (Humphrys 2004: 131), giving rise to frequent assertions that American English exerts a damaging influence not only on English but also on speakers of English around the world (see Yagoda 2011–13 for the contrary perspective). Honey concedes that American English has virtues of its own, but implicitly excludes its speakers from the '[g]uardians of the English language [who] are rightly concerned to try to control the wholesale incorporation of American usages' (Honey 1997: 247). Honey is not alone: on both sides of the Atlantic, speakers of English sometimes blur the distinction between Standard English and British English. If other Englishes have introduced new developments, the corollary seems to be that British (Standard) English remains pure and constant (Saraceni 2011: 280). The other side of the coin is that popular writers and commentators have often seen slang as a distinctively American phenomenon, whether this is something to be celebrated or deplored. For example, Mencken (1937: 567) asserted that '[w]ith the possible exception of the French, the Americans now produce more slang than any other people, and put it to heavier use in their daily affairs', but he offered no explanation as to how he had measured these trends. More recently, Cassidy (2007: 8) asserted that the Irish 'invented slang' through their influence on American English. Although Thorne (Chapter 6) finds a strong current of Irish influence in the language of some groups of British criminals, his survey of the early history of British slang disproves the notion that slang is an Irish or American innovation.

The chapters in this section explore these complementary myths: that Standard English is spoken in its purest form in England and that Americans use more slang. However, they also demonstrate forcefully that the current epicentre of slang influence lies in the commercialization of African-American culture, and these chapters chart its spread outwards from that starting point. Dalzell (Chapter 1) explores the origins and influence of hip-hop slang, with its connotations of urban gang culture. Green (Chapter 5) explores the slang used in Multicultural London English (MLE), arguing that it represents a combination of traditional Cockney English, Black British (largely Caribbean) slang and American slang, particularly terms associated with hip hop. Although hip hop trades upon its gritty 'street' image, Kripke (Chapter 2) demonstrates that its slang does not mirror the slang actually used by inner-city American youths (in New York, at least). Like their inner-city London counterparts, these young people are not passive consumers of commercialized slang: they use it alongside well-established local forms and terms adopted from other varieties of English, notably Jamaican Creole (see Farquharson and Jones, Chapter 10).

Distinguishing between slang and colloquial language is hard enough for native speakers of the variety concerned, but doing so for a variety with which one is not intimately acquainted is next to impossible. As a native speaker of British English, I can assert with some confidence that *afters* 'dessert', *money for old rope* 'an easy profit' and *sod* 'a worthless or despicable person (usually a man)' are (respectively) dialect, colloquial and old-fashioned, but now generally affectionate, though James (2000) includes them in his American dictionary of British slang. This same difficulty in judging the social connotations of de-contextualized language challenges us when we consider the language of groups to which we do not belong. Several chapters in this section describe forms of English that may not seem slangy to their users, but might be considered slang by outsiders. Student slang users may be able to move in and out of their anti-language as the situation demands, but slang is only truly rebellious where it is used inappropriately: in a formal setting or in conversation with a non-slang user. It is probable that the young people whose language is discussed by Kripke and Green are not using slang self-consciously to rebel but (again, unself-consciously) to fit in.

Dalzell sees the influence of prison culture in the low-slung trousers characteristic of hip-hop fashion, and criminality (gangs, drugs, guns and prostitution) clearly feeds into broader aspects of hip-hop culture. Green and Thorne argue that these associations are carried over into the United Kingdom, where MLE is interpreted as a sign of criminality in the press and also criminalized in the legal system by prosecutors whose cases rest on the misinterpretation of slang terms. However, Thorne examines a variety of evidence for criminal slang in the United Kingdom, and finds that different sub-groups use markedly different anti-languages. Prisoners in the category described in police slang as *ordinary decent criminals* continue to use slang and cant documented in dictionaries such as Tempest's (1950). In contrast, Thorne finds that a group of Travellers were using a combination of Shelta, Romany, prison slang, Irish slang, cant and Standard English code words to ensure that prison officers could not understand them, and also to cement their group identity.

Paired chapters by Eble and Coleman (Chapters 3 and 4) examine the slang reported by students in the United States and in England. While there are continuities between them (e.g. *wasted* 'drunk', *banging* 'excellent'), and while the influence of hip-hop slang is evident in both, there are also marked differences, which demonstrate that among these groups, slang continues to vary on a national level: e.g. *bare* 'very, a lot' (at the University of Leicester); *badonkadonk* 'round buttocks' (at the University of North Carolina and also in New York City). Hip-hop slang influences British students in part through the media, just as it influences American students, and in part through the filter of MLE. It is worth noting that most of the students who provided the slang for both of these chapters were female and middle class, undermining the stereotype of the working-class male slang user.

The chapters in this section all demonstrate the importance of the old and new media in disseminating slang within and between English-speaking nations (see Adams, Chapter 15; Coleman, Chapter 18). Several also reflect on how slang and slang users are reported and represented in the media. Stories about slang have provided frivolous column-fillers about Elizabethan cant surviving in twenty-first-century prisons and sensationalized moral panics about the decline of civilization. In contrast, Kripke finds that journalists reporting on an inner-city youth project wrote enthusiastically and informatively about young people's attempts to document their own slang usage. The chapters by Eble and Coleman also use data provided by slang speakers, albeit within an educational setting. Peckham and Coleman (Chapter 16) return to the issue of user-slang lexicography with reference to *Urban Dictionary*.

It is important to remember that even if a term is being used with the same grammatical function and the same referent, its connotations will vary according to the social context. *Whip* 'a car' means something different in the ganglands of inner-city New York than it does among middle-class students in suburban North Carolina. *Sick* 'good' may have been a decisive rejection of social norms when it was used in the early days of hip hop; among students at the University of Leicester it is just one term of approval among many. *Blood* 'a fellow Black man; a friend', also used as a term of address, originated in the Black Power movement of the 1960s. In that context it had connotations of solidarity and masculinity. Neither Dalzell nor Eble cite it in their chapters, but among young people in Britain *blood* is widely used with connotations of affection or (at least) close association. It is non-gendered and used regardless of ethnicity. Knowing the definition of a slang word can be a very small part of understanding its meaning.

The overlaps and parallels between the slang terms and phrases cited in these chapters are so striking as to undermine the notion that 'English slang' and 'American slang' exist as clearly distinct systems. Young people with access to the media on both sides of the Atlantic are exposed to the same music, films and television. They interact with these commercial products through social media and by providing user-generated material to a wide range of websites. While it might once have been true that connectedness was socially stratified, the development of smartphones and the availability of free wireless access in many urban businesses and civic amenities means that students, inner-city youths and criminals can all access the same material online. That they continue to use slang differently is an inevitable result of the nature of slang itself and of its function in expressing and cementing group identity.

1

HIP-HOP SLANG

Tom Dalzell

Hip hop is often seen as new music and a recent cultural movement, especially by those over 40. It is not. We have had hip hop with us for 34 years now, beyond a messianic lifespan. Hip hop has endured, even prevailed, over three decades and three generations of consumer technology, from cassette tape to CD to MP3, all the while employing an earlier generation of technology as part of the rhythm section: the turntable and the record album. Hip hop has been dynamic, reinventing itself from time to time, fighting off co-opting cultural and corporate commercialization on the one hand, censorship and Bill Cosby's finger-wagging criticism on the other. For 30 years, hip hop has supplied a seemingly endless infusion of vibrant slang into the American vernacular. More than any other source, hip hop has informed the slang of young Americans since the later days of the Carter presidency. Like other icons of American popular culture such as blue jeans and rock 'n' roll, hip hop rippled out globally, informing the speech of the young to some extent in all of the English-speaking world and to a lesser extent almost everywhere else.

There is not yet a definitive dictionary of hip-hop slang, and I don't set out here to compile a glossary. Instead, I intend to look at the language of the different components of hip-hop culture, analyze hip-hop slang as an anti-language, and trace previous traditions in black American culture from which the language of hip hop evolved.

Hip hop: the word

Hip hop refers to a subculture that originated in the black and Hispanic youth of America's inner cities, especially New York, specifically the South Bronx, in the late 1970s. Hip hop embraces several art forms in different media. Key elements of hip-hop culture are graffiti, breaking, or b-boying which is known outside the culture as breakdancing, fashion, and rap music, sometimes referred to as hip hop.

The Jamaican dance-hall culture influenced hip-hop culture, but its effect on the language of hip hop has been negligible.

The word *hip hop*, like many of its slang giant peers, has several claimed parents, but no solid evidence supports any of the claims. Disco Fever club DJ Lovebug Starski, Afrika Bambaataa of the Universal Zulu Nation, Club 371's DJ Hollywood, and Keith 'Cowboy' Wiggins of Grandmaster Flash and the Furious Five are all said to have coined the term *hip hop,* but proof is scant. The earliest recorded usage found to date is from nine years after DJ Kool Herc began the experiments that produced the art form, in the Sugarhill Gang's 1979 song 'Rapper's Delight', with 'Said a hip hop the hibbit the hippidibby hip hip hoppa you don't stop.' Out of the scat context, we look to the UK and the 24 December 1981 issue of the *New Musical Express*, where we read about 'pure Harlem black consciousness set to that hip-hop Bronx beat'.

Whoever may have first coined the word, hip hop has carried the word *hip* into its second century of life. *Hip* is the hardest working word in the American slang lexicon, bar none. The 1904 use by George Hobart in *Jim Hickey* stands as the earliest discovered use of *hip* as an adjective meaning knowledgeable, aware, fashionable, stylish. Stories of *hip*'s etymology, all of questionable authenticity, abound – tales involving a keenly aware person named Hip or Hep, hip flasks, boots up to the hip, reclining on the hip to smoke opium, and a possible derivation from the Wolof language of Senegal. In the end, though, *hip*'s lineage is unknown.

What is known is the extraordinary voyage *hip* has taken through American slang over the last 110 years. Just as the fruit of the wild rose is known as a *rose hip* or *rose hep*, *hep* sprang up in the shadow of *hip* in 1908, also meaning knowledgeable or stylish. In 1932 *hip* appeared as a verb, meaning to make someone aware. In 1938 we met the *hepcat*, the stylish and knowing jazz lover, and three years later the same man now known as a *hipster*. In 1953 came the first *hippie*, the jazz aficionado, and then in the mid 1960s the second *hippie*, the flower child members of the post-Beat counterculture. And then in 1979 – *hip hop*.

The lesser elements

Before the main event of rap music, I briefly visit the slangy jargon of the other elements of hip-hop culture, the language of hip-hop dance, art, and fashion.

The dancers known to those outside the hip-hop culture as *breakdancers* never refer to themselves as such; they are *b-boys* and *b-girls*, abbreviations of *break boys* or *break girls*, and the dancing is *b-boying* or *breaking*. Simply put, breaking is a highly stylized, acrobatic, and energetic form of street dance, performed either by individuals or teams, often competitively. It is always a performance, never recreation.

Breaking's vocabulary is largely technical, confined to describing moves and elements of breaking. Like their graffiti compatriots, breakers use *bite* to mean to plagiarize another dancer's moves. If a move is poorly executed, it is *critical*, while a breaker who is excelling is said to *rock* or to be *in power*.

Graffiti is often a key element of popular culture and is by no means original or limited to hip hop. 'Kilroy was Here' is a notable example of widely known graffiti from the World War II era, and 'Bird Lives' scribbled on the subways and subway stations of New York by poet Ted Joans after jazz legend Charlie Parker died in 1955 is an example from the Beat era.

In the beginning was *tagging* or signing a name in a stylized scribble. It was strictly a 'hit it and quit it' operation without artistic representation or even embellishment beyond the swoosh and crown. Tagging persisted in hip-hop culture, but *graf* came to be much more than dashed, stylized signature. Graffiti artists carried sketch books or *piece books*, and planned elaborate, colorful graphics.

Graffiti has spawned a slangy technical vocabulary to describe the craft. Before the technical are the basics – the artist, known generally as a *bomber* or *writer*, and his assistants or *crew*. If experienced and admired, the artist is a *head*, *king*, *president* or *style master*; if completely inexperienced, he is simply a *toy*. To create a work of graffiti art is *to bomb*, *burn*, *tag*, or *write*. The finished product is a *throw-up*.

As is the case with any self-respecting counterculture, hip-hop culture has fashion, and like the language of hip hop its distinctive style of dress – drawn from inner city African-American youth – has had a profound impact on popular youth fashion outside the friendly confines of hip hop and the inner city. There is a more diverse lexicon of hip-hop fashion than is usually the case in a counterculture.

Dress is an element of expressive culture and such is the case with hip-hop fashion, which draws one moment from hyper-materialism with expensive, brand-name clothing and accessories, then from African influences as a nationalistic affirmation, and then from prison culture. No element of hip-hop fashion draws more directly on prison culture than the male wearing his pants low, belt-free, and with expanses of underwear visible. The allusion to prison fashion is direct and represents for some a repudiation of their privileged social status, for others an identification with those in prison. *Sag* is the most common verb to describe wearing pants low, but *jailin' it* is a more direct expression of the origins of low-pants fashion.

Along with the tracksuits, throwback sports jerseys, and big-name brands, the hooded sweatshirt – the *hoodie* – is a ubiquitous piece of fashion gear. There are many terms used for high-end sports shoes, and then there are the accessories such as the gold tooth cap, known as a *front* if permanent or *grill* if removable, and the braided gold or platinum necklace or *rope*.

The main event: rap

The music of the hip-hop subculture, which is based on verbal rhymes over musical beat, is known as hip hop, as neat an example of metonymy as there is, or as an alternative *rap music* or simply *rap*, which is a proud old slang word. As a verb, *rap* first meant 'to inform on or betray someone'. As a noun, it has meant 'a prison sentence' (1900), 'an accusation or criminal charge', and 'a person's reputation'. Meaning 'to talk in an informal and unstructured manner', *rap* was a quintessential piece of American slang in the 1960s, yet was first recorded in 1909. Finally came *rap* as a noun describing the music form and *rap* as a verb describing the performing of rap music, both first recorded in 1979. *Rapping* may refer to the recitation of previously composed and written lyrics, or it may refer to *freestyling* or improvising, which draws on the skills and linguistic dexterity of the ritual insult game of *the dozens*.

Rap lyrics are the central nervous system of hip-hop culture and the engine-room of hip hop as a marketable commodity. The rhymes range from the sublime to the ridiculous and the rhyme tactics from common to obscure; hip-hop lyrics stand, according to Bradley, as 'the most widely disseminated poetry in the history of the world' (*The New Yorker*, quoted in Sanneh 2010).

Taken as a whole, hip hop possesses a 'language with its own grammar, lexicon, and phonology as well as unique communicative style and discursive modes' (Alim 2006: 71). The culture is well aware of its slang's cachet, and there are any number of song titles that refer to the vocabulary of the hip-hop culture. 'Ebonics' (2000) by Big L breaks 'this slang shit down', giving the slang terms for marijuana smoke, a kilogram of cocaine, drug intoxication, fashionable cars, sneakers, money, movies, homes, pay phones, cocaine, and cigarettes. And that was only the first of five verses. This type of self-consciousness undermines the slang's authenticity, suggesting co-opting and commodification in play.

Anti-language

The seminal articulation of the theory of anti-languages is M. A. K. Halliday's 1976 article in *American Anthropologist*. Anti-languages are spawned in criminal and anti-dominant-culture elements. An anti-language, Halliday explains, 'creates an alternative reality' (Halliday 1976: 575). It is not simply a language used by an identified set of speakers:

> An anti-language, however, is nobody's 'mother tongue'; it exists solely in the context of resocialization, and the reality it creates is inherently an alternate reality, one that is constructed precisely in order to function in alternation. It is the language of an anti-society.
>
> *(Halliday 1976: 575)*

Hip-hop culture is an anti-society, and its language is constructed to function in that altered anti-society. In an anti-society, one usually sees a world upside down, with words and phrases given reverse meanings. So it is with black culture and hip-hop culture, connotations and denotations developed in black usage inverted. *Bad*, a staple of black vernacular meaning 'good', is found throughout the lyrics of hip hop, as is *motherfucker*, a term with semantic duality in hip-hop usage, capable of serving as praise or condemnation. *Sick* is similarly in the hip-hop vernacular 'good'.

No word better reveals hip hop as an anti-society with an anti-language than *gangsta*. First recorded in 1988, the term is applied to either a lifestyle or a genre of rap music. Drawing on the reality of violence in the inner-city, *gangsta* is an icon of the old-fashioned organized crime gangster and the youth gang member. The term brings no negative judgment, and in fact the implicit admiration that comes with the term is the epitome of anti-language in that it perfectly reflects an anti-society.

The language found in the lyrics of rap music is controversial, leading at times to full-blown moral panic. In the context of an anti-language, however, the controversial language is simply a manifestation of the alternate reality of an anti-society.

Criticism of hip-hop language, especially African-American criticism, nearly always starts and often ends with the ubiquitous use of the word *nigga*. The word *nigger* is the alpha word in the American hate-speech lexicon. While mainstream African-American leaders have struggled to eradicate use of the word, even threatening boycotts of dictionaries that acknowledge the word's existence, high-profile African-American comics such as Redd Foxx, Dick Gregory, Richard Pryor, and Chris Rock have used the word with impunity, mocking racism and affirming racial self-esteem through its use.

Hip-hop artists too have taken the word *nigger* and through constant use tried to defang it and to normalize it as a term of empowerment. The group NWA (Niggas With Attitude) pioneered the new bold, defiant, self-empowering use of *nigga*, a deliberate re-spelling that was intended to differentiate their term of empowerment from the term of hate. Their song 'Niggaz 4 Life' (1991) is built around the refrain: 'Why do I call myself a nigga?' and is a powerful indictment of racism:

> I call myself a nigga 'cause my skin won't whiten
> I call myself a nigga 'cause the shit that I'm writing
> Hypes me, hypes other motherfuckers around me
> And that's the reason why they want to surround me
> And ask me: why do I call myself a nigger-o
> Ain't none of their fuckin' business …
> You're a nigga 'til you die.
>
> *(NWA 1991)*

Dr. Dre, A Tribe Called Quest, Jay-Z, Geto Boys, DMX, Cypress Hill, Ice-T, Ice Cube, Coolio, and other famous rappers all toss *nigga* around without a care.

African-American elders have not taken kindly to the use of *nigger* or *nigga* by fellow African-Americans. The Reverend Calvin Butts of Harlem's Abyssinian Baptist Church, the National Black Family Empowerment Agenda, and comedian Bill Cosby all campaigned against *nigga*, without much result. Clearly, *nigga* is a flashpoint between generations, with the young seeing the old as accomodationist and assimilationist.

As the use of *nigger* as a term of hate has waned, the use of *nigga* as an affirmation of empowerment has waxed. Correlation does not automatically mean causation, and it cannot be said with certainty that the use of *nigga* with pride has diminished the hate-based reaction to the word. Today, it is a term that is probably used more commonly by African-Americans than whites, but another decade will tell whether either term survives as language of oppression or as anti-language of resistance.

The language of hip hop is often criticized for its misogyny, its masculinist point of view, and its objectification of women. The terms *ho(e)* and *bitch* resonate throughout hip hop. With *ho*, usage conflates a prostitute, a sexually available woman, and an ordinary woman, while *bitch* conflates a mean, despicable woman with an ordinary woman.

The language used by many male rappers when describing women is retrogressive and 'doesn't always side with humanistic values' (Dyson 2007: xxi). Reminding us that there is the map and there is the territory, Dyson places the anti-woman language of hip hop into a social context: 'These things did not spring from inferior imaginations or deficient morals, these things came from our lives' (Dyson 2007: x). Violent masculinity is 'at the heart of the American identity' (Dyson 2007: 93).

And then there are the direct retorts, such as Queen Latifah's 'U.N.I.T.Y.':

> Every time I hear a brother call a girl a bitch or a ho
> Trying to make a sister feel low
> You know all of that gots to go.
> *(Queen Latifah 1993)*

A stranger calls her a bitch in the lyric, in response to which she 'punched him dead in his eye and said, "Who you calling a bitch?"'

The masculinism and misogyny found in hip-hop lyrics reflect attitudes of the anti-society that shaped the language. The language is candid to a fault, using words of disparagement with impunity and without apology.

The language of hip hop is replete with words describing acts of violence, usually by guns, an oft-cited fact in criticism of rap. Rapper Chuck D, leader of the politically conscious group Public Enemy, famously said that rap music is the 'CNN of the ghetto' (Smith 2010: 384). As such, it reflects, and sometimes exaggerates, life in the American inner city, using hyperbole to carry 'us beyond the boundaries of rational thought' (Onwuchekwa 2003: 3). Because hip hop gives a voice to otherwise marginalized African-American youth, the apparent glorification of violence may be jarring, but is it any more jarring than the violence depicted in other aspects of popular culture?

As for the seeming glorification of the gun found in the lyrics of hip-hop music, it is the simple result of the fact that 'the gun is a central part of the iconography of the ghetto' (Dyson 2007: 91). Is the gun any more celebrated by rap than it is by the Republican party or the National Rifle Association? If, as Eric Dyson asserts, 'No other industrialized nation is so consumed by the gun as the symbol of freedom', then rap music is simply an epic ode to freedom (Dyson 2007: 93).

In short, America is a country that is enchanted with violence and enamored with guns. Firearms are a fact of life in American inner cities, and hip hop is a vehicle for depicting contemporary life and society in the inner city as they are, not as we wish they were.

Hip-hop culture is also characterized by a reverence for material success and its objective manifestations. Critics write of conspicuous consumption and Marx's concept of commodity fetishism, while Dyson puts it more succinctly – hip-hop culture 'reeks of materialism' (Dyson 2007: xxi).

The hip-hop lexicon dealing with conspicuous consumption is rich and broad, with no word better capturing the ethos of materialism than *bling* or *bling-bling*. First recorded in 1999, it refers to ostentatious jewelry or in a broader sense to any ludicrously ostentatious display of wealth. Rapper B.G. gave us the hit 'Bling Bling', a celebration of pinky rings, earrings, tooth caps, diamonds and gold, tire rims, cash, luxury cars, private airplanes, summing it all up with 'I got the price of a mansion round my neck and wrist' (B.G. 1999). *Bling* personifies hip hop's commodity fetishism, but it also personifies the culture's linguistic creativity.

Not every anti-language has an anti-spelling, but hip hop does. To the extent that hip-hop language is reduced to writing, alternative spelling or deliberate misspellings are common. Hip hop's non-standard spelling sometimes indicates a difference in pronunciation to approximate dialect, and sometimes simply asserts difference.

A prominent example of deliberate non-standard spelling that simply asserts a different spelling is *phat*. Meaning 'stylish and admirable', *phat* was a primary piece of early hip-hop language. *Phat* was not a hip-hop coining; the earliest recorded usage found to date is from 1963, drawing upon the existing *fat* as meaning fashionable, admirable, and desirable. Yet it became a quintessential hip-hop word and one of the several most prominently re-spelled words.

The substitution of <a> for <er> at the end of nouns is a common hip-hop device that suggests a dialect pronunciation. Other non-standard formulations found in hip-hop spelling are the use of <k> for a hard /k/, <z> for <s>, <da> for *the* and the numerals 2 and 4 as abbreviations for *to* and *for*.

Evolutionary versus revolutionary

The perception that the language of hip hop represents a radical development in black vernacular English is off mark. There is in black America a long tradition of reliance on oral expression, with roots that can be traced to West Africa. The language of hip hop is another example of the high social value placed on verbal ability.

H. Sammy Alim of UCLA has likened hip-hop performers to the traveling poet musicians of West Africa known as griots: 'In a sense, rappers are truly urban griots dispensing social and cultural critiques' (Alim 2006: 21). In an early analysis of rap, Toop (1984: 31) wrote that hip hop has 'clear roots in West Africa' from 'the caste of musicians known as griots'. Similarly, Stavsky et al. (1995: vii) asserted, 'The poetry of rap is innovative oral poetry with ancient roots in African storytelling.'

Griots were reported as early as the fourteenth century; they exist today, existed at the time of the transatlantic slave trade, and it is reasonable to assume that their oral tradition was transported to North America with slaves. Like rappers, griots are more than storytellers. Artisans of the word, they act as historians, genealogists, diplomats, mediators, translators, teachers, exhorters, witnesses, bearers of proverbs, advisors, arbitrators, praise-singers, carriers of gossip, satirists, and political commentators.

Innovative manipulators, they are also instruments for social change and provide 'spontaneous and devastating comment on the passing scene' (Oliver 1970: 98). Playing indigenous instruments, griots blend music and words. The oral tradition of the griots of West Africa was present in African slaves in North America, has been present in African–American culture since the end of slavery, and can be seen in rap and hip hop.

Nothing is more incongruous than the similarities between the secular hip-hop culture and the American black religious tradition, but the similarities cannot be denied. The black experience in the United States has been dramatically different than the white experience, and so there is a black religious experience that is different than the white religious experience. Shaped by the black experience, black religion was 'an affirmation of Black identity, a means of celebrating and supporting Black personhood' (Mitchell 1970: 165).

Central to the black religious experience is the notion that the sermon does not belong exclusively to the preacher, but to the entire congregation. Luther's notion of a priesthood of all believers is personified in the black congregation's joint ownership of the sermon and the notion that the preacher 'does not hold a hieratic monopoly on the word of God' (Crawford 1995: 39). The black congregation joins in the sermon with oral responses, affirmations, encouragement, repetition of whole phrases, question and answer – in shorthand what we name *call and response*.

Call and response is an important feature of rap, with the DJ playing the role of preacher, eliciting response from the crowd. Just as rhythmic repetition gives a pulse to a black preacher's sermon, so does call and response as employed in hip hop provide a pulse to the music. Hip hop is not the first black musical tradition to borrow call and response from the church. Cab Calloway used the technique with his swing band, post-bop jazz musicians would alternate brief solos in a musical call and response known as *trading fours*, and funk performances also drew on call and response.

Beyond call and response, black preachers use rhetorical techniques that have informed the language of hip hop. Timing, the dramatic pause, pace, inflection, a hemistically rhythmic cadence, and other musical qualities of speech are all features of the black religious tradition, and all techniques that are found in the language of hip hop.

The call and response or leader and chorus pattern has a secular ancestor, the field holler, a group work song that is part established, part extemporized, sung by black field workers in the South as they worked. Field hollers featured a lead vocal, the *holler*, that was repeated by other workers and passed down the rows of a field, or met with shouts and commentary by the workers. Improvisation and verbal dexterity were the core of the holler, with a cadence established by elaborated syllables and the singing of a single syllable while moving through several different notes. All are heard in hip hop.

In the 1930s, America discovered swing, big-band jazz that featured improvised melodies developed around a rehearsed, scored melody. The jitterbug craze swept the nation in the late 1930s, leaving American teenagers enthralled by the music and the subculture it represented.

With swing, the jive of urban black America crept into the idiom of America's youth. The early jive lexicon dealt with the music itself, but then in relatively short order spread into a broader vocabulary. In 1938, Cab Calloway published the first of his masterpieces of jive lexicography, pamphlets distributed by his record label to teenagers anxious to understand the use of the language of jazz musicians (Calloway *c.*1938).

One of the seminal adjectives from the language of swing enjoyed a few years as one of seminal adjectives of early rap. *Fly* began its vernacular life in thieves' argot (1724), meaning sly and knowing. It persisted as such into the twentieth century, when it began to emerge as a general term of approval. It was a central word in the swing lexicon, remained quietly embedded in black vernacular English, and then emerged in the early 1980s as praise in the infant hip-hop culture.

For years, black disc jockeys – and their white imitators – on AM radio stations developed a style of 'bandying jokes on air, playfully boasting of their skills, embroidering the music and filling out the interludes with their rhymes and smooth talk, and generally creating a welcoming homey atmosphere for their unseen listeners' (Onwuchekwa 2003: 86): perhaps it was Lavada 'Dr. Hepcat' Durst ('Cool, calm and a solid wig') or Jocko Henderson ('Greetings, salutations, oo-pappa-doo, and how do you do?') or Jerry 'The Geator with the Heater' Blavatt ('Hey yon teenagers, hit that thing, hey hey ho ho'). Talking over the music was, however, 'something no radio DJ dared attempt on air' (Onwuchekwa 2003: 87) The rap that the pioneers of hip hop chanted over beats and music was unmistakably derived from the patter of black DJs. It is no great leap from *oo-pappa-doo* or *hey hey ho ho* to *hippity hop*, and the pulse of 1960s AM radio banter is evident in hip-hop lyrics.

Toasts are a form of performance vernacular poetry that was well known within the small community of black pimps and others in 'the life', but barely known outside. *Hustler's Convention* by Lightin' Rod (1973), born Alafia Pudim, later Jalal Mansur Nuriddin, is the crown jewel of pimp poetry.

Toasts were performed in impromptu settings by pimps, who worked in a profession where verbal dexterity was valued and admired. The toasts celebrate manipulative tricksters who rely on mental and verbal agility to outwit their larger and more powerful foes, as well as coercive badmen who serve as self-appointed guardians of an unseen code of mores. Both are daring and bold.

The celebration of cunning and force, and the themes of alcohol, drugs, sex, gambling, and violence unite toasts and the hip-hop culture, and the stunning use of vernacular in the toasts is a direct ancestor of the vernacular of hip hop.

The language of rap music is short on modesty and long on boast. Similarly, boasting and cadenced rhyming were hallmarks of Muhammad Ali's public persona. Ali was a world champion boxer and self-promoter who conveyed an indifference to authority as well as a confidence conveyed in lyrical boasts. Even his prose sounded poetic. When Ali said, 'Get used to me. Black, confident, cocky; my name, not yours; my religion, not yours; my goals, my own; get used to me' or bragged, 'I'm the greatest, I'm a bad man, and I'm pretty!' he captured the ethos of black folklore that pervades hip hop.

Ali's name was a critical element of his identity. Early in his transition from Cassius Clay to Muhammad Ali, he faced two African-American fighters who continued to call him by his birth name. In both fights, Ali punished his opponents by prolonging his ultimate victory, taunting them with 'What's my name?' In his 1994 solo debut single, rapper Snoop Doggy Dogg engaged in a call and response based on the question 'What's my name?' In 1999, Jay-Z took the question a step further in 'Jigga My Nigga', asking 'What's my motherfuckin' name?'

In analyzing the cultural traditions and icons that came before hip hop, attention should be paid to Ali and his language. Hip hop would have existed without Ali, but there was an Ali, and his persona and language can be seen in the personas and language of hip-hop culture.

Conclusion

Both conservative, assimilationist blacks and militant, Afrocentric blacks repudiate slang and vernacular, placing a higher value on formality and respectability than on humor and linguistic creativity. The language of hip hop rejects this repudiation, enthusiastically embracing the soul of African-American vernacular English with racially positive political overtones. It is humorous, shocking, profane, and artful, making its popularity and influence on youth slang easily understood. Just as black jazz musicians gave American youth a slang lexicon, so have rappers. It may be that the slang of hip hop was been commodified in the US, tamed and neutered for mass consumption, but there was a moment. Our slang is better for it.

2

INNER-CITY SLANG OF NEW YORK[1]

Madeline Kripke

Introduction

New York City slang is historically well documented but underrepresented today both in print and online. In 1942 Zora Neale Hurston (1942: 1001–10) published her wonderful 'Story in Harlem Slang', with its appended glossary of terms; but apparently today there are few works dealing with general or ethnic New York City slang. Works about the city's juvenile slang are absent as well.

But there's an exception, a charming little dictionary entitled *The Dictionary of Street Communications* (O'Connor 2005, 2006, 2008; hereafter DOSC). The dictionary is not only exuberant and endearing; it also presents current slang in use in New York among inner-city youth and supplies evidence in support of the notion that this common, everyday speech is not wholly the same as the language of the hip-hop genre. This dictionary was assembled by teenagers working together at The DOME ('Development of Opportunities through Meaningful Education') Project with the guidance of an adult editor.

The Project and the kids

The DOME Project is a non-profit youth organization that was founded in New York City in 1973 by a young teacher, John Simon. His aim was to help inner-city teenagers – mostly black and Hispanic – in trouble with their schools, the law, and drugs. The kids came, voluntarily, from the Bronx, Brooklyn, Harlem, and the Lower East Side. The DOME Project offered them alternative education, vocational guidance, help in navigating the legal and correctional systems, and substance-abuse counselling.

In the beginning, The DOME's storefront premises on the Upper West Side of Manhattan were run down, and the staff unpaid. But Robert F. Kennedy Memorial grants and other donations eventually allowed The DOME Project to renovate its offices and hire an expanded, paid staff (Chu 1980).

The DOSC

Elizabeth O'Connor was the director of The DOME's Juvenile Justice Program. A graduate of the John Jay College of Criminal Justice with a master's degree in Forensic Psychology, she was also editor of the dictionary. She set out its origins in her foreword:

> As a counselor working with at-risk youth, the idea for this dictionary came about when I realized I was having a hard time understanding what ... these kids were saying in group counseling sessions ... I started jotting things down ... [The] list grew and I thought it started resembling a dictionary ...
>
> [W]ith list in hand, I decided to ... have the kids help me put these words into sentences and start forming our slang dictionary.
>
> At first, [the kids] had a hard time understanding why someone would actually purchase a hand-made book that listed a bunch of words that they use on a daily basis.
>
> *(O'Connor 2008: 1)*

A few of the teens also objected initially to revealing their most secret terms, and they did withhold some. But realizing that detectives and court personnel already knew most of their slang, they became less hesitant to 'give up' their language.

Despite the kids' apprehensions, the DOSC appeared in 2005 and was issued again in 2006 with additions. An enlarged third edition emerged in 2008. All three editions, though not actively distributed, were available at The DOME offices for a $5.00 donation.

Press notices

The DOSC first caught my attention in a *New York Press* article called 'Bust It Down' (Lynch 2008: 10). It was an informative three-page overview of the dictionary that detailed much of The DOME Project's history and activities. Further information was available in a shorter review in a blog (McEneany 2006), which quoted 20 terms from the dictionary. An article in a college magazine showcased the work of Elizabeth O'Connor (John Jay College of Criminal Justice 2008). Chu (1980) talked about Simon's hopes, aims, successes, and failures in founding The DOME Project. The article traced some of the Project's early history. These reviews and articles were enthusiastically supportive of The DOME Project, extolling its founder and its aims; its programs, staff, and kids; and also, especially, its dictionary.

Appearance and structure

A striking feature of the dictionary is its appearance. A computer file of the dictionary's text was printed out on 8½ × 11 inch (21.5 × 28 cm) sheets, which were then each cut into four smaller sheets measuring 4¼ × 5½ inch (11 × 14 cm). The gathered sheets were side-stapled (somewhat haphazardly) in an oblong format with self-covers. Finally, the covers were decorated individually by The DOME Project kids using coloured marker pens, producing vibrant designs.

The 10-point Arial typeface throughout is clearly legible. Each headword is in boldface, with the definition below it in italics. Below these elements, in most cases, there's an example of the term used in a sentence in quoted roman. The layout on the page is visually satisfying.

The leaves making up each of the three editions are unnumbered, with each printed only on the recto. The first edition comprises 36 such leaves; the second, 55; and the third, 78. The first edition contains 166 entries for 157 headwords; the second, 302 entries for 286 headwords; and the third, 375 entries for 355 headwords. The second edition adds 133 headwords to the wordlist of the first edition, deleting only 1 headword. The third edition adds 70 more, also deleting just 1.

The front matter of all three editions consists of a foreword by Elizabeth O'Connor and an unsigned editor's note, presumably also by O'Connor. The first edition's foreword is excerpted above, and a portion of the third edition's editor's note follows:

> Some sentences may have grammatical errors, but they are written that way intentionally ... Some phrases or words may be explicit and even offensive to some readers, but we chose not to censor the kids. It would be dishonest for us to pretend these words do not exist ... A large majority of the kids we work with come from disenfranchised communities and unfortunately, terms that deal with drugs, sex and violence are a part of their everyday lives. We wanted to celebrate their self expression ... And just like Oxford, we keep old words in even though many of our youth tell us, 'That's mad old, miss.'
>
> *(O'Connor 2008)*

The dictionary could easily be faulted – but *should* it be? – for not giving parts of speech or numbering for subentries. Nor is strict alphabetical order always observed. Some confusion is introduced by headwords and subentries which are neither consistently nor clearly organized. There are also a few mildly eccentric spellings, such as <hoop-D> for *hooptie*. Some catchwords are mixed in with the headwords. An outdated example is: *Miss Cleo* 'psychic; fortune teller' "How was I supposed to know that. Ya think I'm Miss Cleo or somethin'?"* Commercials featuring 'Miss Cleo', the well-known scam advertiser, were taken off American television in 2003, but the name was still included in the DOSC in 2008. Another catchword phrase is: *Where's the sniper?* 'What you say when someone is bothering you, and you are joking they should be shot', which refers to the DC snipers, John Allen Muhammad and his teenage protégé, John Lee Malvo. "You're driving me crazy [get on your phone and say] *'Where's the sniper?'*"* The Washington DC shootings occurred in 2002. Though not acknowledged in the DOSC, the phrase was already in use in 1990s hip-hop lyrics, for example, in Volume 10's album *Hip-Hopera* (1994).

Terms unique to the DOSC

The combined wordlist of the three DOSC editions includes 62 terms and expressions not found in other sources studied. In some of these cases the headwords are unique, in others, the definitions.

Examples are: *jaffe* 'a large blunt'; *like it's the 14th* 'sarcastic phrase you say to someone when you think they are smitten or in love with someone'; *men in black* 'uniformed police' (directed by Barry Sonnenfeld, *Men in Black* was a 1997 American action comedy and science-fiction film in which a secret government agency was named Men in Black); *mickey* 'big roll of bills or dollars'; *nufferin'* 'talking about nothing; filling air'; *rockefellered* 'wear something well; more than "rocking it"'; *(take it to the) skybox* 'to have sex'; *spizzy* 'spot where you can get bootleg clothes'; *throw up top* 'beat someone up or kill them (to "heaven")'; *wifey airs* 'Nike Air Force Ones, boys sizes 3.5–5 for girls'.

A few terms in this category merit explanation. For example, *to put a battery in someone's back* 'to instigate or encourage' "If he didn't put the battery in his back, he wouldn't have even done that." The expression refers to the 'Energizer Bunny' series of Energizer Battery commercials on American television since 1998. *Dum dum* is a DOSC term for 'a gun', not the more commonly known name for a kind of ammunition. *Pebbles beach* 'the roof of a housing project building' is a variant of the well-known term *tar beach*, where people without other means must go for their suntan. *Push your wig back,* here 'bust up someone's head; beat up' (literally 'expose the brain by skinning someone's head'), is in Kearse (2006), but defined as 'shot in the head [usually resulting in death]', plainly a different type of mayhem.

Subjects of the vocabulary

Sex, substance abuse, and violence dominate the kids' language. There are also terms for cars, money, and games, as well as the kids' homes, neighbourhoods, and family members. In addition, there are a few calls and terms of address, and some terms describing clothing and sporting activities.

There are several terms for intercourse, including *(got) fixed* 'had sex' "It had been a while, but I got fixed this weekend"; *pop that* 'to have sex' "You gonna pop that or move on?"; and *slid that off* 'had sex'.*† One term for fellatio is *bob scroodles*. The third edition of the DOSC notes that the phrase is pronounced <bop scoodles>. The expression is perhaps too well covered in *Urban Dictionary*. The entries at: <bob scootie>, <Bob Scootles>, <bop scoodles>, <Bob-scroodles>, <bobby scoodle>, and <Bopscrewdles> indicate acts by every possible gender combination, and also an act without specification. Another expression, <bob skootle>, only thinly relates to the other phrases. Further, *Urban Dictionary* defines *bob* as a verb meaning 'to fellate' and a noun meaning 'slutty woman'. In any case, the DOSC is the only source to describe the act as 'sloppy'.

For masturbation DOSC tells us: *wap* 'refers to male masturbation' "My brother gets to wappin' and there's no tellin' when he'll be off the head". For lack of sexual activity, there's *desert dick* 'a dry period of not having sex' "Yo, my man's got desert dick. There anything you can prescribe for that?". The terms *g-mackin'* and *mack* are both defined with reference to flirtation and pursuit of the opposite sex. Homosexuality and homosexual acts are not much acknowledged: *botty boy* 'gay guy' (specific to Jamaican)[†] (see page 33 below).

There are also several notable terms for sexually transmitted diseases, including *bumpy joe* 'a boy who has an STD (refers to bumps on a penis)',[*†] the initialism *house in virginia* 'discreet way of saying someone is HIV positive',[†] and *werewolf* 'someone who has an STD' "Yo, he's a werewolf. He be howlin' all over Harlem".[*] *Willy lump lump* 'genital herpes' "Ya don't talk to him/her, he/she gave out that willy lump lump" appeared first in 1941 in an American radio show, *The Raleigh Cigarette Program,* as the name of a drunken character acted by comedian Red Skelton. It reappeared in the American 1993 drama/hood film *Menace II Society.* The directorial debut of Allen and Albert Hughes, its plot shows urban violence and drug use in the lives of a young hoodlum and his friends in Los Angeles. In one scene, two teenagers riding in a car discuss the driver's most recent sexual encounter. The passenger tells the driver he hopes he was wearing a hat (condom), and the driver answers: 'You know I'm packing the plastic. Shit, I ain't goin' out like Willy Lump Lump … '. *Urban Dictionary* lists both <*Willie*> and <*Willy*> *Lump Lump,* with a variety of definitions, including 'a male with a sexual disease'.

The terms for male and female genitalia are surprisingly unimaginative. The two male terms are *love-stick*[†] and *magic stick* 'penis' "She don't know what it's about until she samples my magic stick". The two terms for female genitalia, also common, are *coochie* and *punani*, defined simply and without examples. There are several terms for large female buttocks. Besides the well-known *badunk* and *ba dunkadunk* these are: *bubble* 'bum, butt, bottom, buttocks' "Shorty got a bubble. How can I git with that?"; and *onion* 'female's buttocks, bum' "He thinks he's gonna peel this onion? We'll see about that. His associate over there looks good". Only one term refers to breasts: *d's* 'breasts'[†]

There are also many terms for promiscuous women, among them:

bird 'a girl who is "loose" sexually and does not respect herself' "His sister is a bird. I be seein' her with mad dudes"
recycled 'a slut' "Don't wife that up cuz she's recycled"[*]
scuzzer 'a slut' "Shorty's a scuzzer. I seen her with mad dudes around my way"
skeet 'a slut' "Son, take that skeet to the back. I don't want her up in my crib like that"
slide 'a person you mess around with sexually, outside of your relationship; someone you're not serious about; similar to the term "slut"'[†]
smuzzin' 'ho (whore)' "This dude in love with a smuzzin'. That's whack"[*]
tip drill 'a girl who isn't considered attractive but has a good body so guys use her for sex but don't admit it in public' (used here in a song by Nelly), "It must be her ass, cause it ain't her face. I need a tip drill"

'Tip Drill' is the name of a 2003 song by Nelly infamous for its blatant and misogynistic sexuality. It is likely the Nelly reference stems from the basketball term for an exercise in which players take rapid turns tipping the ball off the backboard without letting it bounce.

A few terms for women are neutral or positive: *Shorty* 'a girl you hang out with and may have sex with but wouldn't call her your girlfriend. If you have a more permanent relationship with someone else, this may be your girl on the side' "My shorty holla'd at me when I was with my wifey. That was mad disrespectful". This term is not explicitly disparaging. *V-card* 'symbolizes being a virgin' "Matthea's cashed in her V-card. Didn't you know that?" The example here, however, is negative. *Wifey* 'a more permanent girlfriend' "After I finish seeing my shorty, I'm gonna go home to my wifey".

Terms for substances and substance abuse are also well represented:

bust me down 'When you ask someone to give you the rest of their cigarette when they're half done with it' "Before I could even light my cigarette, Wilson asked me to bust him down"

dragon pull 'the act of taking a long drag on a cigarette/cigar/blunt' "Jaquan be takin' mad dragon pulls off the L"

port 'a single Newport cigarette' "Let me get a port. I ran out"

Among many marijuana-related terms are:

did-ime 'a dime bag of marijuana'[*][†]

kush 'a term for good quality marijuana'[†]

L 'a blunt' "Pass that L!"

sour D 'an extremely potent type of marijuana that smells similar to diesel fuel' (*sour D* is short for *sour diesel*)

Terms relating to cocaine and crack include:

bird 'a kilo of cocaine' "He got nabbed with a bird on him. He's goin' away for a minute"

eggs 'drug pellets filled with cocaine, in the shape of jelly beans. They are coated and swallowed by someone to smuggle into the country. They later come out when the carrier goes #2 in the bathroom (see film *Maria Full of Grace*)' "She swallowed like 35 eggs, but they nabbed her at the airport"

Maria Full of Grace, a 2004 Colombian-American film drama written and directed by Joshua Marston, focuses on a few women acting as drug-trade *mules* and swallowing pellets filled with heroin (rather than cocaine as cited in the DOSC).

Terms for 'speed', or amphetamine-based stimulants, are well known: *crank* and *go*. Terms for heroin are also well known: *horse* and *junk*. Some colourful codeine-related terms are: *sizurp* 'liquid codeine'[†] and *tussin'* 'drinking a lot of Robitussin'

"That boy's been tussin' all night. He's bent". Surprisingly few terms, largely self-explanatory, relate to alcohol: *gooked*, *lost in the sauce*, and *saucy*. Quantities of drugs are indicated by: *LB* 'pound' (pronounced as two separate letters) and *O* 'ounce' (pronounced <oh>); *grizzy* 'a gram' "Yo, ya got a grizzy on you? I've got the gouda"; and *packs* 'an amount of drugs' "I just finished 12 packs. I need re-up". Miscellaneous terms for drugs include *(the) spot* 'a place where people sell drugs', *throw one in the air* 'give someone drugs for free when they don't care about money'* and *oofy* 'a head rush'.*

Many entries refer to guns. These include: *backed out* 'pulled out a gun' (specific to Brooklyn) "They fronted on him, so son backed out on him" and *swammy* 'gun' "Cousin got that swammy for them dudes if they keep messing with him". Kids who talk about guns and drugs also need terms for the police and detectives:

DT 'detectives'[†]

jakes 'cops, police' "Watch out, jakes around the corner"

squalay 'the police' (as in The Game's song 'Certified Gangster') "Jay told me the squalay was coming so I passed off the ratchet"

The song 'Certified Gangstas' (the title is inaccurately cited in the DOSC) was the 2004 debut single of Harlem-based rapper, Jim Jones. A remix featuring Jayceon Terrell Taylor, also known as 'The Game', contains the lyrics: 'Yes i fo sho fire, dip low ride, see police slow ride,/ see squalie nigga, cuz they think the rides stolen' (Jones et al. 2005).

Undercover cops are referred to as *time out* "Yo. Time out coming down the block". Terms for arrest and detention are:

knocked 'arrested' "My boy got knocked last night by DT. He's gonna do a large bid fer sure"

the woods 'upstate New York reference for prison (in the country)' "My brother was up in the woods for a minute [translation = 'my brother was in prison upstate for a long time']"*

There are also terms relating to theft, such as *d-bo* 'take; steal [from movie *Friday*, name of the tough guy]'. *Friday*, the stoner-comedy-drama starring Ice Cube (Gray 1995), had a character named Deebo who was a thief. *Juks* 'stab; rob; anything illegal for money' "Chanelle just caught a juks last night for a thousand". A New York City police wordlist (NYC PD 1985, 13–14) gives *Juke* 'holdup, rob, or rip someone off' and *Juke* 'stab'. The DOSC has both verbal senses and adds a noun sense as well. A term used as a boastful verbal threat is *Goonie (goon)* 'dude that doesn't care about himself; your personal muscle' "If you keep talking crazy, I'm gonna send my goonies after you".

As in other collections of slang, salutations and terms of address are also well represented in DOSC:

B or bee 'A greeting to one of your friends' "Yo B, what's good?"

ooh-ooh 'called out in order to get a friend's attention who is far away' (specific to Brooklyn)*[†] *pound* 'the hitting of fists as a greeting; like shaking hands with fists' "They're good. He gave them a pound when he walked in"

what's good? 'How are things?' "Yo. What's good bee?"

yerp! 'a common call out to friends on the street, when said in a specific way that is known to your group of friends, it alerts them that you are nearby and trying to get their attention. (sort of like a code word yelled out so someone out of reach will turn around and acknowledge you)'†

(my) youth 'term of endearment to a friend (maybe younger or less experienced)' "My youth DT's out in force tonight. Get off the block if you wanna stay home with mama"

There are several smaller groups of terms that are also worthy of note. Terms for money are: *fettuccine or fetty, gouda, guap*. A particular denomination is *dove* 'a $20 bill'. Terms for lack of money are *hit a bump** and *on pause.** Terms relating to cars are *blades* 'chrome rims' "I got 22's. It looks like I'm riding on blades" and *whip* 'a car' (referring to the action of whipping it around the corner) "Step out of the whip".

Family-related terms are: *baby mama drama, fams, father unit,* mom dukes, peeps,* and *seeds*. Note that some of these terms have a hypocoristic −*s* suffix. Here *duke* means "parent", a sense also recorded in *Urban Dictionary* (2013). Among the neighbourhood-related terms are *four corners* 'humble surroundings' "That sign makes us look like we're more than just four corners" and *ghetto* 'inner city street savvy; a survivor; term used to describe someone that has a lot of inner city attributes (i.e., wearing a dew rag to a job interview or licking your fingers after you eat something)' "He's mad ghetto because he wears Tims in the summer time".

Among the words relating to home, house, or dwelling are *telly* 'hotel; motel' "When I'm out of town, we stay at the telly" and *free hotel* 'your home'*†; *(The) spot* 'a place where people sell drugs or play dice games. It can also refer to your home'. Examples are given for buying drugs or playing dice, but not for referring to one's home.

Terms relating to clothing are:

boots 'any footwear' "I just got a fresh pair of boots"

fitted 'non-adjustable baseball cap, it must remain crisp to be good' "The fitted that don't look crispy, you can wear *that* in the rain"

Tims 'Timberland boots' "I got my Tims on my toes. I'm out"

Uniform 'clothing and style' "I like guys with the hood uniform. With the low cut Caesar and the deep waves …"*

uptowns 'Nike Air Force Ones' "You have to have a new pair of uptowns for the summer"

Many terms don't easily fall into the categories given above. Among them are:

capital A, capital M 'really early in the morning' "Do you know that he called me at 6:42, capital A, capital M. Who is up then? I told him to call me back at 10 little a, little m" *chirp* 'Nextel beep function' "Don't call me. Chirp me"

flatline 'leaving' "I'm about to flatline. C'ya mañana"*

foo-foo 'bootleg' "He thinks he's doing it, but his whole style is foo-foo"*

Kufi 'head' "Keep messing around, I'ma knock your Kufi off"*

minute 'a very long time' "You've been in that store for a minute. Let's go already"

nufferin', nufferer 'talking about nothing, filling air' "Stop nufferin' me, you have
    nothing to say"*

thraca 'trash' "Those sneakers you bought are thraca. They'll fall apart in a month"

Kufi refers to the skullcap worn by Moslem men. In the DOSC the term is
generalized to mean the entire head.

There's an unusual entry with three definitions referring to 'Jakob the Jeweler'.
Working from his New York City venues at the Diamond District and East 57th
Street 'bling king' Jakob Arabo designed and sold jewellery popular among celebrities,
singers, and hip-hop artists. In 2008 he was convicted of various money-laundering
and drug-related crimes and imprisoned. Later he provided evidence to authorities
in a case in which he himself was swindled.

Jakob 'refers to Jakob the Jeweler, jeweler to the stars' "Where's my mickey? I'm
    out. Take me to Jakob"

—— 'snitch' "Don't give him the 411, he's their Jakob"

—— 'wristwatch' "How do you like my new Jakob?"

An Arabo 'five time zone' signature watch was featured in the video game *Def
Jam Fight for NY,* in which hip-hop characters compete for money to spend with
the jeweller.

Several expressions are labelled *specific to Harlem* or *specific to Brooklyn,* a number
of them imported from Jamaica. One borrowed term is said to be from the
Dominican Republic and one from the American South.

Examples from Jamaica are *bomba clot* 'bitch' and *botty boy* 'gay man'. Dalzell and
Victor (2006) list four spellings of the first term as <bumboclot>; <bumboclatt>;
<bam'clat>; <bumbaclaat>, labelled 'Jamaica' and 'UK'; and *batty-boy*, labelled
'UK'. Green (2010) gives the terms *bumba claat,* labelled 'UK black', and *batty-boy,*
labelled 'West Indies/UK black teen'. In Chen (2002: 7) the term is given as *batty
man*. A term labelled *from the South* is *wawde* 'What's up?' "What do it *wawde*?"*
This term was not found spelled as such in any source, but examples of *what it do*
and *what up* were noted in a variety of online sources. A Dominican term is *tato*
'alright'.† There's *haraca* 'dirty weed; bad quality marijuana', perhaps also a Spanish
term; but the country of origin is unspecified. *Urban Dictionary,* the one other
source to include the term, also fails to specify an origin.

Terms in the DOSC labelled *specific to Brooklyn* are *backed out* 'pulled a gun out'
"They fronted on him, so son backed out on him" and *the V* 'a car' "Once her
father caught us in his house I ran out and jumped in the V". Labelled *specific to
Harlem* are:

time out 'undercover cops (warning to others)' "Yo. Time out coming down the
   block"
skat 'gun' "They tried to jump him but they backed off cuz he had a skat"[*]
SPKs 'stick up kids' "Those them SPKs, don't walk on that block. They'll git ya"[*]
roscoe 'undercover police' "[W]e think it refers to Roscoe, the cop from *Dukes of
   Hazzard*" (East Harlem)[*]

Regarding the last term, Green (2010) gives *stickup kids* and *stick-em-up kids,* both
under *stick-up man,* but not this abbreviation. *The Dukes of Hazzard* was a comedy/
adventure series that aired on American television from 1979 to 1985.

Several acronyms, initialisms, and forms of abbreviation appear in the wordlist.
BITCH 'beautiful intelligent top choice honey'[*] is an acronym perhaps attempting
to justify the use of a stigmatized word. Initialisms are *TNT* 'tactical narcotics
team'; *CWA* 'cracker with attitude' from *cracker* 'a poor Southern U.S. white
farmer' (Green 2010); and *PC* 'protective custody'. There are some creative forms
of abbreviation. A jocular term is *ASPCA* 'like yesterday; now, faster than ASAP'[*],
which blends *ASPCA* 'the American Society for the Prevention of Cruelty to
Animals', with *ASAP*, 'as soon as possible'. Also non-standard is *J.O.* 'job', in
which the first two letters of the standard noun form the new term. Another type
of abbreviation is *PJs* 'the projects'. Here the first letter of each of the two syllables
of the standard noun are taken together to form a new term.

Evaluation and conclusions

A wordlist combining the vocabularies of the three DOSC editions contains 376
senses for 355 headwords. This list was compared with *Urban Dictionary*, Green
(2010), Dalzell and Victor (2006), Kearse (2006) and Westbrook (2002).

The 'crowd-sourced' online *Urban Dictionary* has a very broad scope and an
up-to-the-minute freshness. It also contains a great deal of dubious vocabulary and
is weighted toward extremities of vulgar language. Green has the broadest scope of
the printed dictionaries, including a very wide variety of slang, presented even-
handedly. Dalzell and Victor, not quite as large as Green, has an inclusive, broad
scope also, with a particularly strong coverage of hip-hop terminology. Kearse, a
fairly large hip-hop dictionary claiming to cover vocabulary from the US East
Coast, West Coast and South, is the work of a former drug dealer who operated

TABLE 2.1 Terms included in sources studied

Source	DOSC terms included	Percentage of total DOSC terms
Urban Dictionary	268	71%
Green (2010)	150	39%
Dalzell and Victor (2006)	127	33%
Kearse (2006)	126	33%
Westbrook (2002)	101	26%

out of New York and South Carolina. Westbrook, a comparatively smaller and earlier hip-hop dictionary, does not claim a particular geographical coverage, though it's apparently also exclusive to the US.

Kearse and Westbrook, both dedicated hip-hop vocabularies, might be expected to contain a greater percentage of contemporary New York City street terms than the other works studied, but actually show the opposite result. The fact that the DOSC terms are less well covered in Kearse and Westbrook leads to a conclusion that the current urban speech of The DOME Project kids is not the same as commercially circulated hip-hop slang.

Notes

1 I would like to thank Laura Grandmaison for typing a difficult manuscript and helping me think through this essay. I appreciate her brains and skill and (not least) her good nature.

* Some of the terms unique to the DOSC are listed in a separate section, and others are noted throughout this paper.

† Some of the terms in the DOSC wordlist give a definition but no example using the word in a sentence.

3

AMERICAN COLLEGE STUDENT SLANG

University of North Carolina (2005–12)

Connie Eble

This essay describes and interprets the slang of one seven-year generation of undergraduate students at a large public university in the United States, based on the most frequent words and expressions they contributed to an ongoing collection of college slang from fall 2005 through spring 2012.

The students who volunteered the slang items in this essay were undergraduates at the University of North Carolina at Chapel Hill (UNC–CH), a comprehensive research university with selective admissions and a high academic ranking, enrolling about 18,500 undergraduates and 10,000 graduate and professional students. Most of the undergraduates are 18–22 years old, live on or within a short bus ride from campus and complete a bachelor's degree in four years. Approximately 85 per cent are residents of North Carolina, 85 per cent are white and 60 per cent are females. Intercollegiate sports are important, particularly men's basketball and women's soccer. Nicknamed in sporting competitions The Tar Heels, or simply Carolina, the university fields 28 varsity teams. Traditionally, private social organizations of males and of females have also been an important part of non-academic life, and about 15 per cent of undergraduates are members of 54 fraternities and sororities. The students who contributed slang items to this collection were overwhelmingly white, female, residents of North Carolina, 18–22 years of age and majoring in English or education.

Carolina students have much in common with undergraduate students throughout the United States and, judging from the entries in the University of Georgia slang glossary (McCreary et al. 2012), use much of the same vocabulary in social interactions. American college and university students are not a marginalized group. Their identity as students is deliberately temporary, and completing their education admits them to the socioeconomic mainstream. They envision themselves as leaders in public and private enterprises; as the powerful, not the powerless. They use standard varieties of English almost all the time, except when relaxing with friends in social situations. They know that the language of their prosperity will not be slang, and even if the network connections they make with peers during their student years persist, other markers (like annual income) will displace slang as signs of in-group status.

American college students of the twenty-first century are sensitive to embracing diversity and including people unlike themselves in their social circles, and most belong to several different networks. Unprecedented numbers study in other countries and learn to speak a language other than English. Not only do they interact with other students on their local campus, they also live their non-academic lives and use their slang for social purposes on a global scale. Technology makes less important some of the factors of group inclusion or exclusion that traditionally operate on college campuses. The current generation of college students who use slang in internet communication to include others at a distance in their social sphere often do not know, or do not care about, such information as the ethnicity, socioeconomic status, or physical appearance of their fellow bloggers, game players, or YouTube creators.

In each semester, students in my introductory English linguistics courses are asked to bring to class on a designated day and in a prescribed format at least ten items they judge to be 'good, current campus slang', written out on separate index cards. The assignment is not graded. Some students turn in more than ten cards and others just two or three. Some students give citations, and others do not. Of their own volition, students censor submissions and seldom turn in, for example, offensive racial slurs. A subset of the cards that these Carolina undergraduates turned in for the fourteen semesters from fall 2005 through spring 2012 forms the corpus for this study.[1] A glossary of the 117 terms reported on these cards is appended.

Over the most recent seven academic years, about 600 students contributed almost 5,000 different words and expressions, from *adorkable* 'charming but socially deficient' in fall 2005 to *zooted* 'drunk' in spring 2012. Each semester, I compiled a list of slang items that were submitted by at least three students that semester. In every semester, the slang types submitted by only one or two students greatly outnumbered the terms enjoying popularity. For example, in fall 2007, 472 of the 510 were submitted only once or twice. In no semester did even as many as one-third of the students submit the same item. *Sweet,* which holds the record in fall 2005 for the greatest number of submissions in a single semester, was offered by only 13 of 60 students, and *yolo,* the most popular of spring 2012, by only 11 of 56. By using submission by three or more students in a single semester as the criterion for popularity, 117 slang words and phrases achieve the status of 'the most popular' over the past seven years. Only *sketchy/sketch* retained popularity for all 14 semesters, and only 10 others reached the mark for at least half of the semesters – *sorostitute, own/pwn, legit/legitimate, dank, fratastic, baller, chill/chill out, creeper, totes* and *word.* Slightly more than half, 60, met the criterion for only one semester (these are not included on the table of most frequent submissions, but their semester of popularity is noted at the end of their glossary entries). Some of these are still used and recognized but no longer project trendiness, for example, *bling* and *ghetto.* Some – *friend, google, my bad* – may no longer be considered slang at all. Others are tied to an event or cultural moment that has passed, like *Black Falcon* and *badonkadonk*. Still others have not had their chance at longevity, as they are new arrivals in college slang, for example, *duckface* and *herpderp*. When popularity is gauged by number of submissions regardless of reaching a threshold of three in a particular semester, the list is similar (see Table 3.1). *Sketchy/sketch* at 107 occurrences is far ahead of second place *sorostitute* at 67, and *legit, dank, totes, own/pwn, creeper, chill, fratastic* and *crunk* finish out the top ten. Not surprisingly, more than half of the 117 slang items were submitted by six or fewer students during their semesters of popularity. The vocabulary by which students connect with each other, as opposed to the Standard English that they use in their role as students, is filled with hundreds of new and infrequent forms and just a handful of popular ones that remain in use for longer than a semester. For students, acquiring and passing along vocabulary from this constant swirl is an important part of having a life on campus beyond the classroom.

The meanings of the 117 most frequently submitted items also show that slang is a vehicle for traveling the social highways and byways of college life. Looking at the entries and their definitions in the glossary, it would be hard to deduce that the users are full-time university students. No term refers to an academic subject or to studying – nor to faculty, administrators, or parents. Instead students' slang depicts the emotional and social context of their academic experience. In my analysis of UNC–CH slang 1972–93, I discussed the limited range of meaning of college slang and the predictable categories into which the meanings fell; the top ten then were 'excellent', 'socially inept person', 'drunk', 'attractive person', 'to insult', 'to relax', 'hello', 'attractive', 'to do well' and 'fraternity or sorority member' (Eble 1996: 49–52). The slang of the current generation still tends to proliferate in these categories, which account for about one third of the 117 items. 'Excellent' continues to give rise to the largest number of synonyms, about 10 per cent of the corpus: *banging, clutch, crucial, dank, dope, epic, legit, ratchet, sick, straight, sweet* and *tight*. 'Drunk', however, seems to inspire less productivity than formerly, exemplified here by only *crunk, shwasted* and *wasted*. None of the top 117 refers specifically to drugs.

Judgments of approval (*swag*) or disapproval (*whack*), acceptance (*word*) or rejection (*fail*), are implicit or explicit in most of the vocabulary and aid students in responding to behavior and maintaining group solidarity. A sizeable set of the slang terms pertains to types of people (*baller, cougar, creeper, douchebag, emo, fratstar, hipster, ho, noob, random, sorostitute, tool* and *troll*) and the relationships between and among people (*biffle, boo, bro, bromance* and *shorty*). A range of prefabricated expressions fits the situation automatically when a response is required: *haters gonna hate, my bad, obvi, shake my head, snap, that's what's up, whatevs, word* and *w.t.f.* Getting into and out of conversation is made easier too with terms for 'hello' (*'sup, what's good?*) and 'goodby' (*deuces, holla, lates, peace out*). The ups and downs of emotions are conveyed by the exclamations *lehgo, yolo, ef, f.m.l.* and *w.t.f.*, and three slang terms function grammatically to intensify adjectives or adverbs, *hella, mad* and *totes*. Physical attractiveness is always important in human relations. A *dime/dime piece* is 'a female of perfect beauty', and a *butterface* has 'a perfect body but an unattractive face'.

TABLE 3.1 Most frequent submissions by academic year

Slang item	2005–06	2006–07	2007–08	2008–09	2009–10	2010–11	2011–12	Cumulative reportings	Semesters reported
sketch(y)	13	18	18	19	14	14	11	107	14
sorostitute	7	12	13	7	9	7	12	67	11
legit(imate)	0	0	6	11	15	11	6	49	9
dank	4	6	7	14	13	0	0	44	8
totes	0	0	0	7	8	9	18	42	7
own/pwn	5	5	9	11	8	0	3	41	9
creeper	0	0	0	15	10	9	5	39	7
chill (out)	5	9	8	7	8	0	0	37	7
fratastic	9	5	5	3	4	5	4	35	8
crunk	10	6	11	3	4	0	0	34	6
baller/balla	0	8	10	11	4	0	0	33	7
sweet	13	10	3	3	4	0	0	33	5
holla(r)/holler	11	12	9	0	0	0	0	32	5
word	3	9	4	10	6	0	0	32	7
cray(cray)	0	0	4	0	11	0	13	28	4
facebook	12	9	3	0	0	0	3	27	6
sick	7	0	4	0	4	0	7	22	5
hot	6	9	0	4	0	0	0	19	4
obvi/obvs	0	0	3	7	4	0	5	19	5
swag(ger)	0	0	0	3	3	0	13	19	4
(epic) fail	0	0	0	6	12	0	0	18	3
beast	0	7	4	0	5	0	0	16	3
bangin(g)	0	0	8	7	0	0	0	15	3
bromance	0	0	0	0	12	0	3	15	3

TABLE 3.1 (CONTINUED)

Slang item	2005–06	2006–07	2007–08	2008–09	2009–10	2010–11	2011–12	Cumulative reportings	Semesters reported
butterface	0	9	0	5	0	0	0	14	3
hook up	5	5	4	0	0	0	0	14	3
w(h)ack	0	3	0	3	4	4	0	14	4
dime (piece)	0	5	4	0	4	0	0	13	3
pregame	0	0	6	0	0	3	4	13	4
s(c)hwasted	0	0	5	5	0	0	3	13	3
straight	7	0	0	6	0	0	0	13	2
hella	3	5	0	0	0	0	4	12	3
peace (out)	0	12	0	0	0	0	0	12	1
tight	8	0	0	4	0	0	0	12	2
cougar	0	0	3	0	4	4	0	11	3
epic	0	0	3	0	5	0	3	11	3
noob/newb	0	0	0	0	4	3	4	11	3
shorty/shawty	0	4	4	0	3	0	0	11	3
yolo	0	0	0	0	0	0	11	11	1
presh	0	0	0	3	0	4	3	10	3
trip	0	0	3	3	4	0	0	10	3
bling (bling)	9	0	0	0	0	0	0	9	1
boo	0	0	3	3	0	0	3	9	3
hashtag	0	0	0	0	0	0	9	9	2
hot mess	0	0	3	3	0	3	0	9	3
Top-o	0	0	6	0	3	0	0	9	2
busted	0	0	4	4	0	0	0	8	2
chillax	0	4	0	4	0	0	0	8	2

TABLE 3.1 (CONTINUED)

Slang item	2005–06	2006–07	2007–08	2008–09	2009–10	2010–11	2011–12	Cumulative reportings	Semesters reported
douche(bag)	0	5	0	0	3	0	0	8	2
hipster	0	0	0	0	4	4	0	8	2
sexile	0	0	5	0	0	0	3	8	2
b.t.dubs	0	0	0	0	3	0	4	7	2
crucial	0	7	0	0	0	0	0	7	2
lol(z)	0	0	0	0	0	3	4	7	2
biffle	0	0	0	0	0	3	3	6	2
gank	0	0	3	3	0	0	0	6	2
ghetto	6	0	0	0	0	0	0	6	1
ridonkulous	0	0	3	3	0	0	0	6	2
shake my head/s.m.h.	0	0	0	0	0	0	6	6	1
tool	0	0	3	0	0	3	0	6	2
whatev(s)	0	0	0	6	0	0	0	6	2
yo-po	0	0	3	0	3	0	0	6	2

A *badonkadonk* is a female's 'large, round buttocks'. *Cankles* are 'thick ankles', and *muffin tops* are 'rolls of midriff fat hanging over waistbands of trousers or skirts'. 'Unattractive' members of either sex are *busted* or *fugly*. Three terms refer directly to sex, *hook up*, *sexile* and *sext*, and two do so obliquely, *awkward turtle* and *that's what she said*.

Not surprisingly, the slang of the current generation of university students reflects the incorporation into daily life of cell phones, Google, the internet and social media sites. During the seven years spanned here, the verbs *Google*, *facebook* and *friend* all had short lives of feeling slangy to college students but have now passed into unremarkable general usage. Electronic media continue to inspire student slang, however. *Noob* came from playing video games; *lolz*, *biffle* and *s.m.h.* came from the practice of abbreviating in electronic communication; *pwn* came from a typographical error; *heart* and *hashtag* came from the pronunciation of graphic symbols. *Duckface* came from the practice of uploading photographs to social media sites, and *troll* from mean-spirited behavior online.

Slang has always been a vehicle for navigating social networks. American college students' social networks are likely now to stretch around the globe. Today's university students are so connected to the world electronically that almost none of their slang originates locally or is exclusive to college students in general or to their campus. They learn it from cable television channels, YouTube, Twitter, Skype and even *Urban Dictionary*, and try it out among friends face to face and electronically. Already they have self-mockingly expressed their twenty-first-century frustrations in their slang – *first world problems*!

UNC–CHAPEL HILL SLANG FALL 2005–SPRING 2012

Glossary of most frequent submissions (*n* = 117)

Guide to Glossary

/	indicates a form in free variation
b.t.w.	Points within the entry indicate a letter by letter pronunciation of an abbreviation.
S11	indicates the semester (S = spring and F = fall) and year of a term submitted only once.

adorbs [<*adorable*] 'adorable' "Those puppies are totally adorbs." S11

awkward turtle 'acknowledgement that a situation is socially uneasy' "That conversation with my ex was an awkward turtle [usually accompanied by a gesture of hands placed on top of each other, palms down, with the thumbs moving in a circular motion]." F09

badonkadonk 'female's large, round buttocks' "Did you see that fine badonkadonk on that girl [popularized in 2005 by the song 'Honky Tonk Badonkadonk' by country and western singer Trace Adkins]?" S07 *ball (out)* 'to spend excessive amounts of money freely' "We balled out at the mall on Jimmy Choo shoes." S12

baller/balla 'someone admired for style, knowledge, and skill' "He's really good at writing up chem labs *and* with the ladies. What a baller!"; 'skillful, stylish, admirable' "That concert last night was balla."

bangin(g) 'exciting, lively, fun' "That party was banging!"

bank 'a lot of money' "I worked for only four hours yesterday, but I made bank." S10

beast 'to prevail over something or someone decidedly' "I beasted the Engl 314 test."

biffle [expansion of acronym *b.f.f.l.*] 'best friends for life' "She's my biffle. We're inseparable."

black falcon 'used as a nickname for Carolina's sophomore basketball star Harrison Barnes' "Black Falcon dropped twenty points last night [bestowed by the media in 2012 and taken up by students]." S12

bling (bling) 'flashy, shiny jewelry' "You could see his bling from a mile away." F05

bomb 'to do poorly on, fail' "I think I bombed both of my midterms." S11

boo (boo) 'male or female sweetheart' "This box weighs a ton. Hey, boo, can you give me a hand?"

bro [<*brother*] 'term of address among males' "X: 'I got that girl's number for you.' Y: 'Wow! Thanks, bro.'" F11

bromance [<*brother* + *romance*] 'close relationship between two heterosexual males' "Those two boys went shopping together – that's a total bromance [popularized in 2009 by Brody Jenner's MTV reality show *Bromance*]."

b.t. dubs [<acronym *b. t. double-u*] 'by the way' "I'll be ready at three, b.t.dubs."

b.t.w. [<*by the way*] 'by the way' "My friend will be joining us for lunch, b.t.w." S11

busted 'ugly, unattractive (of people or things)' "I couldn't date him – his face is busted."

butterface [<*but her face*] 'female with an attractive body but ugly face' "I thought she was hot until she turned around. Total butterface."

cankle [<*calf* + *ankle*] 'thick ankle' F11

cheese 'to smile broadly' F08

chill (out) 'to relax, do nothing' "I should have been doing my homework, but I was chilling."

chillax [<*chill* + *relax*] 'to take it easy, experience calmness or diminished stress' "During Spring Break I'm gonna chillax at the beach."

clutch 'admirable, spectacular, prevailing in a tense situation' "Kendall Marshall's three-pointer at the end was clutch." S12

cougar 'older woman interested romantically and/or sexually in younger men' "My roommate's mom is such a cougar – she dates guys in their twenties."

cray (cray) [<*crazy*?] 'outrageous, ridiculous, unbelievable' "We lost to Florida State! That's cray [popularized by Jay-Z and Kanye West in the song 'That Shit Kray']."

creeper 'someone who makes others feel uncomfortable or unsafe, sometimes by gaining knowledge about them via internet social network sites' "The current Chapel Hill creeper broke into a girl's room while she was sleeping and just stood there rubbing her leg."

crib 'room, apartment, house' F07

crucial 'difficult' "That test was crucial"; 'important' "That dunk was crucial"; 'exciting, impressive, interesting' "Did you see the Pit Break Up on YouTube? It was crucial."

crunk [<*crazy* + *drunk*] 'extremely drunk or exciting' "This party is about to get crunk."

dank 'particularly excellent or admirable' "This steak is dank."

darty [<*day* + *party*] 'to participate in an intense social event (often outdoors) during daylight hours' "Spring Break was wonderful because we could darty every day." S12

deuces 'goodby' [said while holding up two fingers in a V shape, the peace sign] F07

dime (piece) 'female who scores ten out of ten for beauty or sex appeal; supreme example of physical attractiveness' "That blonde in the mini-skirt is a dime."

dope 'attractive, exciting, excellent' "Your t-shirt is dope/the dope ticket." S07

douche (bag) 'someone who is impolite, annoying, mean' "Bob kept interrupting with the most inane, pseudo–intellectual crap – what a douchebag."

duckface 'facial expression of puckering and pouting the lips in imitation of a duck's beak, usually made by adolescent girls who photograph themselves and post the pictures on social networking sites' "She's making a duckface in all of her facebook pictures." S12

eff [<*fuck*] used to express extreme negative emotion "Eff! I left my wallet at home." // "X: 'Somebody just backed into your car.' Y: 'Are you serious? Eff my life!'" // "I have so much effing homework."// "Why don't you shut the eff up?" F09

emo 'person who wears black (including makeup and hair), listens to angry music, and may have lots of piercings and tattoos; melodramatic, depressing' S08

epic 'amazing, impressive' "Dude, that kick flip was epic! Your skateboarding skills are amazing."

(epic) fail [<*failure*] 'disappointment, failure to achieve or meet expectations' "That party was such a fail." Also used in response to failure or disappointment "X: 'That party wasn't what I expected.' Y: 'Fail.'"

facebook 'to use Facebook to browse other people's information anonymously or to establish a social connection' "I'm totally gonna do some facebooking tonight to see if I can find that hottie from math class." // "Lauren facebooked Sarah the morning after she met her."

first world problem 'annoyance caused by an abundance of technology or possessions not experienced by most inhabitants of the planet' "X: 'My stupid iPod isn't connecting to the wifi so I can't see when the bus is coming.' Y: 'First world problem.'" S12

f.m.l. [<*fuck my life*] used to acknowledge a bad or unfortunate situation "Candy machine ate my money. F.M.L. [popularized by *fuckmylife.com* website]" S10

fratastic [<*fraternity* + *fantastic*] 'exhibiting the stereotypical qualities of a fraternity member, e.g. short khaki shorts, polo shirt, backwards cap' "He's so fratastic in his silk bowtie and pastel shorts – and he's probably wearing Vineyard Vines underwear."

fratstar 'male who epitomizes the stereotypes of fraternity life in clothing, habits, and attitudes' "He was wearing salmon shorts and drinking Bud Lite at 8 AM – such a fratstar." S12

friend 'to request the status of friendship on Facebook' "I friended him after the party last night, but he hasn't responded yet, so I'm afraid he doesn't remember me." S08

froyo [<*frozen* + *yogurt*] 'dessert similar to ice cream' "Do you wanna get some froyo after dinner?" S12

fugly [<*fucking* + *ugly*] 'exceedingly unattractive' "Dude, your haircut is pretty fugly." F07

gank 'to steal' "My bike just got ganked."

ghetto 'unpleasant, distasteful' "This club is ghetto. Let's get outta here." F05

google 'to find information using Google' "The concert starts at 10 – I googled it." F07

grill 'teeth; cosmetic, metal mouthpiece worn in front of the teeth and often decorated with diamonds' "I bought a platinum grill." F05

grub 'food' "Let's get some grub"; 'eat, usually a lot or fast' "That girl is grubbing." S07

hashtag 'used as the spoken equivalent of <#> on Twitter to categorize a tweet as a brief summary of the statement to which it is attached' "O.M.G., I have no cell reception. Hashtag: first world problem."

haters gonna hate 'used as an expression of disregard for the negative comments or gestures of another' "X: 'Girl, you wear too much makeup.' Y: 'Haters gonna hate.'" S12

heart 'to like or love' "I heart Nordstrom. They have the best clothes." F07

hella 'very' "This soda is hella sugary."

herp derp [<from cartoon characters Herp and Derp made popular in online rage comics] 'mundane, boring, trivial, stupid or incoherent task or action' "This essay assignment is a bunch of herp derp." Also used as an interjection: "I totally just poured orange juice on my cereal! Herp derp"; 'act stupidly' "He's herping and derping everything." S12

hipster 'person who subscribes to a philosophy of irony, e.g. wearing clothes from thrift stores mixed with designer labels, who is interested in obscure music and topics no one has ever heard of, and who often has an attitude of superiority' "Tom says he doesn't even own a television – he's such a hipster."

ho (-bag) 'promiscuous female' "Do you see how tiny that skirt is? What a ho-bag!"; 'among females, affectionate address for a friend' "You ho-bag! I can't believe you ate my Cheetos!" S08

holla(r)/holler 'used to express excitement' "X: 'We're in the Final Four!' Y: 'Holla!'"; 'get in touch, phone' "I have to go to class now. Holla [used as a farewell]!"

hook up 'to engage in sexual intimacy of any degree' "After she fought with Adam, she hooked up with some random at the club."

hot 'sexually appealing' "The new grad student discussion leader is pretty hot."

hot mess 'someone who looks frazzled and disorganized but is still attractive' "Girl, you're a hot mess tonight [usually said of and by females]."

jelly [<*jealous*] 'jealous' "I'm so jelly of your new iPhone." S12 *jorts* [<*jeans* + *shorts*] 'tight jeans shorts, especially cut-offs' "You look great in those jorts." S12

lates [<*see you later*] 'goodbye' "I'm leaving now. Lates!" F08

legit(imate) 'actually, truly' "I legit didn't get any sleep last night"; 'wonderful, excellent' "Your new watch is legit." Also used as an interjection "X: 'I got an iPad.' Y: 'Legit!'"

lehgo! [<*let's go*] 'used as an optimistic expression of determination to succeed' "I have two hundred pages to read before my mid-term test – lehgo!" S12

lol(z) [<*laughing out loud*] 'to find something highly amusing' "I lolled when I saw you singing and dancing by yourself in our room."

mad 'extremely, intensely' "I'm mad hungry"; 'large amount' "I've got mad homework tonight." S10

muffin top 'ridge of flesh overhanging the top of tight trousers or skirt' F07

my bad 'my error or fault' "X: 'The ice cream is gone!' Y: 'My bad.'" S09

nom(s) 'food' "I'm hungry. Where can I get some noms?" F08

noob [also spelled <newb>] 'new or unskilled, particularly at computer games' "This quest would be much easier without the noobs"; 'stupid, unintelligent, lacking knowledge or common sense' "That noob thought they speak Brazilian in Brazil."

obvi/obvs [<*obvious(ly)*] 'evident' "Your motive is so obvi"; 'evidently' "I obvi can't write this paper by tomorrow."

own/pwn [pronounced either [on] or [pon]] 'to dominate an opponent, often in a video game' "I pwned those guys in Starcraft." Also used as an interjection, "I just shot him down. Pwned [*pwn* is from a typographical mistake for *own*]!"

peace (out) 'to go, depart' "She makes me so angry. Next time I'm just gonna peace out"; 'goodby' "Gotta go. Peace." F06

pregame 'to drink alcohol with friends prior to a planned event elsewhere' "Let's pregame at my apartment before going to the beach"; 'gathering for drinking prior to an event' "Where's the pregame tomorrow?"

presh [<*precious*] 'adorable' "Look at that little girl's tutu – she's so presh."

random 'person who is unknown or out of place' "She's always bringing home some random." F07

ratchet 'out of control, wild, excellent' "That spring break party was totally ratchet. [popularized by YouTube video 'Ratchet Girl Anthem']." S12

real talk 'honest discussion' "We need to have some real talk about your relationship with your boyfriend"; 'truthfully' "X: 'I'm gonna lifeguard this summer.' Y: 'Real talk? I thought you couldn't swim.'" F08

ridonkulous [<*ridiculous*] 'outrageous, unbelievable' "That three-pointer that Dewey Burke made at the buzzer was ridonkulous."

roll 'to leave' "Are you ready to roll?" S09

sexile [<*sex* + *exile*] 'to evict from one's quarters so that a roommate can have sex' "When I came back last night I found I had been sexiled."

sext [<*sex* + *text*] 'to send sexually explicit or provocative text messages' "My boss was totally sexting with one of the female employees." F10 *shake my head/s.m.h.* 'used to express disbelief' "She ate all of my Lucky Charms without asking. Shake my head." S12

shorty/shawty 'female, girlfriend, attractive woman'

s(c)hwasted [<*shit faced* + *wasted*] 'extremely drunk'

sick 'excellent, admirable' "X: 'That biker is about to jump over that bench again.' Y: 'Sick!'"

sketch(y) 'dubious, questionable, threatening, scary' "I left the club early because this sketchy guy was staring at me."

snap! 'used to express surprise, disbelief or consternation' "He's going to skateboard down this ramp. Oh, snap! That didn't work so well." S08

sorostitute [<*sorority* + *prostitute*] 'scantily dressed, drunken college-age female, considered to be available for sex' "There are a lot of sorostitutes on Franklin St. tonight."

straight 'fine, acceptable, O.K.' "X: 'Sorry I can't come to the meeting.' Y: 'It's straight. I'll take notes'"; 'really' "You're straight crazy."

sup? [<*What's up?*] 'used as a greeting' F08

swag(ger) 'combination of stylish appearance and confident attitude' "That girl with the yellow diamond earrings and Coach purse has some serious swag."

sweet 'good, agreeable' "That was one sweet shot Danny Green made to turn the game around." Also used as an interjection, "X: 'No class tomorrow.' Y: 'Sweet.'"

that's what she said 'used to indicate unintended sexual innuendo' "X: 'What did you think about that test yesterday?' Y: 'It was so hard.' X: 'That's what she said' [popularized by television program *The Office*]." F08

that's what's up 'used to express approval, agreement, or admiration' "X: 'I'm majoring in photo journalism.' Y: 'That's what's up.'" F08

tight 'impressive, enviable, exciting, stylish' "Your new black jacket is so tight." Also used as an interjection, "X: 'My uncle is going to give me his Playstation 2 and all his games.' Y: 'Tight!'"

tool 'graceless, boorish person who often tries hard to appear cool' "That tool just took up two parking spaces."

Top O 'Top of the Hill, restaurant and bar upstairs at Franklin and Columbia Streets' "I'm gonna watch the game at Top O tonight."

totes [<*totally*] 'positively, absolutely': "I totes aced my math exam this morning." Also used as an interjection "X: 'Are you going to the mall with us?' Y: 'Totes. See you there.'"

trip 'to act dramatic, inappropriate, or crazy' "She was tripping when she found that note."

troll 'form of internet bullying in which one purposefully makes an inappropriate joke or belittles the posts or photos of another' "He was trolling my facebook page, so I blocked him from my account"; 'someone who interferes with another's internet posts' "I can't believe some troll posted that racist joke on my facebook page." S12

wasted 'drunk' S12

w(h)ack 'bad, difficult, absurd, undesirable' "That test was whack."

whatev(s) 'used to express indifference or indecision' "X: 'You need to clean your room – it's disgusting.' Y: 'Whatevs.'"

what's good? 'used as a greeting' F06

whip 'automobile' S07

word 'used to express acceptance or agreement' "X: 'We're going to meet at Josh's to pregame.' Y: 'Word.'"

w.t.f. [<*what the fuck*] 'used to express surprise, confusion or disgust' "A pop quiz! W.T.F.?" S08

yolo [<*you only live once*] 'to act impulsively or on a whim' "I plan for two minutes. Then I yolo the rest of the day." Also used as an interjection, "Should I buy these shoes or pay rent? Yolo! Shoes it is [from rapper Drake's 'The Motto']." S12

yo-po [<Yogurt Pump, frozen yogurt shop on Franklin St.] 'any frozen yogurt or ice cream' "Wanna grab some yo-po after dinner?"

your mom 'used to challenge or cast doubt on an assertion when inserted as the subject of a repeated sentence' "X: 'I go jogging every day.' Y: 'Your mom go jogging every day.'" S08

Note

1 A fuller description of the university, its students and its culture, as well as a discussion of methodology, are included in Eble (1996). Beginning in 2014, the entire collection of alphabetized index cards (1976–2012), glossaries by semester, and my papers and publications based on the collection will be available to researchers at the Southern Historical Collection of the UNC Libraries in Chapel Hill.

4

SLANG USED BY STUDENTS AT THE UNIVERSITY OF LEICESTER (2004–11)[1]

Julie Coleman

The publication of student slang glossaries began slowly during the nineteenth century and reached its peak in the United States during the 1960s. During and after this decade, scholarly and popular attention shifted towards youth slang in general (Coleman 2004b: 247–58; 2009a: 132–5, 195–216; 2010: 181–230). Eble (1989, 1996) and Munro et al. (1991) revived the study of student slang by adopting a sociolinguistic perspective and treating students as representatives of their age group as a whole rather than as members of a cloistered society speaking in unique ways (see also McCreary et al. 2001). They also demonstrated that studying their own usage was an engaging way for students to learn about linguistics. This chapter and the module it refers to were inspired by Eble's and Munro's work.

Having taught an optional module on slang to final-year undergraduates since 2004, I have been surprised by how often students have claimed at the beginning of the course that they and their friends do not use very much slang. This has always proved to be inaccurate: students have never had any problem coming up with 100 slang words for their assessment. This might suggest that untutored students cannot distinguish between slang and Standard English, but the absence of slang from assessed essays undermines this supposition. Students do not tend to use slang when they are talking to me or even to one another within my hearing. Even during seminars for the slang module, students tend to talk about slang rather than using it unself-consciously. This indicates that although they are aware, on some level, that some of the terms they use are not appropriate to formal conversation or writing, they do not necessarily think of them as slang or use them for conscious effect. Perhaps more importantly, their use of slang belongs within friendship groups rather than acting as an act of rebellion or rejection of those outside the group. In other words, their slang is much more about fitting in than standing out.

The slang module requires students to produce a glossary of around 100 slang terms used in a selected context of their choice. Of 68 students who have completed the module, 36 opted to make their glossaries freely available online.

A further 23 gave me permission to access their glossaries for the purpose of this study. These 59 glossaries can be divided into three types: first, studies of the slang of the student's own university friends; second, studies of the slang used by groups of friends or co-workers outside the university setting; and third, studies of the slang of a group in which the student is not a member. The third type of glossary offers a fascinating insight into the slang of a range of professions and interest groups, but their contents are often so specialized that they would distort the figures if they were included here. For that reason, the following account is based on the first and second groups of glossaries. The data from a small number of these had to be discarded because their file format had become inaccessible.

Forty-six glossaries belonging to the first and second groups provided 4419 citations in total, a figure that excludes spelling variants and citations of closely related terms by a single individual. In order to make any sense of this mass of data, it is necessary to group terms together, and the list below represents the most frequently cited root forms. An individual who understood any one of the cited terms under each heading would be able to interpret the others and also to produce them independently without having heard them before. This means that although some of the separate forms and phrases in the list below were cited only once, the root form is widely known. Many students cited several realizations of the same root form. Forty-one root forms were cited by 10 or more students, and they are listed in descending order of frequency:

ming v. 'to be disgusting, smelly, unhygienic or unattractive'
   minger, ming-troll n. 'an unattractive person'
   minging adj. 'disgusting, smelly, etc.' [24 glossaries]
gay, ghey adj. 'homosexual; bad, annoying, stupid, unfair, despicable'
   gay, gaybag, gaybo, gayboy, gaylord n. 'a homosexual or effeminate person; (less often) an idiot'
   gaydar n. 'the ability to identify a (fellow) homosexual'
   gayface n. term of endearment [23]
waste, waster, wastegash (f.), *wasteman* (m.) n. 'someone who is lazy, relies on other people's efforts or drinks too much'
   waste adj. 'bad, poor, unpleasant'
   wasted adj. 'drunk or stoned' [23]
arse n. 'the bottom; an idiot; nonsense'
   the arse n. 'a bad mood'
   arsey adj. 'bad tempered, uncooperative'
   what's up your arse? phr. 'what's wrong with you?'
   arsehole, arsewipe n. 'an idiot'
   arsehole adj. 'incompetent'
   arsebandit n. 'a gay man; an idiot'
   arsed adj. 'bothered (usually negative)' [20]
piss n. 'urine; alcohol'
   to piss v. 'to urinate'

on the piss prep. phr. 'engaged in drinking alcohol'

pisshead n. 'a frequent or excessive drinker'

piss-up n. 'a drinking bout'

pissed adj. 'drunk'

to piss about v. 'to mess about'

to piss (it) down v. 'to rain heavily'

to piss off v. 'to go away (usually imperative)'

pissed (off), pissy adj. 'angry, annoyed'

pissy-fit n. 'an instance of anger or annoyance'

to take the piss v. 'to ridicule, tease or take advantage of'

to piss on someone's chips v. 'to spoil someone's day' [20]

shit (on it) interj. expressing fear or disgust

to shit oneself/it/a brick v. 'to be scared'

shitter n. 'a toilet; an unpleasant place or situation'

shithole n. 'a disgusting place'

shithawk n. 'a person who does not prevent bad behaviour'

shithead n. 'an idiot'

to shitstir v. 'to stir up trouble'

in the shit prep. phr. 'in a bad situation'

this/that shit just got real, the shit's going to hit the fan phr. 'there are going to be unpleasant consequences'

shitfaced, shithoused adj. 'drunk'

shitting intensifier

shitload n. 'a lot'

the shit n. phr. 'the very thing'

for shits and giggles phr. 'for a laugh'

shit-hot adj. 'excellent' [19]

sick, sicky adj. 'excellent; very unlucky'

sicko n. 'a pervert' [18]

bare adv. 'a lot; very' [17]

fit adj. 'attractive; good'

fittie/fitty n. 'an attractive individual' [17]

fuck v. 'to have sex (with)'

fuckable adj. 'sexually attractive'

fuckbuddy n. 'a regular partner for uncommitted sex'

fucking a interj. expressing approval or agreement

fuck (a duck), fuck it, fuck me (sideways), fuck you (right in the eye) interj. expressing annoyance, surprise, disappointment, rejection or excitement

fuckbag, fucker, fuckwit n. 'an annoying or stupid person'

fuckery/fuckeries n. 'a situation in which someone is insulted, affronted or hard done by'

to fuck up v. 'to make a mistake or mess (something) up'

fuck-up n. 'a mistake; a messed up person'

fucked adj. 'intoxicated; unwell, tired; in trouble; broken'

fucked-up adj. 'messed up'

fuck off v. imp. 'go away'
   to fuck over v. 'to take advantage of'
   fucks adj. 'completely pointless'
   fuckload n. 'a lot'
   fuck off adj. 'obvious' [17]
bang v. 'to have sex with'
   banging, bang tidy adj. 'good; attractive'
   to bang out v. 'to beat (someone) up; to do (something) quickly' [16]
chav, charva(r), charver, charv, chav(v)a n. 'a working-class person, typically in a tracksuit and ostentatious jewellery'
   chavalicious, chavvy adj. 'like or characteristic of a chav'
   to chav it up v. 'to behave or dress like a chav' [16]
skank, skanky n. 'an unattractive or promiscuous woman; an unreliable or untrustworthy person; a scrounger'
   skank, skankariffic, skankaroo, skanking, skanky adj. 'unattractive; promiscuous; disgusting; unreliable'
   to skank v. 'to let someone down; to betray, take advantage of, cheat or steal from' [16]
wank v. 'to masturbate'
   wankathon n. 'an extended period of masturbation'
   wankbank n. 'a collection of sexual memories and thoughts'
   wanker, wankstain, wankstate n. 'a masturbator; an idiot'
   wank n. 'something boring or bad'
   wankered adj. 'drunk'
   wank off v. imp. 'go away' [16]
lol(s/z) interj. expressing amusement or (in later use) a failure to amuse
   lollage, lolgasm n. 'something that is funny'
   lolcat, lolrus 'an amusing picture of a cat/walrus'
   lolspeak 'the style of language used in producing *lolcats*' [15]
rank adj. 'disgusting, horrible' [14]
safe interj. indicating agreement and as a greeting or in parting
   safe adj. 'good, reliable'
   safety interj. expressing approval [14]
gash n. 'a vagina; sex with a woman; woman collectively; anything bad or worthless'
   gash adj. 'bad'
   gash interj. expressing disapproval or dismissal [13]
pussy n. 'a vagina; a weak effeminate male; a coward'
   (pussy)whipped adj. 'dominated by one's girlfriend or wife' [13]
screw v. 'to have sex (with); to cheat'
   to screw over v. 'to cheat'
   to screw up v. 'to ruin'
   screwed adj. 'in trouble'
   to screw at v. 'to shout at or be angry with'
   screw you/it (etc.) interj. expressing dismissal or rejection [13]
bad adj. 'excellent; intimidating, aggressive, untrustworthy'

badass, badman n. 'an intimidating person'

bad egg n. 'an untrustworthy person'

baddy/baddie n. 'a minor injury' [12]

blag v. 'to achieve (something) with little effort or expense, to avoid doing something; to lie; to steal or rob'

blag-artist, blagger n. 'one who blags' [12]

cock n. 'a penis; an idiot'

to cockblock v. 'to impede a sexual relationship'

cock-blocker, Captain Cockblock n. 'one who impedes a sexual relationship'

cock-blocking n. 'the act of impeding a sexual relationship'

cockfest n. 'a event or gathering dominated by males'

cock-holster n. 'a vagina'

cocksucker n. 'a fellator'

cockbag, cock-knocker, cocksucker n. 'an idiot'

cock interj. expressing disappointment or frustration

cocky adj. 'arrogant; brash' [12]

lush adj. 'good, attractive, tasty' [12]

pull v. 'to pick up; to seduce, kiss or have sex with'

on the pull prep. phr. 'seeking a sexual partner' [12]

sound (as a pound) adj. 'excellent'

sound interj. expressing agreement [12]

hot adj. 'attractive'

hot stuff, hottie n. 'an attractive person' [11]

mint, mintus adj. 'good; attractive; tasty' [11]

tight adj. 'good; close (of a friendship); unfair; miserly; careful (of a gambler); rude'

tight-ass/-arse, tightwad n. 'a miserly person' [11]

ball n. 'a testicle'

ball-bag n. 'the scrotum'

ball-bag interj. expressing disappointment or frustration

to go balls out v. 'to do something with full commitment'

ballache n. 'an annoyance or irritation'

to ball v. 'to flaunt one's wealth'

baller n. 'one who flaunts their wealth'

balling n. 'the act of flaunting wealth'

balls n. 'nonsense; courage'

balls up n. 'a mistake' [10]

bitch n. 'an unpleasant female; one who indulges in scandalous gossip; any female'

bitchy adj. 'given to scandalous gossip'

to bitch (about) v. 'to spread scandalous gossip'

bitching adj. 'good'

bitchpiss n. 'alcopops'

bitchslap n. 'a slap'

to bitch(slap) v. 'to slap; to defeat'

in a bitch phr. 'in a bit' [10]

blood, blad, blud n. 'a friend'; also as a term of address [10]

chillax v. 'to calm down; to relax' [10]

cool adj. 'excellent; trustworthy'

   cool interj. marking greeting or parting

   cool, cool beans, coolio interj. expressing approval [10]

fugly adj. 'very ugly' [10]

hammered adj. 'drunk' [10]

munter n. 'an ugly person'

   munted, munting adj. 'ugly'

   munted adj. 'drunk or stoned' [10]

smash v. 'to do something well or with enthusiasm; to destroy; to win'

   smashed adj. 'drunk or otherwise intoxicated' [10]

sweet (as) adj. 'excellent'

   sweet interj. expressing approval or pleasure

   sweetie-pie, sweetpea n. 'terms of endearment'

   sweet sixteen n. 'a young person spoilt by rich parents' [10]

tit n. 'a breast; an idiot'

   to titwank v 'to stimulate a penis with one's breasts'

   titwank n. 'an act of stimulating a penis with one's breasts; an idiot'

   to get on someone's tits v. 'to irritate or annoy someone' [10]

well intensifier [10]

Grouping words in this way makes it possible to provide some generalizations about slang usage among these students. Even when related terms are clustered as explained above, 75 per cent of word groups are evidenced by a single citation (see Figure 4.1). There is no single cohesive body of 'student slang' and none of the frequently cited root forms listed above is restricted to students.

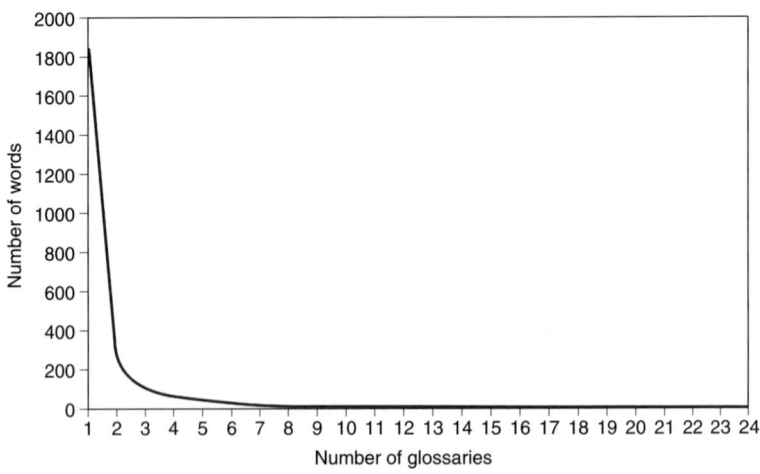

FIGURE 4.1 The distribution of root forms across glossaries

Students on this module also have to design a website and put their glossaries online as part of the assessment. From 2005 onwards, students have had access to the glossaries of earlier students, which has certainly led to an improvement in quality. The effect this has had on the contents of students' glossaries is less clear. For example, browsing through an earlier glossary might remind a student of a term that they also use with their friends, which they could then add to their own glossary. This would tend to decrease the variety of terms cited. On the other hand, seminar discussions indicate that many students strive to document unusual usages within their group, and access to information about other students' slang would enable them to avoid well-documented terms, which would tend to increase the proportion of terms supported by a single citation. We would also expect to see changes through time. Figure 4.2 shows that the average percentage of overlaps between glossaries tends to decrease in relation to the number of years between them, but the effect is slight and averaging obscures marked differences in the degree of overlap between glossaries, which ranges from 0 to 32 per cent.

Asking students to document only 100 of the slang terms they use will also tend to reduce repetition, in that each group of friends undoubtedly uses more slang, including many terms that are employed only infrequently. Students are thus documenting a limited selection of the terms they use and a variety of factors may have influenced their decisions, including the knowledge that their glossary would be accessible online. For example, some students may have chosen to omit drugs slang and offensive terms dealing with gender, sexuality and ethnicity. Many students have opted not to include swear words on the grounds that their group does not swear in a particularly innovative way and that there would, therefore, be relatively little new to say about these words. Nevertheless, swear words and other obscenities are well represented among the highly cited terms because they are used with grammatical and phrasal flexibility. Their inclusion in the high-frequency list is thus, in part, a result of the cumulative treatment of their less frequent variants.

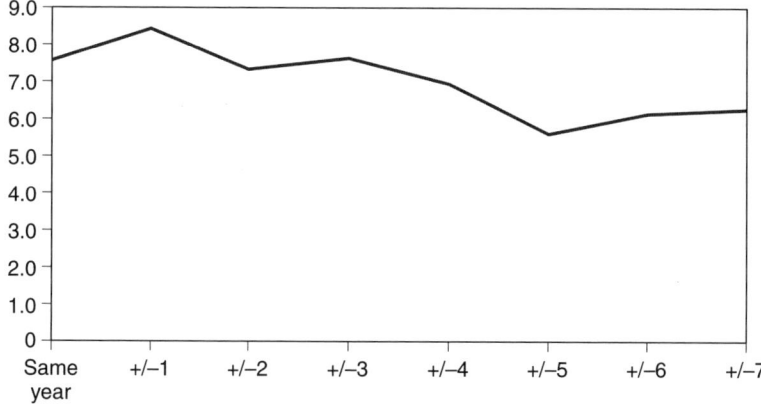

FIGURE 4.2 Average percentage of root forms shared between glossaries according to the time (in years) between their composition

Examination of less frequently cited terms does not suggest that students are parti-cularly innovative slang users. Terms cited only twice include *bender* 'a prolonged drinking session' (1846), *booze* 'alcohol' (1859), *grand* '£1000' (1921), *to nab* 'to steal; to take' (1794), *pal* 'a friend' (*c*.1770), *to scoff* 'to eat quickly' (1798), and *to waffle* 'to talk too much' (1900). In each case, the *Oxford English Dictionary* (OED) first citation date, provided in brackets, indicates that these terms have been in slang usage for at least a century and are likely to be known to more students than reported them, as well as to non-students. Students may have chosen to omit such widely used terms as colloquial rather than slang, and for this reason the frequency of citation for some terms may actually operate in an inverse correlation with their frequency of use.

For the purposes of this chapter, then, we have to understand 'student slang' to mean not 'slang that is common to and created and used only by students', but 'slang that students on this module chose to report'. Some of the single-cited terms may represent exclusive in-group slang, but these are not used by the student body as a whole and thus cannot meaningfully be characterized as 'student slang'. *Zanzibopping* 'dancing at the Zanzibar (a nightclub, now renamed)' is one of very few terms specific to Leicester, and none of these was reported more than once.

Our students do not generally arrive at university speaking Standard English in all social settings. Even those students who do not have a distinctive local dialect use colloquial and slang terms when they are in informal situations. The informal terms they use will have been influenced by their family and friends at home, and there is thus an annual re-injection of slang and colloquialisms into the student body. Student halls represent a linguistic melting pot for first-year students and each individual's slang usage develops under the influence of their evolving friendship groups. This means that no single individual's slang can be assumed to represent the whole student body. On the other hand, social stratification and geographical recruitment aside, there is no reason to think that slang used by a selection of students at the University of Leicester is markedly different from that used by a comparable range of students at universities around the United Kingdom.

Despite these reservations, the conditions under which these glossaries were produced have not changed from year to year. They are therefore broadly com-parable with one another. They provide an insight into general trends in youth slang, albeit the slang of those young people who did well at school and were able to continue their studies at university. These students, disproportionately white, middle-class and female, are one of the conduits by which MLE slang discussed by Green (see Chapter 5) and other types of slang enter wider usage. It is certainly the case that much of the slang they cite has been in use for several decades. It may no longer be in use by the more marginal groups that created it, but its appearance in these glossaries shows slang transmission in action.

It should come as no surprise that certain themes bulk large in the slang reported by students. Alcohol is an important feature of the social life of many British students. The harmful effects of alcohol are jocularly acknowledged in many of the adjectives meaning 'drunk': *annihilated, badgered, battered, bladdered, bollocksed, buzzing, cunted,* destroyed, *fucked, gassed, hammered, lashed, legless, licked, mashed, mash-up, messy, mortal, munted, off one's face/head/trolley, out of it, paralytic, pissed, plastered, quadra-spazzed, rat-arsed, shit-faced, slaughtered, slizzered, sloshed, smashed, sozzled, steaming, stonking, tanked, trashed, trolleyed, twatted, wankered, wasted* and *wrecked*. Many of these terms are used with general reference to the after-effects of both drugs and alcohol, suggesting that the state attained is more important than the means by which is it effected.

Students' glossaries also feature a great many words and phrases relating to sex, usually excluding emotional involvement and tenderness. Transitive verbs with the sense 'to have sex with' include *bang, beat, boink, bone, bonk, dick, drill, frig, fuck, knob, mash, nail, pork, put one through, screw, shag, shine, tap* and *thump*. Intransitive verbs meaning 'to have sex' tend to be less violent and sometimes imply more reciprocality: *do it/the deed, willy-waggle, get jiggy, get laid* and *get one's end away*. *Cop off with, get off with* and *pull* tend to refer to initial encounters whether or not they lead to future involvement. Although there is a general expectation that students will drink and have sex, the double standard persists in the reported terms used to refer to promiscuous females (*bosh, cumbucket, cumdumpster, ho, hobag, scuffer, skank, sket, slag, slapper, slut, spunkbucket* and *tramp*) and males (*lad, manwhore* and *player*). *Dirtbox, filth* and *scrubber* were reported as gender-neutral terms for a promiscuous person. They imply, as do many of the terms for promiscuous women, that promiscuity is unhygienic and unattractive.

Students also reported a great many verdictive terms: adjectives and adjectival phrases with the general sense of 'good' and 'bad', including *ace, acetastic, awesome, bad, banging, bitching, boss, bum, class, classic, cool, cracking, dro, epic, fan-fucking-tastic, glossy, grand, heavy, immense, leg(end), leng, live, lush, mad, major, mega, mental, mint, mucky, nang, nifty, off the hook, peng, phat, proper bo, pukka, quality, razz, ridic, sexual, shit-hot, sick, slamming, sound (as a pound), spiffing, spigging, standard, street, supercool, super super, swedish, sweet (as), swish, tidy, tight, top, uber, unreal, valid, wavy, wicked (bad)* and *wizard*. Something that is good can also be described as *the dog's bollocks, the sex, the shit* or *the shizzle*. These terms tend to be used with great frequency in conversation, with the terms favoured by one individual or group of friends shunned by others, or even used with their meaning inverted. Negative adjectives included *crap(py), dirt(y), dutty, filth, gammy, gash, gay, gnarly, grim, lame, mank(y), minging, munted, munting, pants, rank, rare, ridonk(ulous), rough, rubbish, scabby, shite, skank(ing/y), sucky, trashy, vadge* and *waste*.

Clearly it is not necessary to have so many different terms to indicate approval and disapproval. There are no reliable shades of difference between these terms: their function is to signal and cement group membership and shared attitudes. The status of the individual who chooses to use *mental* for 'good' when their friends are all using *swedish* is going to depend on where *mental* is on its arc of usage within that group. Individuals who continue using a term once their friends have stopped using it will tend to be those who are peripheral to the group or less influential within it. The terms that are picked up by a group will tend to be those used by individuals who are most central and influential.

It should not be assumed that all terms will follow a bell curve of usage: there will always be some terms that are used idiosyncratically within a group, becoming identified with the speech of a single individual to an extent that precludes their wider adoption. Neither will terms follow the same trends across the whole student body: *mental* may be on the rise in one group and simultaneously falling from use in another. Similarly, a student who began using *swedish* with their friends at home might find that it became symbolic of the growing distance between them. Whether they chose to persist in their use of *swedish* or revert to terms originally or currently used among those friends would demonstrate their commitment to that friendship group. In this way, as we shall see below, slang terms often ebb and flow in pockets of limited usage rather than falling into complete obsolescence. Because I am looking at relatively small numbers of students, it would be unwise to attempt to document these ebbs and flows of usage (but see Eble, Chapter 3).

The primary function of intensifiers is also to signal social cohesion and shared attitudes. Intensifiers reported in these glossaries include *bare*, *chuffing*, *dead*, *fricking*, *fully*, *horribly*, *mad*, *mega*, *proper*, *pure*, *right*, *shitting*, *totes* and *well*. While there is no difference in denotation between *pure cool* and *proper cool*, each term will not only function as an identifier of group-membership but also acquire local connotations by association with the people who use it. For example, for a group of friends who habitually use *bare* and *proper* as intensifiers, the terms *pure* and *well*, preferred by a more adventurous contiguous group of friends, may acquire associations with excess. Thus for the original group, *pure cool* may come to seem more forceful than *bare cool*, while the second group may feel that *pure cool* is neutral and *bare cool* a weaker alternative. For other groups their relative strength might be inverted.

A Pearson correlation analysis of the mean percentage overlap between glossaries identifies geographical location, student status and social focus as significant variables. Glossaries documenting slang used in Leicester, slang used among students and slang used in a social situation rather than in an activity-based context all have a significantly higher rate of overlap than those documenting slang used outside Leicester, by non-student groups and in activity-based contexts (all $p = 0.01$). This suggests that network density plays a more important role than gender in slang usage.

Writers on slang often assert that it is characteristically masculine: that women do not innovate in language and that it is men who revel in the vulgar and offensive (e.g. Jespersen 1922: 247–8). If this ever has been true, these glossaries suggest that it is no longer the case. Of the 46 glossaries discussed here, 34 were compiled by female students and 12 by male students. The first column in Figure 4.3 reflects this gender imbalance, in that approximately two-thirds of the terms that are cited only once were cited only by female students. For those terms that are cited more than once, as might be expected, a progressively higher proportion of terms were cited by both males and females, including *boomting/bumting* 'an attractive person (usually female)', *dog* 'an unattractive person (usually female)', *poon(tang)* 'the vagina; sex with women; women generally' and *whipped* 'dominated by a sexual partner (usually, but not always a female)'. In these examples, female students are sometimes accepting the double standard (as in *poon(tang)*), but sometimes using terms that

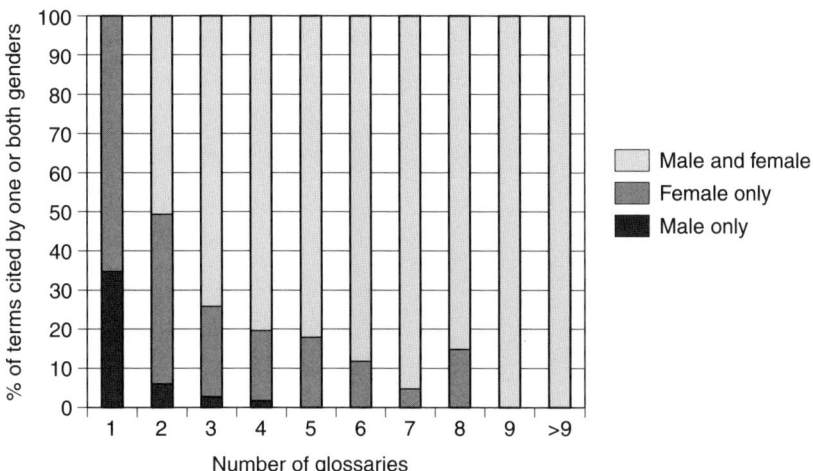

FIGURE 4.3 Gender and slang citation

originally referred only to women to include men as well (as in *boomting/bumting, dog* and *whipped*).

Because of the gender imbalance among students on this module, we cannot read too much into infrequently reported terms. However, four terms were cited by three or more male students and not by female students: *kip* 'a short sleep', *ponce* 'an effeminate or gay male', *schlong* 'the penis; an idiot' and *immense* 'excellent'. Eight terms were cited by six or more female students and not by male students: *def(fo)* 'definitely', *spaz* 'an idiot', *tramp* 'a disgusting person; a promiscuous woman', *moob* 'the flabby chest of an overweight man', *beef* 'a problem or complaint', *buff* 'attractive, well-toned', *trolleyed* 'drunk' and *whatever*, used as an interjection expressing disinterest or rejection or (less often) approval or acceptance. Neither group of terms is original to Leicester students, so they cannot be considered indicative of creativity in either case. Moreover, the addition of another year's worth of glossaries would undoubtedly remove some of these terms from their single-sex categories, but it is tempting to speculate that male students might still retain some potentially offensive terms, such as *ponce* and *schlong* for male-only conversations. Male-only terms cited just twice (and therefore even less stable in this category) include *banjo-string* 'the skin joining the foreskin to the penis', *clunge* 'vagina', *prozzie* 'prostitute' and *nail* 'to attack; to set to (a task); to have sexual intercourse with'. Female-only terms also deal with sexual behaviour and attractiveness (*tramp, moob, buff*), but the presence of *beef* and *whatever* in this list suggest that female-only conversations deal with other aspects of interpersonal relationships too, such as conflict and compromise.

Although more female than male students compiled glossaries, many documented the slang used in mixed-sex groups. Figure 4.4 indicates that the proportion of uniquely cited terms was similarly distributed among female-only and mixed-sex groups, suggesting that it is the presence of women that determines the way slang is

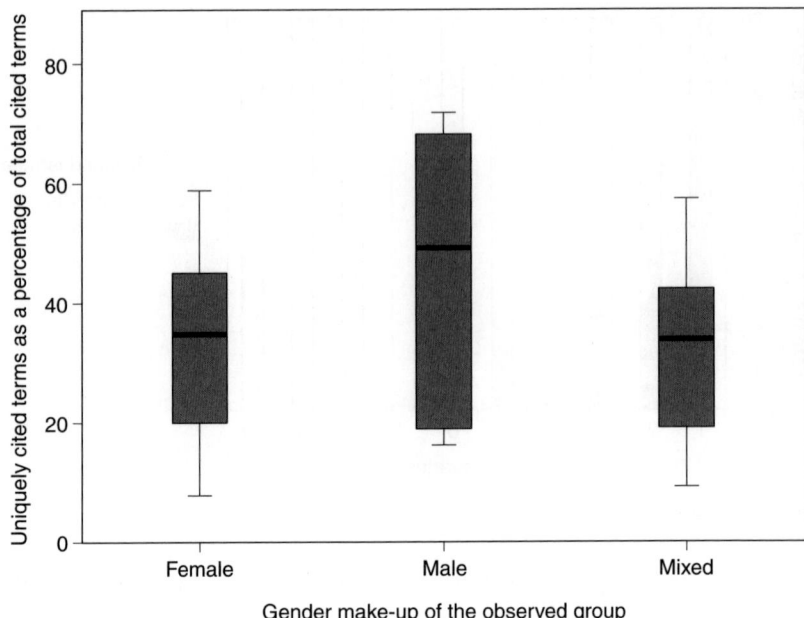

FIGURE 4.4 Percentage of uniquely cited terms in glossaries of mixed and single-sex groups

used to create social identity in these groups. Male-only social groups provide a considerably higher proportion of uniquely cited terms, suggesting that verbal competitiveness is more characteristic of male-only groups (but see Cameron 2007: 62–4).

The glossaries suggest that some semantic changes are predetermined by the parallel meanings of synonymous terms. For example, many terms meaning 'penis' also mean 'an idiot' (e.g. *bell-end, chode, cock, dick, knob, penis, prick, schlong* and *tool*). Terms for gay men (e.g. *fudgepacker, gay* and *knobjockey*) are also reported in use as generic insults. Terms meaning 'vagina' sometimes develop the sense 'bad' (e.g. *vadge* and *gash*) or develop the verbal meaning 'to do (something) badly or indecisively' (e.g. *faff, fanny* and *muff*). OED dates for these senses suggest that this last development has changed direction or become bi-directional:

muff n. (1699) → *to muff (about/around)* v. (1846)
fanny n. (1879) → *to fanny (about/around)* v. (1971)
faff n. (not in OED) ← *to faff (about/around)* v. (1874)

The sources of the slang reported by Leicester students will be evident from the chapters elsewhere in this book. Some of it is in general informal usage in the UK, some is from MLE (see Green, Chapter 5) and much is shared with the slang of US students (see Eble, Chapter 3), probably from shared musical, online or media influences.

There is no cohesive body of 'UK student slang' used by all UK students and only by UK students. The slang used by one group of students will not be common to all, even within the same course at the same university. Each social network will have its own preferred terms and students may modify their own speech as they move between social networks. Neither are students particularly prolific creators of new slang: on the whole their slang is an amalgam of widely used terms largely originating in Britain and the United States. These provisos may beg the question 'Why study student slang at all?' and the answer lies in students' dense (if temporary and shifting) social networks: that they study with other students goes without saying, but they often also live and socialize with other students, and each contact with another user of a slang term will tend to cement their own usage. Students are thus ideal subjects for a study of the general slang of their age group.

Note

1 I would like to thank the students who allowed me to refer to their glossaries in this paper.

5

MULTICULTURAL LONDON ENGLISH

The new 'youthspeak'

Jonathon Green

Multicultural London English (henceforth MLE) represents the 'state of the art' of London 'youthspeak' for many young people, a substantial proportion, but by no means all of them born to Caribbean or Asian immigrant families. First noted by Kerswill (2005: 50–1), it was seen as transcending many previous forms of youthful speech by incorporating elements of a number of cultures, and by 2008 was billed as a 'new transcultural idiom' (Abley 2008: 11). It is perhaps impossible to measure, but the cultural crossover extends not merely between races but also classes, and MLE can also be found among young middle-class white speakers.

To outsiders its accent sounds 'black' (i.e. West Indian or specifically Jamaican) and as such it is distinguishable from its London-based predecessor, 'Estuary English', a modified form of cockney, the traditional language of (mainly white) East Enders which flourished in the 1980s and since. Among the differences noted by Kerswill (2011) is that MLE speakers 'talk proper'; in other words, unlike their Cockney or Estuary peers, they do not drop the initial /h/. MLE speakers see it simply as 'slang' because its lexis is predominantly composed of slang terminology, and they consider it to be a separate linguistic phenomenon to 'cockney', which is seen as the 'slang' of an older generation. MLE may move with its speakers as they grow older, but at the moment it does not exist outside the young.

A brief history of black speech in the UK

The UK had hosted a tiny black population for centuries, primarily imported either as servants or, occasionally, as flesh-and-blood souvenirs of distant lands, brought home by explorers and paraded before gawping Londoners. Grose (1785) noted a few 'negroe' terms, although these were from the plantations. In 1919, Britain's first race riots focused on ports where the black population had expanded.

After World War II, successive governments began looking outside Britain for new workers to help the steadily improving economy of the 1950s, which could no longer be serviced by the indigenous population. They began recruiting in the Commonwealth, notably in the islands of the West Indies, and found that the black populations were more than willing to make the journey.

The arrivals did not, as yet, impinge on English speech. If they spoke slang, which for most listeners would have been hard to distinguish from island patois, they kept it to themselves. For the first decade it was a mainly male society, and without women there were no children and without children far less cross-cultural mixing. Such immigrant narratives as Selvon (1956) remained rare and looked inward. Selvon uses 85 slang terms: over half of those are from the Caribbean, and there is no sense that the whites with whom his characters worked and sometimes socialized picked them up. The process was more likely to have gone the other way: the remainder of Selvon's terms are mainstream white slang.

A decade later, there was little sense of change. Black slang had arrived in the UK, but it was African-American, not Caribbean. Those who actually enjoyed Caribbean culture, in the form of ska and bluebeat, reggae's musical prequels, were the white working class, ironically the racist subgroup known as skinheads. There were more black children by now, and it was the embryo skinheads and not the middle-class hippies who had shared classrooms with these second-generation British-born blacks. Skinhead slang, however, remained either traditional and homegrown or, again, imported from America.

The popularity of reggae, spearheaded by Bob Marley, whose first crossover hit album, *Catch a Fire*, was released in 1974, brought a few words into white speech, but essentially as postcards from a strange, if fascinating land. They were not Jamaican patois, as spoken in Brixton, but the quasi-religious intonations of Rastafarianism: *dread, Jah, I-and-I, irie* and of course *Babylon*, for the white man and all his works, specifically the police.

The work of the Brixton-based poet Linton Kwesi Johnson (1978, 1979, 1980), appearing in the late 1970s, revealed more terms – among them *juke* 'to stab', *mauger* 'thin', *yout* both 'a young man' and a generic term for the increasingly disaffected community of young working-class black Britons – but it was Johnson's heavily accented delivery that was as potent an indicator of the arena in which he worked as his vocabulary.

Transition and translation: Smiley Culture

The first inkling of what would become MLE came in 1984: the release of the record 'Cockney Translation' by black British dancehall DJ Smiley Culture. Born David Emmanuel, he was the son of a Jamaican father and Guyanese mother, and lived in Stockwell, next door to the black centre of Brixton in south London. The music business sidelined it as a novelty song, but the lyrics laid out a bilingual glossary of words used by young Cockney tearaways and their black peers:

Cockney's not a language, it's only a slang
And was originated yah so inna England
The first place it was used was over East London
It was respect for the different style pronunciation
But it wasn't really used by any and any man
Me say strictly con-man also the villain
But through me fill up of lyrics and education
Right here now you a go get a little translation.
...
Say cockney fire shooter, We bus' gun
Cockney say tea leaf, We say sticks man
You know dem have wedge while we have corn
Say cockney say be first, my son! We just say Gwan!
Cockney say grass, We say outformer man
When dem talk 'bout iron dem really mean batty man
Rope chain and choparita me say cockney call tom
Say cockney say Old Bill, We dutty Babylon
(Smiley Culture 1984)

He was not alone. Tippa Irie's 'Complain Neighbour' (1985) pointed up a similar cultural clash, underpinned by the singer's alternation of 'roots' and 'Cockney' voices. These two artists both worked with 'fast-style' reggae, sometimes characterized as 'British rap'.

Hebdige (1990: 50–51) suggested that far from representing a commercial 'novelty', 'Cockney Translation' pointed up an important social one:

> Smiley Culture is part of a new generation of young black British MCs who are talking their way into a new sound and a new identity. 'Cockney Translation' is about this process. In the record, Smiley Culture seems to be two separate people. Although he is a Londoner he is also a *black* Londoner. He isn't a white, working-class Cockney. But he isn't a rootsy Jamaican 'yardy' either. He can speak both languages – Jamaican patois and cockney rhyming slang – but he doesn't fully *belong* in either camp. He hops back and forth between the two roles when he needs to in order to keep out of trouble and earn a living.

> 'But sometimes me shake out and leave me home town
> And that's when me travel a East London
> Where I have to speak as a different man
> So that the cockney can understand.'
>
> *(Hebdige 1990: 50–1)*

Smiley Culture was seemingly the first songwriter to combine black and white slang. Yet there is still no suggestion of crossover. His whole point is difference, even if, if Hebdige's analysis is correct, Smiley Culture is suggesting that one person can use both vocabularies as and when required. His delivery accentuated the very different speech rhythms of his two groups, and as the singer pointed out it was meant as a social tourist guide or, more practically, a survival mechanism.

The translation worked both ways: blacks as well as whites were being educated. In the video that accompanied the record, in which he plays a teacher, Smiley Culture's class is composed only of black pupils. The singer was also noting his own code-switching, which stood for that of many peers: black in Brixton, cockney in the East End.

Two-Tone

Coming from the other direction, again via music, was Two-Tone: a cover-all term for bands such as Madness, the Selecter and the Specials. Often mixing black and white musicians, they returned to the ska and bluebeat classics of twenty years earlier, reinterpreting music that had been wholly Caribbean for a white audience. Again, it was not yet crossover, more an acknowledgment: many of the songs were effectively covers, and if they used black slang, they did not comment on it. Launched in 1979, Two-Tone flourished briefly into the 1980s; it collapsed when the same skinheads who had enjoyed the original music saw it as a useful backdrop for far-right politics. The bands, appalled, faded away.

'Young England, Half-English'

MacInnes (1957: 11–18) coined the phrase 'Young England, Half-English'. The young England in question was the pop singer Tommy Steele and his fans; the other 'half' was America. A music-hall fan, MacInnes was lamenting American influence, but unconsciously and, with quite a different focus, the phrase was prescient. American influence would only increase, but what would form MLE was a blurring between the two varieties of English young: native white and immigrant black. With reference to his research in the West Midlands in 1985, Hebdige (1990: 158) suggested that '[t]he old national culture and national identity have started cracking at the seams. There is an army of in-betweens and neither-nors out there who feel they belong to no given community'. He noted that '[i]n some parts of Britain, West Indian patois has become *the* public language of inner-city youths, irrespective of their racial origin' and suggested that '[p]erhaps there is another nation being formed for the future beyond the boundaries of race. If that nation can't yet be visualised, then it can perhaps be heard in the rhythms of the airwaves, in the beat that binds together histories, cultures, new identities' (Hebdige 1990: 158).

Like many aspects of 'youth culture', this was driven by musical taste. If the 1980s and even more the 1990s offered London's white speakers a way into blackness, it was via this code-switching. Not between class but between colour. A switch that was encouraged not so much by home-grown music, but by the new and increasingly powerful agency of what began as hip hop and moved on, as what had begun as disco-originated party music transformed into something far angrier – not to mention slangier – with the advent of gangsta rap. The source, in common with that of most slang since World War II, was America. If one wished to understand this increasingly ubiquitous form, one had to understand its vocabulary. And having understood, the likelihood would be that just as the beats and hippies had twenty years before, one would incorporate that language into one's own.

Wiggas: Ali G and Londonstani

The rapper Kanye West, talking in 2006, described the white man's fascination with black speech as 'diction addiction' and joked that there should be an obligatory moratorium of twelve months before white teens were allowed to start using the ghetto's latest coinages (Green 2006: 99). It was far too late. Nothing epitomized the white incorporation of this black culture more than the character Ali G, created by the UK comedian Sacha Baron Cohen. Ali G, the 'voice of da yoof', came not from the mean ghetto streets but from the dormitory town of Staines, outside London. The character, self-styled leader of the 'West Staines Massive', debuted on TV in 1998; eventually there would be a movie. The joke was that he saw himself as black, dressing like a rapper, brandishing gang signs and speaking accordingly. His scripts were seeded with the obligatory cliches: *big up yaself, booyaka, for real, punanny, chill, batty-boy, respect, wa'g'waan* and most ironically *keep it real*. The references, despite *batty-boy* and *punanny*, both staples of Jamaican sexual 'slackness', and the greeting *wa'g'waan*, looked to the States.

Ali G was a fictional creation. The real-life type persisted. In 2007 he was, as it were, made print, in Gautam Malkani's debut novel *Londonstani*, set in another west London dormitory, Hounslow, home to a substantial and rooted Anglo-Asian community. It takes the book's entirety for us to discover that the narrator, who runs with a second-generation Asian immigrant gang, is in fact white. The language, as expected, veers to MLE, using such terms as *blood* as a term of address, *bruck up* 'to assault', *flex* 'to show off; to intimidate', *garms* 'clothes', *peeps* 'people' and *yard* 'one's home', although the 150-odd terms bypass some of the primary vocabulary – no sign for instance of *nang* 'good', *sket* 'a promiscuous female', *shotter* 'drug dealer', *mandem* 'a group of friends; one's gang; men in general', also used as a salutation – and look as much towards America as they do to the Caribbean, Bow or Brixton.

Jafaikan

In 2006 the British press noticed a new form of youth speech. It came with a name: *Jafaikan*, which seemed to be a journalistic invention: a neat and punning blend that combined the proper name *Jamaican* and the dismissive adjective *fake*. *The Guardian*, hot on the multi-culti bandwagon, referenced television's Ali G and offered readers the chance to 'learn jafaikan in two minutes', and in the way of half a millennium's slang expositors, offered both a short glossary and a few sample sentences: 'You lookin buff in dem low batties. Dey's sick man. Me, I'm just jammin wid me bruds. Dis me yard, innit? Is nang, you get me? No? What ends you from then?' (Ashton 2006). The paper's columnist Zoe Williams (2006) predictably railed against it two days later, noting but failing to understand slang's best-established trope, and thus wondering why women were so vilified in the new lexis. The *Daily Mail*, worrying as ever about what Margaret Thatcher had once termed the immigrant 'swamping' of indigenous culture, announced that 'Jafaican [sic] is wiping out inner city accents' (Clark 2006).

It was left to Quinion (2006) to make a little sense. Although he perhaps erroneously threw 'African' into the mix, on the basis of the ultimate origin of the Caribbean-born parents of its first speakers, he noted that, as ever, the journalists had got it wrong. Jafaikan did not refer to a language or a youth dialect, but was a London slang term used by working-class black teens to deride their middle-class, though equally black peers, posing, just like the equivalent white *wiggas, wannabes* and *waspafarians*, as hardcore proles, all the way from Trenchtown with a Rasta tam, waist-length dreads and a spliff-ful of sensimilia. The earliest recorded usage is from 2004.

The Jafaikan bubble, being ephemeral, duly burst. MLE did not. It took root, strengthened and spread. At the moment, it is the default speech of young Londoners and it may be that since the young grow older and take their speech patterns with them, it may move beyond the current identification with a single generation. To quote Thorne (2006), it appears 'that the use of slang is becoming much more than a stylistic preference, is more than a transient phase in adolescent behaviour. If you think about it, the constraints that formerly induced people to abandon slang are no longer there. The family, the school and the workplace are no longer in a position definitively to restrict and censor this kind of language.'

Researching MLE

There was, certainly, a form of language, but it had quite another name. Quinion (2006) explained that 'a team of linguists are investigating this emerging speech form, as a three-year project led by Professor Paul Kerswill at Lancaster University. They prefer the neutral term Multicultural London English (MLE).' He quoted Kerswill (2005): 'A clear new vernacular is emerging in inner London, linking ethnicities, and forging shared identities – often around music like rap, hip-hop, grime or bangra' (Quinion 2006). There were certain changes in pronunciation, notably the shortening of traditional London vowel sounds, and the diminished stress of the Cockney's trademark, the glottal stop. It also appeared that MLE was overtaking the last 'new' London language: Estuary English, itself a mix of Standard English and traditional Cockney pronunciation and vocabulary, and spoken by an older generation as their rejection of 'pure' cockney. This had become especially popular among those who wished to appear linguistically 'classless'. Whatever its roots, MLE is innately British and fundamentally London, although it has been suggested that in other cities, where the immigrant community arrived from areas other than the Caribbean, there is a sprinkling of terms that reflect those origins, typically the appearance of Somali terms in Cardiff.

The language of the Caribbean, and particularly of Jamaica, remains central. Its immediate roots lie in the language of a wholly British creation: grime, a musical style that appeared, at least for the wider public, in 2002. Like other youth slangs, music, or more properly the lyrics that accompany it, has provided the primary impulsion for its adoption, and if MLE has had a single driving engine, then this is it. Grime, most easily, if inaccurately, described as British rap, draws on a variety of roots, including US rap itself, but more locally UK garage (pronounced 'garridge') and West Indian dancehall. It came out of east London, particularly Bow, and was initially promoted via the flourishing world of pirate radio stations, often broadcasting a mere few hours per week on kit thrown together in tower block apartments. It enjoyed various names: 8-bar (which referred to the verse patterns) and Nu Shape (with more complex 16- and 32-bar patterns). It could also be Dark Garage, Sub-Lo, One-Step or Esky or Eskibeat (a nod to slang's veteran term *cool*), which blended in dance and electro styles and was created by Wiley (Richard Cowie). Wiley, alongside Dizzee Rascal (Dylan Mills) – perhaps the most successful of all its stars, and now a far more mainstream performer – was the first to move the form from the underground to a wider audience.

Compared with the juggernaut of mainstream rap, grime has remained a niche creation, still not so far removed from the hand-distributed tapes and one-on-one DJ 'battles' that typified its early incarnation. It is very much home-grown, and there is little celebration of the bling that typifies its American cousin. Grime lyrics reflect what Skinnyman (2004) (Alexander Holland; Leeds-born, but north-London-raised) neatly expressed as 'a council estate of mind'. There is no concept of 'ghetto fabulous'. The lyrics underline the problems of life – unemployment, police harassment, racial prejudice. The overriding emotion, as the Sex Pistols (1977) put it 30 years earlier, is that there is 'no future'.

If grime has an overriding characteristic it is that of being music put together by the young for themselves – taking advantage of new technology even if their products remained spurned by major labels. MLE, which has nothing like the worldwide spread of rap slang, seems a parallel phenomenon: a London creation that has sprung wholly from the street, blending linguistic sources just as grime has combined musical ones. It reflects the immigrant communities: poor, multilingual, family based and self-reliant. Rock, for all its careful posing, is often more middle class than it likes to admit. No wonder that its slang was second-hand. Grime is not, and the language seems, even if it borrows widely, to be a genuine creation.

Skinnyman is white; so too, one more among many, is K Koke (Kevin Georgiou), Greek-born and resident on the notorious north London Stonebridge estate. His lyrics are as saturated with MLE as are any of his black peers'. The video that accompanies his near-incomprehensible 'diss track' 'Are You Alone Fam' with its gang-sign flashing hoodies and grim, urban wasteland backdrop, is as mixed-race as might be desired. Colour is no longer the issue; and the language is what binds, not race.

Grime will never be world-shattering. It is simply too 'London'. For the same reason, if MLE has any cultural 'showcase', it is in this streetwise, cross-cultural music.

Fear of language

In August 2011, London erupted in a series of violent, destructive riots, spearheaded by youngsters from both black and white working-class communities. The immediate trigger was the shooting by police of Mark Duggan, whose image was either pillar of the community or minor gangster, depending on the biases of the speaker. Aside from the narrative of the riots themselves, variously characterized along a spectrum ranging from mindless violence and greedy looting to an outcry by justifiably angry young people forgotten by society, one of the biggest stories came not from the street, but from the ivory tower. Speaking on BBC-TV's *Newsnight* (broadcast 12 August 2011), the conservative academic David Starkey pronounced that:

> Whites have become black. A particular sort of violent, destructive, nihilistic, gangster culture has become the fashion. And black and white, boy and girl, operate in this language together, this language which is wholly false, which is this Jamaican patois that's been intruded in England, and this is why so many of us have this sense of literally a foreign country.
>
> *(Starkey 2011a)*

Starkey was not original: in 2006 the former chief inspector of schools, Chris Woodhead, claimed that slang 'contaminates and subverts'. Writing a couple of days later, Starkey extended his theme. While 'good' blacks showed their acceptability by speaking Standard English, 'bad' ones spoke what he persisted in terming 'Jafaikan'. In so doing, they had corrupted susceptible members of the white underclass, the so-called chavs, who, as Starkey explained, 'have integrated into the pervasive black "gangsta" culture: they wear the same clothes; they talk and text in the same Jafaikan patois; and, as their participation in recent events shows, they have become as disaffected and riotous' (Starkey 2011b).

Speakers

MLE speakers are primarily working class, both black, white and 'brown', i.e. Asian. There are no statistics but it appears that the lexis has also been adopted, probably to a lesser extent, by middle-class speakers, in the same manner that some took on Estuary English and before that 'Mockney'. MLE has thus become something of a lingua franca for those under 30. Middle-class users, however, are far more likely to code-switch, in the same way that white users of rap slang/ebonics will also have other alternatives available. As has always been true of slang speakers, the further one is from 'good' society, the more dense will be one's use of 'bad' language.

Lexis

Like all slangs MLE is not a separate language. It has no rules and, again like slang, is essentially a lexis. Its themes echo those of slang: sex, drugs, violence, money, personal insults and so on. It need not be the sole slang in a given context. A Skinnyman lyric, 'Little Man' (2004), set in prison, mixes MLE – *parro*, *feds*, *blud* – with terms such as *lockdown*, *hang up* and *sweatbox* that originated in American prisons.

The accent of MLE, irrespective of the speaker's colour, is perceived as 'black' and the lexis, as much as it can be assembled, is heavily influenced by black use: part taken from the Caribbean, part from American rap, and part home-grown in London estates with a high second- or third-generation immigrant population such as those of Bow, Brixton, Stonebridge and Tottenham. Drawing mainly on published glossaries, the lyrics of grime, media coverage and a range of interviews, including those with grime stars such as Dizzee Rascal, I have assembled just over 220 terms. There is no suggestion that this is a definitive list, nor that all terms are used by all speakers. Slang has grown increasingly localized and like campuses, which both share the general usage of their generation and employ localisms, each estate will have items unused elsewhere, albeit referring to the same things. These break down into 39 terms from the Caribbean, usually Jamaica (including *cotch* 'to relax', *nang* 'good' and *stoush* 'arrogant'); 35 from US black slang (including *balling* 'making money', *jack* 'to rob' and *whip* 'an automobile'); 41 from US white slang (including *beef* 'an argument', *kicks* 'trainers' and *sick* 'excellent'); and 35 from white London slang or cockney (including *cushty* 'first-rate', *nab* 'to arrest' and *papers* 'money'). In addition, 74 home-grown terms (including *beanie* 'an attractive girl', *fuckery* 'nonsense' and *shotter* 'a drug dealer') are used as the core vocabulary of MLE and have evolved independently of Caribbean, US or 'cockney' roots. Although London hosts many families from Asia (primarily Pakistan and Bangladesh) and Africa, such languages do not seem to have contributed. Presumably, black usage is seen as more cool.

Conclusion

MLE, with its cross-race, cross-class adoption, stands among the most interesting manifestations of 'youth slang' since that phenomenon began to be analysed and recorded. That said, I offer a pair of questions. The first of these regards MLE's exceptionality; the second its actual existence as a discrete linguistic phenomenon.

Although MLE was touted as something new, its arrival was surely quite logical. The all-male immigrant society of the 1950s had long been replaced; children and grandchildren were now living in the UK and, certainly as regarded the working class, were being schooled with their white contemporaries. It was hardly surprising that there would be an increasing overlap in the way that these youths spoke. In addition, the allure of black culture has been promoted by those who merchandise 'urban style' as de facto rebellious: 'hard', more masculine, more 'sexy'. The novelty, if there is one, is the adoption of MLE by an increasing section of the white middle class, but again, one can see this in the previous popularity of Estuary English. The terror of being perceived as elitist, let alone 'posh', holds serious power among those whose credo is 'authenticity'. In the local context of the East End, whose latest 'immigrants', in the wake of the artists of the 1990s, have turned out to be the gentrifying and well-off white middle classes, it is perhaps unsurprising that these new 'East Enders' have opted to take on the predominant linguistic coloration.

As for question two, MLE surely exists, but I also think that it is dangerous to isolate and simplify, however much this may suit the media. Slang is a continuum, half a millennium old at least, and MLE is simply the latest version, a development and not a side-track let alone a parallel creation. MLE is the name that has been given to the current set of words to fulfil the role of 'youth slang', mainly as sourced within the confines of London. That the roots of much of that slang were originally black and have crossed both race and class (not merely to whites but, given the current demographics, also to Asians) is not a wholly new phenomenon: one saw that, though less consciously, in the middle-class adoption by the beats and then hippies of black American slang in the 1960s. The difference there, again because of demographics, is simply that the UK now has a substantial young native-born black population, whose slang production is strengthened by their fulfilling the primary role of social outsiders/'cool' rebels. This has created a home-grown input that did not hitherto exist. This was not through choice, but because those who provided the slang did not yet exist in the UK. So what we are seeing is a perfectly logical development. Perhaps the adoption of black speech sounds is different, but then that seems to me to echo Mockney, where the sounds adopted were those of the white slang speakers, again by a social group – the young white middle-class – who would never hitherto have used them.

But outside temporary labels and subsets, slang in its most broad-brush form remains a continuum. It has been collected for half a millennium and very likely spoken for longer. We have slang's themes and indeed users – the dispossessed, the marginal – in 1531 and have been seeing them one way or another ever since. The marginality is what counts, not the drugs, the clothes or the music. To an extent MLE exists because the media shone its light and lo! it was there. It is perhaps the latest form, at least in the UK, but it is still, just as is the succession of synonyms that form slang's evolving lexis, more of what we have already seen and, surely, a precursor of what is to come.

6

THE NEW CANTING CREW[1]

Tony Thorne

'Tis no Disparagement to understand the Canting Terms: It may chance to save your Throat from being cut, or (at least) your Pocket from being pick'd.

(Coles 1676: 4)

Introduction

This chapter was prompted by a linguistic curiosity – the assertion that modern-day criminals in custody in the UK had revived the cryptolect (the secret code, or 'cant', as it was known) employed by their Elizabethan predecessors five hundred years earlier. Investigating this claim was perhaps an unusual task for a linguist and lexicographer, but not a unique one. I have also encountered at first hand the language of criminals in several other contexts, and it seemed to me that bringing these instances together might provide interesting examples of current usage to compare with earlier accounts and also illustrate similarities or differences in the way that such language has been reported.

The chapter first examines in detail the words and phrases used by convicts and recorded by prison officers in one particular prison in the north of England. It then considers the language used by transgressive youth, in the contexts of civil disorder and of gang crime, often characterized as 'Multiethnic London English' or MLE. I go on to contrast this mixed vocabulary with samples of language given to me by an older member of the white, 'working-class' criminal fraternity.

Slang and criminality

Categorizing the speech patterns, and occasionally the written language, of the British criminal classes is not straightforward. The word 'slang', familiarly applied today, was not recorded until 1756. Before that, successive collections of criminal vocabulary, compiled not by trained linguists but by amateurs or enthusiasts, used the word *cant* from Latin *cantare*, 'to sing or intone', in the transferred sense of '(uttering) wheedling, seductive or deceptive words' ascribed to beggars and cheats. In modern Standard English, the same word has come to mean 'hypocritical or insincere speech, typically professing high ideals'. A full account of the early cant collections is provided by Coleman (2004a).

The most comprehensive compendium attempted thus far was published in 1698. B.E.'s *New Dictionary of the Terms, Ancient and Modern of the Canting Crew* was the first publication to resemble a modern dictionary in format, as opposed to the shorter and sketchier pamphlets that preceded it. The 'canting crew', the speech community which 'B.E., Gent', the otherwise anonymous compiler, was reporting on, consisted, he wrote, of 'several tribes of gypsies, beggars, thieves, cheats, etc.'

In the caption expanding on his title, B.E. declares that the work is 'useful for all sorts of people (especially foreigners) to secure their *money* and preserve their *lives*; besides very diverting and entertaining, being wholly new'. Here we have the typical rationale offered up as justification for glossaries of cant. The ostensible purpose is to warn the public of the activities of ne'er-do-wells and enable the innocent to protect themselves, at the same time intriguing the reader with the novelty of the language on display and the notion of a horde of evildoers preying upon respectable society. These works, in Coleman's words, 'represent knowledge and understanding that will protect the purchaser from crime, but also titillate him with forbidden glimpses of immorality' (Coleman 2004a: 183).

A new canting crew?

On 8 June 2009 a news item was published in some UK newspapers and on news websites that held out a fascinating possibility for anyone interested in slang and non-standard varieties of language. The report, which also featured in *Have I Got News for You*, a satirical TV quiz, claimed that inmates at a prison in the north of England were using archaic slang in order to pass clandestine messages. Under the headline 'Convicts Use ye Olde Elizabethan Slang to Smuggle Drugs Past Guards into Prison', the mid-market *Daily Mail* tabloid observed, 'You might think that prison officers would be delighted that their inmates were becoming well-versed in Elizabethan dialect. But far from any self-improving study of the works of Shakespeare, criminals are instead becoming fluent in thieves' cant, a dialect used by 16th-century rogues to keep their plans secret' (Tozer 2009). The *Mail* printed a glossary of 'Rogue Words' collected at Buckley Hall Prison in Rochdale (a 381-prisoner 'category C' establishment for low-risk offenders) and added 'the Ministry of Justice is so worried about the use of the code that it has issued a security alert to governors at jails in England and Wales'.

The wordlist in the order in which it appeared was as follows:

Chat/Onick 'Heroin'
Cawbe 'Crack cocaine'

Inick 'Phone/SIM card'
Grade 'Money'
Fein 'Man'
Soolbick 'Mate, friend'
Lakeen 'Woman'
Bure 'Girlfriend'
Keenya 'House/flat'
Wid 'Talk'
Warbs 'Police'
Shades 'Prison officers'

I was asked in a radio interview to give an instant reaction to the report and was able to identify several examples of Shelta, the mixed Anglo-Irish language used by nineteenth-century tinkers and other travelling communities. The online *Wikipedia* 'encyclopedia' has an entry which gives an introduction to Shelta, and specific Shelta terms are listed in lexicons at the *Traveller's Rest* website. They included *grade* (also spelt *greid*) 'money', *fein* 'man', *lakeen* 'a woman' (a re-ordering of the syllables of Irish Gaelic *cailín* 'a girl') and *soolbick* (also *sublich, subilee* or *sooblik*). *Soolbick* was described by an informant in 2011 as 'a word used instead of boy in Ireland particularly the Carlow area', with the illustrative example "See that sublich over there – if he looks at me Air Max [trainers] again I'll dance on his head". I was later told that at Rochdale the word always specified 'close male friend'. Other terms were more obscure and required more careful investigation.

It took some time to determine the circumstances in which the prison wordlist was produced and publicized, especially since the first press article was the result of a leak of restricted information by persons unknown. It transpired that the list had been sent by Sean McNicholas, the senior prison officer who had compiled it, to Paul Williams, editor of the *Monthly Security Bulletin*. This publication, circulated only within the Ministry of Justice and restricted to that readership, was the 'security alert' referred to in the press reports.

Access to the prisoners who had used the language in question was not possible – in any case Buckley Hall had in the meantime converted from a women's prison (a fact ignored by press reports, giving the lie to any assumption that slang is exclusively a male preoccupation) to an all-male establishment – but with the help of the Ministry of Justice I was able eventually to contact the prison staff and question them by telephone and email over the period December 2010 to August 2012. They readily furnished more details of their attempts to 'break the code' and provided background information on the setting and circumstances. It then became easier to assess the code in question by examining the remaining words in turn.

Chat 'heroin' has been used since at least the seventeenth century to mean 'a body louse'. *Urban Dictionary*'s contemporary collection of mainly youth slang from the Anglosphere records its use in Australia and the US since 2003 as noun and adjective to denote '(something or someone) dirty or disgusting' and as a synonym for 'shit'. Transgressive slang often equates drugs with excrement, so this may relate to recorded instances of *chat* meaning '(a tablet of) ecstasy' (*Urban Dictionary* 2004) or 'hashish' (*Irish Slang* website). The current Irish lexicon also lists it with the meaning 'a thing', and Harman's cant pages from 1567 contain *cheat*, 'a thing'.

Onick 'heroin' like *inick* 'Phone/SIM card' is probably originally an arbitrary coinage, a nonsense word used when the thing referred to cannot or must not be given its correct name. On the *Irish Slang* website (a very useful compendium of mainly user-generated contemporary material) *inic* is defined as 'a thing, object' with the exemplification "Give me that inic there". Romany speakers today use *inox* to mean 'an (unnamed) item' and one commentary describes this as a borrowing from *Gammon*, a word used since at least 1781 (*Oxford English Dictionary*) to mean 'talk, chatter', sometimes narrowed to 'deceitful, deceptive talk' and now heard only in Ireland.

On *cawbe* 'crack cocaine', Sean McNicholas later commented, 'I was initially told that 'cawbe' is crack cocaine, but I have since been told that it means 'fight'. A term used when violence is inflicted is 'give someone a crack', so it's possible that 'cawbe' means crack, and could refer to either hitting someone, or to cocaine' (Thorne 2012). *Corb* and *corp* are indeed used in contemporary Irish slang to mean 'chastise' or 'assault', but their derivation is obscure (the former might even have begun as an Irish pronunciation of the standard verb 'curb', for example). In Anglophone slang, heroin is commonly known as *smack* (though that is from Yiddish *schmeck*, 'sniff'), and *hit* denotes 'a portion of a drug, usually powdered' in slang.

Bure (also *byohr*, *beoir*, *buor*) 'girlfriend' is from Irish. A prison officer later clarified, 'I asked one [male] prisoner why they referred to a woman as a *lakeen* and a *bure* and he told me that the first is a general term for a woman, but *bure* is a reference to a girlfriend'.

Warbs is a prisoners' term for police officers, and I have heard the same word used by English so-called chavs with the same meaning. It derives from *warbie*, a Scottish dialect term for a maggot, whence also the Australian slang *warb*, recorded there since 1933 with the senses 'a dirty person' or 'a no-hoper'.

Shades 'prison officers' is contemporary Irish slang for the Garda Siochana, the Republic's police force, derived by some from the fact that their uniforms are of two different shades of blue, but this may be a folk etymology, as MacGreine (1932) and Share (1967) derive it from Irish Gaelic *seideog*, 'a policeman'.

This leaves two terms that might truly be characterized as relics of 'Elizabethan' slang or cant. *Keenya* 'house/flat' is likely to be related to *ken*, 'a house', listed in Harman in 1567. The word, which might be related to the noun kennel ('a shelter for a dog'), and the verb form which could then also mean 'to lurk', which were first recorded at roughly the same time, has a long history, sometimes denoting a house where thieves congregate. In Irish slang today *kenya* can refer to an unoccupied property or somewhere that is easy to break into (*Irish Slang* website). *Wid* 'talk' appears to be related to *whid* 'word', first attested in Harman (1567) along with *whids* 'words' and *whiddle* 'to talk or reveal'.

There was a very obvious Irish dimension to most of the terminology recorded, and much was consistent with glossaries of Shelta. Sean McNicholas confirmed that virtually all the prisoners who spoke 'in code' were Travellers, and 'nearly all of the

Travellers I have had dealings with had Irish connections and some spoke broad Irish and others didn't. The majority of Travellers lived in and around the Oldham, Rochdale and Manchester areas (in their words, settled people) and came from large families' (Thorne 2012).

Irish Travellers operating in the Republic of Ireland and across the UK are an originally 'nomadic' or itinerant minority population which some see as a distinct ethnic sub-group within Ireland, although their early history is unrecorded. As well as Standard English, they speak a mixed language based on Hiberno-English with significant Irish Gaelic elements and influences, the language often called by commentators Shelta (the label, first appearing in 1882, is probably an anglicization of Irish Gaelic *siul(toir)* 'walk(er)'). Members of this community may refer to their own speech patterns as *(the) Cant* (see below) or as *(the) Gammon* (see above).

Travellers are distinct from the Roma or Romany-speaking gypsies with whom they have often been confused (we do not know, for instance, the ethnic makeup of the 'gypsies' referred to in the early cant glossaries). As well as sharing many aspects of lifestyle these two groups sometimes intermingle language items, so that Irish-based Shelta terms appear in Romany glossaries and Romany words, many ultimately deriving from Indian dialects, are often included in Shelta lists. Romany terms are listed at the online *Freelang Romany Dictionary* (Figueiredo 1997–2013).

Prison staff informed me that inmates under discussion did not refer to their code as slang or as Shelta, but as *cant*. In subsequent correspondence and telephone conversations the staff provided more cant terms used by female and by male prisoners (Thorne 2012).

Wonga for 'money' is a Romany word for coal and has been used to mean money since the nineteenth century (*cole* – an archaic spelling – was recorded as a synonym for money by Greene 1591). The Romany word was recorded as *wongur* in England in 1888 and became fashionable in raffish UK slang in the 1980s, also in the form *womba*. It is now familiar enough in colloquial usage to serve as the name of a web-based money-lending company.

Mush 'man, mate' is also from Romany, where it means man, and has been used with this sense in UK slang (first attested in 1936), often, too, like 'mate', as a term of address. Powis (1977) listed it in his field manual for police and ascribed it to 'South Country thieves'.

Cushti, kushti or *cushdy* 'good' is from Romany *kushto* or Hindi *kush, kushi*, ultimately from Persian *khosh*. It means 'excellent', 'wonderful' or 'comfortable', and is a familiar slang word in the UK, not least owing to its popularization since 1981 by the TV comedy series *Only Fools and Horses*.

Chavvi 'child' is a word used by Romany speakers to mean 'child' or 'friend', and is a variant of *chav*, the label famously applied to members of a spectacular, stigmatized 'underclass' by the UK media from around 2004. According to the *Oxford English Dictionary* (OED), it may derive ultimately from Sanskrit *śāva*, 'the young of any animal'.

Del has not been recorded in cant, either archaic or contemporary, with the meaning 'dark' ascribed to it at Rochdale. As *dell* it has appeared in a number of English cant wordlists in the sense of 'virgin' or 'strumpet'. However, Romany has a word, *dolimi*, defined by Stewart Macalister (1937) as 'the dark of night', possibly from Greek. *Divvus*, meaning 'day', also recorded in the forms *deves* or *d'ives* in modern glossaries, is Romany.

Pooker 'speak' would be a northern English pronunciation of *pucker*, which does appear in Romany glossaries with the definition 'talk'. Significantly, though, Mayhew (1851: 251) recorded it as showmen's slang, defining it as 'to talk privately'. The surrounding text suggests that it actually had the sense of 'talk in a way unintelligible to onlookers'.

Gop 'kiss' is a reversal, a technique often used by Shelta, as in English back-slang, so *gop* is formed from Irish *póg*. *Taken*, for 'swallowed (drugs)', is simply a narrowing of the standard sense of the word where take means 'ingest'. Although *bugged* 'received' is a highly polysemous slang word, I have not previously come across it in this sense. Vaux (1812) listed the verb *to bug* in a vocabulary of Flash (thieves' slang) with the sense 'hand over', 'give'. Nowadays *bugged* can also mean '(to have had something) inserted in the anus', which might conceivably apply in this context. *Pavee* is probably the most common term by which Irish Travellers refer to themselves. It seems to have no antecedents and to be a Shelta coinage. *Goijer* is a form of the Romany term *gadje* or *gaje*, used to denote a non-Roma or non-Traveller. *Settled people* is Travellers' designation of the members of their broad community who are no longer itinerant. It can also refer to non-Travellers, members of the public at large, sometimes pejoratively.

The prisoners also used longer sequences of Standard English as part of their cryptic code. *Bring the children* was an instruction to deliver drugs; *lots of hair on the children* was a demand for large quantities of drugs. They would also make reference to clothes which had another meaning relating to drugs, including *brown T-shirt* 'heroin', *white T-shirt* 'cocaine' and *green trainers* 'cannabis'.

The exchanges recorded at Buckley Hall prison are a very specific instance of the use of an 'obscure' code to confuse outsiders, evade detection and commit illegal acts. They not only represent a modern counterpart of the canting activities of earlier generations, but confirm the longevity of the designation *cant* itself as a keyword for insiders. The glossaries compiled by prison staff resemble the cant wordlists of old, but they are targeted at a professional readership only and their aim is not to titillate. Once they are leaked to the popular press, however, an element of titillation does come into play.

The Buckley Hall data illustrates language use by a sub-group with a distinct identity and self-ascription. Just as there are other communities of circumstance engaged in law-breaking and antisocial behaviour, so there must be other codes in play in the UK's underworld today. Logic suggests that two of the players in question will be those representatives of a younger generation widely blamed for gang crime, drug use and other forms of delinquency, and the members of an older generation of 'white working class' criminals associated rightly or wrongly with the traditional practices of armed robbery, burglary, pickpocketing, etc.

Youth crime and MLE

Press reports of the civil disturbances, the 'urban riots,' which took place in the summer of 2011, mentioned young rioters' reliance on instant messaging on mobile phones to coordinate and report on their activities. Lists featured in press reports, and records of phone intercepts which I was asked by the police to comment upon, confirm the presence of the youth slang known as Multicultural London English or MLE (see Green, Chapter 5). Another way in which I have several times come into contact with the authentic speech of younger miscreants is in the context of prosecutions where evidence turns upon interpretations of their terminology, drawing on verbal depositions, phone intercepts and secret recordings of conversations. A typical example involved murder in the context of gang-related disputes among adolescents. The gangs concerned frequently have Afro-Caribbean, and in some cases 'Asian' (in UK usage actually South Asian, a problematical category in that it may encompass a variety of ethnic, religious and cultural identities), origins or connections, and invariably communicate using a high level of MLE vocabulary.

In the case in question the prosecution hoped to show that the youth accused of murder had issued a direct death threat to his victim, employing the words 'waste' and 'man' in a declaration along the lines of 'You (are) waste, man!' This, they claimed, made use of the US slang verb 'to waste' meaning to kill. In a witness deposition I made the following observations.

> One of the phrases which is in widespread use among young people across London is *waste-man*. This compound is typically used as a term of contempt or derision of a third party or may be delivered as a direct insult or 'put-down'. It may carry considerable force, thus function as a provocation or wounding comment, or may be employed lightly, in passing, as a dismissal of someone considered pitiable, or even jokingly to an associate. 'Waste-man' is based on the notion of someone being 'a waste of time', or a 'waste of space', and presumably originated as an alteration of these colloquial phrases … I would therefore not be at all surprised to hear the term *waste-man* used by a London teenager in 2008. If the formulation in question is 'your [*sic*] waste man', 'you're [a] waste-man' or similar, this would be a typical way of expressing derision, contempt (whether mild or extreme), dislike or dismissal to another person, presumably a male. It would mean something like 'You are a worthless individual', or simply 'I don't like you/disrespect you'.
>
> In North American slang, as used by criminals and members of the armed forces, for example, and in the inauthentic 'tough-guy' slang used in TV and cinema dialogue, the verb *to waste* can be a synonym or euphemism for 'to kill'. It is always … used as a verb and used transitively, e.g. 'waste him'/'they got wasted'. In the USA, *waste* is not used as an adjective to mean 'dead', nor is the noun *waste* used to mean 'a dead person', or 'person marked for death'. It is impossible to state with absolute certainty that the terms have

never been used thus, as slang operates in contexts where it may go unrecorded by outsiders, but I consider it very highly improbable indeed that the terms could be used in this way in London in 2008.

(Tony Thorne, witness statement to defence counsel, 1 October 2009)

A lag's lexicon

Although their language is no longer a novelty and has not been publicized recently, there is another class of criminal, caricatured in films and TV series from the 1940s on, quaintly characterized in police slang as *ODCs* ('ordinary decent criminals'), who habitually commit 'acceptable' crimes such as theft and deception, rather than taboo crimes relating to drugs and sex. The same group, when they are convicted and re-offend, are in colloquial English dubbed *old lags* (Vaux 1812), itself from prison slang. These criminals are likely to belong to, or exhibit behaviour and language usage typical of, the so-called 'traditional white working class'. Their slang has been collected in works such as Tempest (1950) and Morton (1989) and in the lexicon of prison slang compiled by the English Project at Winchester Prison (Mulvey 2010).

I was recently provided with samples of language employed by this older generation in an extended correspondence with a professional criminal of the baby-boomer generation from the Elephant and Castle district of South London. 'J.T.' made contact initially in order to correct errors I had made in publications and to share his enthusiasm for his peer group's colourful but perhaps obsolescent vocabulary.

> I thought I would report the contents of an actual conversation I had today. I met someone who used to be a pickpocket and got talking about things in general. We spoke about how the game used to be and about how the firm working 'the Under' (Underground) were 'cake-o' (rich) and about the fact that they 'had a licence' (were allowed to work by the Transport Police). I think I have already told you about 'losing one off the back'. This is where the firm allows one of their members to be arrested. Obviously if the police did not arrest any of the gang it would become clear that they [the police] had been straightened.
>
> *('J.T.', e-mail to Tony Thorne, 3 March 2012)*

Cake-o is a version of *caked-up*, where *cake* (1968) denotes '(an abundance of) riches, luxury and pleasure'. *Firm* (1809) is well known with the meaning 'criminal gang or organization', while *straightened out* (1937) is a euphemism for 'bribed, suborned or otherwise corrupted'. Dates for criminal slang terms of the twentieth and twenty-first centuries are from Green (2010). The dates given are first citations in print; as slang is firstly and primarily oral the terms are of course likely to be older.

'J.T.' also confirmed the generation gap in criminal usage. Presented with samples of the current MLE slang relating to stabbing and shooting from my own archive – *skeng, shank, wetter* and *shiv* for 'knife', *leng* and *strap* for 'gun', *to slump* meaning 'to stab' – he was able to contrast with his own vocabulary.

> On young black slang I have been told that the new word for stabbed is 'nanked'. I know it used to be 'jerked'. I would have probably said 'plunged' as in 'he copped for him and plunged him' or I may have said 'He pulled a blade and livened him up.'
>
> *(J.T.', e-mail to Tony Thorne, 20 April 2012)*

'J.T' knew *shiv* as *chiv*: as *chive* it dates from 1673, the 'sh' spelling and pronunciation is the preferred one in the USA (recorded since 1915) whence the younger speakers may well have acquired the term.

There is a degree of crossover: the Jamaican and MLE terms *hench* and *margar* (1910 in Caribbean usage), meaning 'well-built' and 'skinny' respectively, figured on the list of prisoners' slang recovered from Winchester Prison, while black gang members told this writer that they might use 'white' slang, picked up sometimes from fellow prisoners while on remand, such as *blag* 'to steal, rob or defraud' (1930) and *screw* for 'prison officer' (1812).

Folk-devils and moral panics

The pamphlets and canting dictionaries of the past, seeking to portray a hierarchy of criminal types organizing itself against the hapless citizen-victim, do not have precise modern equivalents. It is nowadays the print and electronic media rather than pamphleteers who report, mediate and foment the 'moral panics' that have for centuries served to demonize the 'other' and reassure the majority. An example of a recent moral panic based on the evocation of such a 'folk-devil' (a stigmatized, stereotypical 'other'), promoted by the press and publishing industry, was the 'chav' scare of 2004–5. Chavs – an underclass category characterized by fecklessness, shamelessness, aggression and petty criminality (equating roughly to Australian *bogans*, US *trailer trash*, Norwegian *Harrys*, French *lascars*) – were said to be identifiable by dress, accessories and to some extent by their language. The examples of 'chavspeak' put forward were not derived from any sort of serious research, but their deployment in a class-based representation of an outcast group has been analysed elsewhere (Bennett 2012).

Travellers and Gypsies in the UK did also become the objects of ambivalent and fairly sensationalist media attention in 2010 and 2011 when the reality TV series *My Big Fat Gypsy Wedding* was broadcast; and the *Daily Mail*, among other newspapers, ran reports of the eviction of Travellers from an illicit site. Language however was not focused upon, apart from the glossing of a few terms.

In addition, newspapers regularly present lists of youth slang ('yoofspeak', 'teen-talk') as evidence of intergenerational misunderstandings and of the frivolous or antisocial tendencies of the younger generation; and this, too, can be seen as a less spectacular, somewhat less sensationalist construction of an 'other' of whom the mainstream is invited to disapprove.

Conclusion

If the disparate material presented here demonstrates anything meaningful, it is that there is no uniform criminal slang but at least three distinct language varieties, or sociolects, being used by transgressive groups – the 'several tribes' – operating in the UK today. Direct comparisons with the ne'er-do-wells of previous centuries and their codes is difficult, not least because we have no reliable evidence concerning ethnicity, intergenerational differences or the authenticity of data for those groups. It is a truism to state that criminals today pursue some of the same activities as the rogues, beggars and vagabonds of Old England, and have the same need to use language to conceal those activities and confuse the representatives of law enforcement. It would be nice to imagine that there is a direct line of transmission whereby contemporary malefactors have inherited or actively acquired the language of their very distant predecessors, but this is not straightforwardly the case. So-called Shelta, dating back to the nineteenth century and probably older, is indeed still in use, retaining many features a century old, including admixtures of Romany. The slang shared on the street and in prison from the nineteenth to the twenty-first century by 'Cockneys' and what might be called 'mainstream' criminals persists, too, if only in the recollection of its users, but is not currently thought fashionable or deserving of media attention. Unsurprisingly, the multicultural youth vernaculars, comprising influential new intonations and new vocabularies, encompass an updated lexicon of violence, intoxication and lawlessness and, just like cant, allow users to play on their opacity when potentially hostile outsiders are listening in.

Note

1 My very sincere thanks to Paul Williams, Sean McNicholas, 'J.T.', Jonathon Green and Julie Coleman for the information and advice they have kindly provided.

Conclusion:

PART II

Slang in other English-speaking countries

Julie Coleman

This section discusses the slang used in a disparate range of other countries in which English is spoken. Some, such as Australia and New Zealand (Chapters 7 and 8), are often thought of as monolingual despite the survival of the Maori language, for example, along with others which are part of the rich linguistic variety that existed before colonization. These are countries that belong to Kachru's (1985) inner circle, in that English is the dominant first language. In other postcolonial contexts, such as India (Chapter 11), English co-exists alongside numerous other languages, largely functioning as an aspirational language, but also as a minority first language. Indian English is not a codified variety, so speakers of English in India look to other national forms for standard usage, largely British English. India thus belongs to Kachru's outer circle. In other national contexts, different varieties of English co-exist and challenge one another for local standard status. In Jamaica, for example (Chapter 10), there is a continuum between Standard English and Jamaican Creole; in Scotland (Chapter 9), Scottish English is the dominant form, although Scots and Scottish Gaelic are acknowledged as national vernaculars. Kachru's model is less helpful for these varieties of World English.

Given the difficulty of pinning down the standard language in these contexts, the challenge of identifying slang usage is harder still. In each case, the definition of slang is strongly influenced by the local history of English. For example, Moore notes that while general Australian dictionaries do not tend to use *slang* as a usage label, popular dictionaries of Australian slang abound. This dichotomy results from the changing status of Australian English: while British English provided the standard, anything distinctively Australian was seen as slang. When Australians began to take pride in Australian English, *slang* was avoided by some because of its negative connotations, but embraced by others as a linguistic emblem of the social solidarity, irreverence and informality inherent in the conception of Australian national identity. Scott observes similar patterns in the use of the label 'slang' with reference to non-standard forms in Scottish English. In both of these contexts, a conflict of interests discourages the labelling of marginalized varieties as slang. Identifying slang usage emphasizes the differentiation found within Scottish and Australian English, demonstrating the richness of the local linguistic situation, but it might also play into the hands of those who want to dismiss all distinctively national forms as slang.

There are a number of similarities between Moore's chapter, on Australian slang, and Bardsley's, on the slang of New Zealand, and these are in keeping with parallels between the history and development of English in these countries. Both chapters observe that the greater informality of everyday discourse in these contexts complicates the task of distinguishing between slang and colloquial language. Both also note that the group identity defined by this slang is on a national level, though Bardsley notes that New Zealand slang is receptive to Australian influence as well as to the influence of British and American slang. In both of these countries, the use of short-lived global slang is particularly characteristic of the language of young people.

Scott's focus is on the fascinating question of the contextuality of usage: what could be standard Scots in one context can function as slang in another setting. Within a functional continuum from Scots to Scottish Standard English, the identification of a single lexical item as slang requires a well-informed reading of the social context. Scottish slang creates group identity on an aspirational national level and may also indicate the political orientation of the speaker regarding the question of Scottish nationality. Not all of the slang used in Scotland is Scottish slang: distinctively national slang forms are found alongside the slang used in the rest of the United Kingdom (not all of which, in turn, is restricted to British slang).

Farquharson and Jones identify slang usage within the creole continuum found in Jamaica between Jamaican Creole and Standard English. They find that existing lexicons avoid the label 'slang', but that, nevertheless, numerous lexical items do function as slang within Jamaican Creole. This challenges the chronology of Schneider's (2007) last two stages in the evolution of World Englishes, in that differentiation has occurred before endonormative stabilization. While many of the semantic categories of Jamaican slang overlap with those noted in other chapters in this book, the lexis of homophobia appears to be particularly well developed in this context.

Like Jamaican slang, Indian slang has received little serious attention. Without a detailed codification of the local standard form, slang usage might seem trivial and barely worth commenting upon to speakers of Indian English, with the result that the meanings and social functions of Indian slang remain entirely inaccessible outside India. Lambert's chapter makes a useful distinction between unmarked forms in Indian English (some of which are slang elsewhere) and those terms that function as slang in Indian English. These are extremely various in origin, including borrowings from British, American and Australian slang alongside loans from indigenous languages and innovations from within the lexis of English.

It is clear that not all English slangs are equal in terms of their influence on one another. The influence of American slang has a global reach. All of the chapters in this section acknowledge the on-going influence of American slang in the country under discussion. However, this influence has by no means wiped out local differences. While some American slang may feed into the national slang idiom, it is often restricted to the transitory language of popular culture and youth, where it is used in conjunction with local forms. Several chapters refer to 'global slang': to slang that transcends national boundaries on the wings of globalized commerce and culture and, presumably, the internet. The last section of this volume returns to these issues, but for now it is sufficient to note that much of what could now be identified as 'global English slang' originated in Britain or, particularly from the mid twentieth century, in the United States, and that it is seasoned with terms from Jamaican slang to differing degrees in different locations.

It is, unfortunately, beyond the scope of this volume to survey slang usage in all English-speaking countries around the world. In addition to several popular publications on Irish slang (e.g. Share 1967; Murphy and O'Dea 2004), a number of papers have provided a starting point for more scholarly work (e.g. Lillo 2010). Some work has been undertaken on Canadian slang (e.g. Preston 1973), but documenting general national usage in Canada remains a priority (see Dollinger 2006–). The slang of English-speaking countries in Africa is also ripe for further research. For example, Kouega (2003) documents the multilingual slang used in English in Cameroon. Bembe and Beukes (2007) consider the use of slang in projecting personal identity among young English speakers in South Africa, and Sanga (2011: 192) notes a similar practice among musicians in Tanzania. Mesthrie (2013) also studies slang usage in South Africa, but in this case with specific reference to speakers of South African Indian English. In each of these geographical, linguistic and social contexts, a form of slang has emerged that combines distinct terms and features with a selection of those that are more widely used.

Publications on slang from around the world often focus on what is unique to their local context. It can be unclear whether this means that more widely used slang terms are omitted because they are not used or because they do not fit within a patriotic sense of what the national slang ought to be. It is also possible that they are not commented on because writers assume that their readers already know that these terms are used everywhere: they are not commented on, in other words, because there is nothing interesting to say about them with regard to the local context. This is one respect in which a sociolinguistic approach can be more successful than a citation-based approach, in that its focus is on the slang used in specific social situations. The pit into which sociolinguistic studies have sometimes fallen is the assumption that the slang observed is peculiar to that context. This is a mistake that speakers, learners and scholars of English also make on a daily basis: I have evidence of this slang term being used by an Australian, so it must be Australian slang.

7

AUSTRALIAN SLANG

Bruce Moore

To mention the topic 'slang in Australia now' is to be confronted with a challenging paradox. According to the two major Australian dictionaries, the *Australian Oxford Dictionary* (Moore 2004) and the *Macquarie Dictionary*, there is no slang in Australian English, unless it be slang of specified kinds – as *rhyming slang*, or *military slang*, occasionally *teenager slang*, and sometimes *US black slang*. No Australian words are given the label 'slang' in these dictionaries. And yet, while mainstream Australian lexicography will have no truck with the term *slang*, there is another flourishing Australian tradition of popular lexicography, which delights in the term 'Australian slang', and which produces numerous books that are all variants on the ur-title *The Book of Australian Slang*. Outside of the Cockney rhyming slang industry, there can be no other variety of English that has generated slang books in such quantity. Thus we have a seeming paradox: for mainstream Australian lexicography there is no Australian slang; for popular Australian lexicography, Australian English is full of slang.

In this chapter I draw on my research on Australian English as director of the Australian National Dictionary Centre from 1994 to 2011. This research includes work on a new edition of the *Australian National Dictionary* (Ramson 1988; hereafter AND), a dictionary based on historical principles, modelled on the *Oxford English Dictionary* (OED), and with only Australian words and meanings, as well as on various editions of the *Australian Oxford Dictionary* (including Moore 1997 and 2004). In the first part of the chapter I outline some representative areas of Australian slang; in the second part I address the issues raised by the paradox noted above.

The semantic coverage of Australian slang

As with slang in all Englishes, the human body and sexual activities are predictable areas of lexical density in Australian English. For 'arse, backside', AND included *acre*, *blot*, *bronze*, *dinger*, *freckle*, *ort*, and *quoit*. We can now add *bracket*, *clacker*, and *ginger* (from *ginger ale*, rhyming slang for 'tail'). A *browneye* is 'the obscene gesture of bending over and exposing one's buttocks and anus to someone', and the activity is typically described as *chucking a browneye*. For 'penis', AND had *old fellow* (used elsewhere but primarily Australian) and *sausage* (now known not to be exclusively Australian). We can now add *donk, percy* (from *point percy at the porcelain* for 'urinate'), *tockley, tonk,* and *tossle/tossil* (a variant of *tassle*). The scrotum can be called a *lolly bag* (literally 'a bag of sweets'); the testicles (via rhyming slang for 'knackers') can be called *jatz crackers* (a brand of dry biscuit) or *Kerry Packers* (from the name of the media businessman); semen is *sprog* (one step back, as it were, from the standard sense of 'baby/child'); and the female genitals and pubic hair are the *map of Tasmania*. *Root* in the sense 'sexual intercourse' generates *root rat* 'a sexually promiscuous male' and *root ute* 'a vehicle, usually a utility truck or panel van, regarded as a convenient place to have sex'. A 'male masturbator' is a *rod walloper*, to *flip oneself* is 'to masturbate', and a 'habitual masturbator' is a *flipwreck*. *Spunk* in the Australian sense, 'a sexually attractive person', is a good example of the way a term from Standard English (where it has the meaning 'courage, mettle' alongside the slang meaning 'seminal fluid') can develop local meanings. A *spunk bubble* in Australian English is also a sexually attractive person, and *spunk rat* is used to describe a young male who is handsome and sexually promiscuous (or so imagines himself). A sexually attractive person is also a *hornbag*. A sexually promiscuous person *bangs like a dunny* (or *shithouse*) *door* (where a *dunny* is 'an outdoor toilet').

Plonk and *grog* are two common Australian terms for alcoholic drink, although the international terms *booze* and *piss* are also widely used. *Plonk* is possibly an alteration of French *vin blanc* (but perhaps a form of *plinkety plonk*), and while it is now used in British English it is originally Australian. *Grog* ('alcoholic liquor of any kind, especially beer') is a generalized use of British *grog* 'a drink consisting of spirits (originally rum) and water'. *Amber fluid* is another term for 'beer'. Beer that is consumed outside a pub can be bought in a *tinnie* or *tube* 'a small can', a *tallie* 'a tall bottle', or a *stubbie* 'a small squat bottle'. In Australian Aboriginal English in the 1960s the word *goom* (sometimes spelt *goon*) appeared as a term for cheap alcohol (often methylated spirits), and this word came from a Queensland Aboriginal language where it meant 'water'. The word has spread into the slang of Standard Australian, and generated such terms as *goon cask* or *goon sack* for 'wine cask' and *goomie* or *goonie* for 'an alcoholic'. For the party drinking-game *goon of fortune* (a play on the name of the television quiz show 'Wheel of Fortune'), *goon sacks* of various kinds of wine are attached to a rotary clothes hoist, the players are positioned around the perimeter, the clothes hoist is spun, and the players must drink an agreed amount of alcohol from the cask that is nearest to them when the clothes hoist stops spinning. A great thirst for an alcoholic drink can be expressed by such idioms as: *dry as a dead dingo's donger, dry as a kookaburra's Khyber,* and *dry as a pommy's bath towel* (*pommy*, often abbreviated to *pom*, is 'a British, especially English, migrant' and more generally 'any British person'). Drunkenness can be expressed by a variety of words and idioms: *off one's face, pissed as a parrot, rotten, shickered, stonkered*; and especially by a series of idioms beginning with *full as* (and with *full* potentially standing for 'drunk', 'replete with food', or 'overcrowded'): *full as a bull, full as a family po* ('chamber pot'), *full as a footy final, full as a goog* ('egg'), *full as a pommy complaint box, full as a state school hat-rack* (a state school is a 'public school'), *full as a tick*, and so on. After a night of heavy drinking you might find that you have *a mouth like the bottom of a cocky's cage*.

Slang terms are de rigueur for those regarded as outsiders. Immediately after the Second World War, migrants who were not *poms* usually came from other European countries, and they were often called *reffos* (from 'refugee') and *balts* (from 'Baltic States'). The most common term, however, is *wog*. The most recent Oxford University Press dictionaries from the UK label *wog* as '*British, offensive*' with the definition 'a person who is not white'. This definition is not satisfactory for Australia, where the word had taken a somewhat different direction. In the 1950s and 1960s in Australia *wog* came to be used to describe migrants of southern European origin, especially those from Italy or Greece. Later, the usage expanded to include migrants of Middle Eastern origin. *Wog* would not be used in Australia to describe a person from India or Pakistan, whereas this is not the case in Britain. Partly because migrants themselves have often taken ownership of the term (especially through plays and television programmes with titles such as 'Wogs Out of Work') it does not carry in Australia the degree of offensiveness that is present in British usage. Australian English has developed a number of compounds based on *wog*. Soccer is often called *wogball*; *wogspeak* describes a variety of Australian English that includes pronunciations influenced by Greek and other migrant languages; a *wog mansion* or *wog palace* is a large and vulgar house, often using southern European architectural features such as elaborate columns; *wog telly* is television broadcast by SBS (the Special Broadcasting Service that has programmes in many community languages); a *wog chariot* (or *wogmobile*) is a hotted-up car; *wog food* is cuisine of southern European or Middle Eastern origin.

Australian English is rich in words for fools. *Boofhead* (and its abbreviated form *boof*) come from a Standard English word *bufflehead* meaning 'fool', in turn from *buffalo head* – which helps to explain why Australian *boofhead* can refer either to a person with a large head or to a person with a head that has very little in it. *Dill* is Australian for 'a fool' and comes from a British dialect adjective *dilly* that meant 'strange, cranky'. *Drongo* was an unsuccessful racehorse in the 1920s (perhaps named after the black bird called the *drongo*), and by the beginning of the Second World War the word *drongo* was being used for a raw and inexperienced Air Force recruit; it soon spread into the wider community as a term for a fool or a hopeless case.

Folly is expressed in many idioms, including *as mad as a gumtree full of galahs, not the full two bob* ('a two shilling coin' in pre-decimal currency), *to have kangaroos in the top paddock, as silly as a two-bob watch*, and *barmy as a bandicoot*. *Mad as a cut snake* and *mad as a meat axe* are double-barrelled in that 'mad' can refer to folly or to anger. Incompetence is part of the field of folly: *couldn't train a choko vine over a country dunny* (the *choko* is a green pear-shaped vegetable); *couldn't organize a chook raffle* (a raffle with the prize of a frozen chicken, usually held in a pub); *couldn't knock the dags off a sick canary* (a jocular transfer of the standard Australian sense of *dag* 'a lock of wool clotted with dung on the hinder parts of a sheep').

Madness and eccentricity are conveyed by variants on the idiom *short of* (as in the worldwide variant *a sandwich short of a picnic*). Although this is now an idiom that is known and used throughout the world, the most recent research reveals that it had its origin in Australia. Australian variants include: *a couple of tinnies short of a slab* (a *tinnie* is 'a can of beer', and a *slab* is 'a carton containing 24 cans of beer'); *a few snags short of a barbie* (a *snag* is 'a sausage' and a *barbie* is 'a barbecue'); *a sheep short of a paddock*; *a stubbie short of a sixpack* (a *stubbie* is 'a small squat-shaped bottle of beer').

A distinctive suite of Australian slang words occurs with the numerous terms for 'a pair of close-fitting male swimming briefs made of stretch fabric such as nylon or lycra'. Speedo was originally an Australian company, and the swimming costume became known both in Australia and internationally as *speedos*. For many years some form of *speedos* had become the standard male swimming costume, but fashions change and in the 1980s *board shorts* (or *boardies*) became very popular among the young, initially because of their associations with the surfing tradition. Real surfers wore *boardies*, whereas *speedos* were worn by what the surfers called *clubbies* – the members of surf lifesaving clubs who controlled the beaches and tried to make things difficult for surfers (according to surfers!). It seems to have been during this period of conflict between *speedos* and *boardies* that the *speedo* variety developed an extraordinary number of risqué or simply curious synonyms: *blue pointers* (with allusion to the shark), *dick daks* (*daks* is an Australian term for 'trousers'), *dick pointers* (sometimes abbreviated to *DPs*), *dick pokers, dick stickers, dick togs* (sometimes abbreviated to *DTs*), *fish frighteners, lolly bags* (cf. the sense 'scrotum' noted above), *noodle benders, scungies, sluggers, sluggos* (with allusion to *slug* meaning 'penis'), *slug huggers*. The 'cheeky' term *budgie smugglers* made its first appearance in Australian English in 1998, and within a few years had become the dominant term.

The suffix -ie (or -y) and -o

Use of the –ie (or –y) and –o suffix with abbreviated forms of words is not exclusive to Australia, although it is more common in Australia than elsewhere, and is used in distinctive ways in Australia. Elsewhere such forms are typically hypocoristics (as *birdie, doggie*), but in Australia they serve primarily as markers of informality, and among speakers they operate as a code of familiarity, common understanding, and solidarity.

AND listed over 100 words with the –ie suffix, including *barbie* 'barbecue', *coldie* 'a cold drink of beer', *kindy* 'kindergarten', *mossie* 'mosquito', *prezzie* 'present', *sickie* 'a sick day off work', *tinny* 'a can of beer' or 'a boat with an aluminium hull'. More recent examples include *firie* 'a firefighter', *leaguie* 'a rugby league supporter', *meatie* '(in rugby) a try' (from rhyming slang *meat pie*), *parkie* 'a homeless park dweller', *shockie* 'a shock absorber', *tradie* 'tradesman', *vollie* 'a volunteer', and *wettie* 'a wetsuit'.

The synonymous –o suffix (which has its nineteenth-century origin in sellers' calls, as *milk-oh/milk-o* and *rabbitoh/rabbit-o*) is not used as much as –ie, but it has produced significant words in the past (AND includes *arvo* 'afternoon', *compo* 'compensation', *demo* 'demonstration', *garbo* 'garbage collector', *muso* 'musician', and *salvo* 'a member of the Salvation Army'). The suffix continues to be productive: *ambo* 'ambulance officer', *bowlo* 'bowling club', *gyno* 'gynaecologist', *lammo* 'lamington' ('a small chocolate and coconut-covered cake') and *touro* 'tourist'.

Rhyming slang

Australian rhyming slang developed during the first decades of the twentieth century and was especially productive during the Second World War. Names have always been a popular source for rhyming slang; AND included *Adrian Quist* 'pissed' (Australian tennis player, 1913–91), *Captain Cook* 'a look', *Ned Kelly* 'belly', and *Oscar Asche* 'cash' (Australian actor, 1871–1936). Shortened forms are common: *Noah's ark* 'shark' now usually appears as *noah*; *on one's Pat Malone* 'on one's own' often appears as *on one's pat*; *septic tank* for 'Yank, an American' is now usually abbreviated to *septic* (and sometimes further altered to *seppo*).

Recent research has documented many examples of rhyming slang that were not included in AND. Examples from names include *Harold Holt* 'a bolt; a quick exit' (Australian prime minister who disappeared while swimming in 1967), *Sydney Harbour* 'barber', and *Wally Grout* 'shout' in the sense 'paying for a round of drinks' (Australian Test wicketkeeper, 1927–68). Other kinds include *billy lid* 'kid', *dapto dog* 'wog' (after the greyhound racetrack at Dapto), *dropkick* 'prick', *juicy fruit* 'a root; sexual intercourse' (from the name of a chewing gum), and *sausage roll* 'goal'.

Australian English has continued to produce new rhyming slang, but not as much as in the past, and to many Australians it feels old-fashioned. Of relatively recent creation are *Barry Crocker* 'shocker' (Australian entertainer), *Lionel Rose* 'nose' (Australian boxer, 1948–2011), and *Reg Grundys* 'undies' (from the name of the Australian television producer Reg Grundy), with variants *grundies*, *reginalds*, and *reggies*. *Stuart Diver* 'survivor' (the sole survivor of the landslide at Thredbo ski village in 1997) provides a rare example of the name being thematically linked in some way to the rhyming slang meaning.

Slang's banishment

Here, then, is a veritable 'God's plenty' of slang. Even in this brief sampling, one can see that there is plenty of material to fill those numerous books of Australian slang. Indeed, in the popular imagination there certainly was and is a category of 'Australian slang'. In the late nineteenth century there appeared the anonymous *Sydney Slang Dictionary* (1882) and Crowe's *Australian Slang Dictionary* (1895). In the mid twentieth century Sidney Baker produced three editions of *A Popular Dictionary of Australian Slang* between 1941 and 1943. Since 1990 more than 20 such books have been published. Any study of these slang books would confirm the richness of the field, and the predictable fact that it is male-dominated in both its semantic categories and its actual usage. Some of it is in the process of disappearing, as with old favourites such as *cobber* 'friend' and *bonzer* 'beaut, great'. While the fading of individual items prompts some to predict a general demise of Australian slang, this is not supported by the evidence. Similarly, Australian English takes in numerous slang terms from American English or global English, and while these might in their early use be obviously marked for 'Americanness', they are soon naturalized. A regular complaint tradition has it that Australian slang is being swamped by American slang, with the blame usually being levelled at the susceptibility of the young. This tradition has been regularly heard since the beginning of the twentieth century. It was especially strong in the 1950s when young males were called *bodgies* (from Australian *bodgie* in the sense 'something flawed, inferior, secondhand') because of their imitation of American style, culture, and language. Australian slang, however, has survived all this.

Given this widespread evidence of slang, and the popular embracing of slang in numerous books, why does mainstream Australian lexicography not use the term 'slang' to describe the terms and idioms that are included in these popular books? There are a number of reasons. Some are historical and cultural; some have to do with the special nature of the Australian lexicon; and some derive from the difficulties modern dictionaries have in drawing lines between the labels *colloquial* and *slang*, and overlaying these with other labels such as *derogatory*, *offensive*, and even *jocular*.

The historical and cultural reasons have to do with attitudes towards Australian English, especially those current in the first half of the twentieth century. In the nineteenth century, 'Australianisms' were typically designated as *colonial slang*, *colonial language*, *colonial phraseology* and occasionally as *Australian slang*. While these designations were primarily descriptive of new and unusual elements in the language, they often suggested a falling away from a perceived British standard. What was occasional criticism in the colonial period became ubiquitous in the post-colonial period, when Australian slang was often the target of criticism by people visiting from Britain. Within Australia, such views became internalized, and Australian words and meanings across a wide-ranging register were judged as being sub-standard and 'incorrect', by reference to British models (Moore 2008: 131–52). There is nothing especially surprising in this, and it fits neatly into Schneider's predictions about the 'complaint tradition' in a postcolonial society (Schneider 2007: 43). What is surprising, I think, is that even when most elements of the complaint tradition disappeared, and when Australian English became largely naturalized and accepted, the causes and instruments of the complaint tradition were not forgotten or forgiven. The British imperial linguistic yoke might have been cast off, but the Australian cultural memory still carries with it the whips and shackles of its British-controlled past, and especially the assumptions about social class that drove the linguistic model.

Something of this cultural ball-and-chain lay behind the decision of the editors of the first edition of the *Macquarie Dictionary* (1981) to use *colloq.* for a range of words that would normally attract labels such as *slang*, *vulgar*, and *coarse*. One of the editors comments in the introduction:

> In this dictionary no word is labelled slang, vulgar, coarse, illiterate. Sub-standard or nonstandard ... We may be thought to have ducked a responsibility, but our view has been that it is unrealistic in a lexicographer to interpose

personal judgment or even committee judgment, on the basis of taste, between a man and the words he swears by, thus departing from those canons of compromised objectivity which are all the lexicographer, poor harmless drudge that he is, has left to defend himself with.

(Macquarie Dictionary 1981: 15)

While this sentence is pitched in terms of general principles, there is a bristliness about the rejection of terms such as 'slang' and 'vulgar', and an incipient egalitarianism in the embrace of the 'man and the words he swears by'. The general principles could be applied to the slang/colloquial element of any 'new' English, but they have a special resonance in Australia because of the earlier commonplace equation of 'Australianism' and 'slang'.

In addition to these issues, there is also evidence of a persistent and widespread belief within Australian lexicography that the Australian lexicon does not fit neatly into the conventional boxes of *slang* and *colloquial*. In the introduction to his *Australian Language* Baker wrote: 'If we class as slang every Australian term that sounds strange to English ears, practically the complete body of our language will fall into that category' (Baker 1945: 18). The first general dictionary edited in Australia was Johnston (1976), which added much Australian material to the English text on which it was based. Unlike the dictionaries that followed, Johnston gave some Australian words a *slang* label and some a *colloquial* label, even while admitting in the introduction how problematic these pigeon-holings are:

> The abbreviation (Aust. sl.) has been used with a wide range of meaning, and some expressions so labelled will be found in formal contexts: many Australians make no sharp distinctions between formal and informal speech.
>
> *(Johnston 1976: xxi)*

It was much the same argument about the range of contexts in which a word might be used that in part led W.S. Ramson to eschew register labels in the AND:

> We have taken the view that, while it is sometimes a proper part of the descriptive process to use a subject label to indicate that a word is restricted to a particular field of activity, there is a danger that using labels to indicate register can be over-interpretative and over-restrictive. This seems particularly true of Australian English, which allows easy movement between formal and informal usage ... Labels like *coarse, colloq., derog., slang*, and *vulgar*, which tend unnecessarily to categorize, have therefore been omitted.
>
> *(Ramson 1988: vii)*

The second edition of *The Australian Concise Oxford Dictionary* (Ramson et al. 1992; hereafter ACOD2) used the standard range of register labels, including *colloq., sl., coarse sl., derog.*, and *offens*. Ramson's attitude towards the Australian material can be gauged by comparing it with the first edition (Turner 1987; hereafter ACOD1).

ACOD1 marked the following Australian words as *slang*: *bludger* 'a loafer', *bonzer* 'beaut, great', *bung* 'broken, ruined', *chunder* 'vomit', *dag* 'an amusing person, a character', *drongo* 'a fool', *furphy* 'a rumour', *ocker* 'an uncivilized Australian', *plonk*, *pommy*, *rort* 'a trick, a racket', *sheila* 'woman, young woman', *snag* 'a sausage', *wog*. In ACOD2, these words are marked *colloq.* or are unmarked, with the exception of *sheila* (labelled *sl. offens.*) and the racist sense of *wog* (which is labelled *sl. offens.*). Whereas the *slang* label is quite common in ACOD1 for Australian words, it is rare in ACOD2 except for words that have the extra label *offens*. Thus *root* 'to have sexual intercourse' is *coarse sl.* in ACOD2 (and *vulgar sl.* in ACOD1).

When I came to the editing of ACOD3 (Moore 1997), I took these discernible trends to their logical conclusion – a conclusion that was in harmony with the cultural imperative of not denigrating the distinctively Australian elements of the language. In the preceding decade, and continuing into the 1990s, there was clearly an increase in the number of terms regarded as *offensive*, especially on racist grounds. *Coarse slang* had become a label applied to the taboo group that included words for sexual parts of the body, sexual activity, and bodily functions. Once the *offensive* and *coarse slang* words were accounted for, a distinction between *slang* words and *colloquial* words for what was left was not especially illuminating or useful (languages of particular groups are signalled, as is customary, by subject labels such as *Horseracing* and *Two-up*). I replaced *sl.* with *colloq.*, and as a consequence *coarse sl.* became *coarse colloq.* In these cases, the solution to practical issues of lexicographical methodology and theory coincided with the imperatives of overt or latent nationalism. The *slang* label was banished.

What is a slang group?

Because slang is often the language of a minority group, a group that must negotiate its identity in relation to a wider society, it now seems self-evident to us that the language of such a group will embody and express the values of the group in a manner that often seems aggressive and over-lexicalized to outsiders. Of course all language encodes cultural values, but in a large group it will hardly be necessary for slang to have such an overt identity-defining function. It is no doubt for this reason that it never occurs to us to ask what 'British' values are encapsulated in British slang or what 'American' values are encapsulated in American slang. We ask such questions only when we examine the language of minority groups within those cultures, often describing their language and the values it expresses as being in a state of conflict with the dominant culture.

It seems to me that the question of what slang *is* becomes much more complex when we are dealing with postcolonial societies such as Australia which, unlike the United States, still have problematic ties with the mother country and the mother tongue – for example, Australia remains a constitutional monarchy and Queen Elizabeth II is Queen of Australia. When we look at the tradition of popular books of slang in Australia, it soon becomes clear that the range of words included is much wider than would be contained in any usual definition of slang. A clue to what is going on here is found in the typical comments in the introductions to the books. Baker called his first book *A Popular Dictionary of Australian Slang*, but in the opening words of his 'Author's Foreword' he signals the issue of category distinctions:

> Slang is too small a word to describe the evolution of a new way of speaking, of a national idiom. But it is a flexible term, and for the purpose of this brief dictionary it must be taken to include many Australian expressions that have long since ceased to be slang in the strict sense of that word and have become 'standard'.
>
> *(Baker 1941: n.p.)*

Hunter (2004: introduction) writes: 'Slang is the casual, spoken language of a country ... and generally reflects the personality and history of a country'. Similarly, Dawson (1999: vii) writes that 'Aussies coined and adopted slang with great gusto, no doubt as a means of cocking a snook at authority and at social niceties favoured by the mother country.' In such accounts, 'Australian slang' is very much coterminous with 'distinctive Australian words', and distinctive Australian words are those that encapsulate Australian values and attitudes, and are also carriers of Australian history – the 'national idiom', as Baker called it in 1941. These words fulfill the function of being markers of national identity in a way that is hardly distinguishable from the identity-forming functions of language in smaller groups.

In the final paragraph of *Speaking Our Language: The Story of Australian English* (Moore 2008: 206), I offered a 'baker's dozen' of the main words that I feel carry and embody a history of Australian values and attitudes: *battler* 'a person who struggles valiantly to make a fair living', *bludger* 'a person who lives on the efforts of others', *dinkum* 'genuine, true', *dob* 'to inform on someone', *larrikin* 'a person who acts with disregard for social convention', *mate* 'a very close friend', *no worries* 'no bother, no trouble', *ocker* 'a boorish Australian male', *rort* 'a dishonest practice', *she'll be right* 'all will be well', *tall poppy* 'a successful person who attracts envy', *true blue* 'genuine, Australian', and *wowser* 'a puritanical fanatic, a killjoy'. I would probably now replace *ocker* with *bogan* 'an uncultured and unsophisticated person'– *bogan* has been the most 'successful' Australianism of the past decade. Those who accept the usual international divisions of the English lexicon would no doubt say that we have here a collection of the standard, the colloquial, and the slang. Yet it is what unites the words in this list, rather than what divides them, that makes them significant markers of Australianness. They are all in the popular slang books.

If slang is typically the language of a sub-group, then a national lexicon that continues to position itself in contrast to the language of the wider international group certainly presses all the buttons of one commonly accepted definition of 'slang' – even when the gatekeepers of the national lexicon, the harmless drudges, know that this definition is *a stubbie short of a sixpack*.

8

SLANG IN GODZONE (AOTEAROA–NEW ZEALAND)

Dianne Bardsley

> New words or words used in a new way can sharpen our wits, coruscate what would otherwise be dull, or enliven our means of communication.
>
> *(Rose 1995: 6)*

Slang has been regarded as such a feature of New Zealand English that for many decades the variety's distinctiveness was reputedly based on its informal and slang content, rather than other features such as its Maori loanwords. But while slang and colloquial terms are often seen to represent a national character or identity, lexis from all registers and contexts, together with phonology, has set New Zealand apart from Mother Britain and other colonial Englishes from early settlement times and into the twentieth century:

> The young colonial naturally laughs at the dialect of the new–chum who is so frequently met on the Quay.
>
> *(New Zealand Free Lance 5 September 1908: 12)*

In the twenty-first century, newcomers from Britain and other nations are still perplexed at vocabulary items not previously encountered. Sampling *electric puha* 'cannabis', being a *poozler* 'fossicker' and having the *dry horrors* 'hangover' leave the uninitiated completely lost. The source of terms and citations used here is the 40,000 headword database of New Zealand English held in the New Zealand Dictionary Centre, Victoria University of Wellington, which is the provenance of material for numerous dictionaries and thesauruses, including those of Orsman (1997), Deverson and Kennedy (2004) and Deverson (2012).

The beginning

It is likely that Maori and Moriori ocean voyagers discovered and settled the islands that make up New Zealand around the thirteenth century. Other than missionaries, the first Europeans to have substantial interaction with Maori were the eighteenth-century whalers and sealers, who brought with them a style of life and a Western culture, language and value system that were to change the Maori and Maori culture forever. The southern whalers introduced a form of slang known as 'whaler's Maori'. Of the whalers, Wakefield wrote:

> their whole language is in fact an argot, or slang, almost unintelligible to a stranger … every article of trade with the natives has its slang term, in order that they may converse with each other respecting a purchase without initiating the native into their calculations. Thus pigs and potatoes were respectively represented by '*grunters*' and '*spuds*;' guns, powder, blankets, pipes, and tobacco, by '*shooting-sticks, dust, spreaders, steamers*,' and '*weed*;' A chief was called a '*nob*;' a slave, a '*doctor*;' a woman, a '*heifer*;' a girl, a '*titter*;' and a child, a '*squeaker*.'
>
> *(Wakefield 1845 I: 318)*

The exploits of these southern seafarers earned dysphemistic slang terms for Russell, the principal settlement, which was widely known as the *Hellhole of the South Pacific*, *Blackguard's* or *Blaggard's Bay* and the *Devil's Playground*. While New Zealand has always been known as the Antipodes of Britain, as Britain's geographic opposite, it is essentially an English-speaking nation with predominantly English customs and culture among its *Pakeha* 'European' and Maori citizens.

With a land area approximately equal to Great Britain (27 million hectares), the population of New Zealand is still less than five million. Significant for a tiny isolated island nation is the number of slang names it has attracted – including *Godzone,* 'God's own country', *Kiwiland, Maoriland, Moaland, Pig Island, Quaky Isles, Shaky Isles, the Shakies, Wowserland*, 'puritanical nation' and, from the nineteenth century, *Fernland* and *Fuller's Earth*.

Although pioneer groups belonged to particular occupations that all developed their own slang, such slang was actually distinguishable from technical language or jargon. Dalmatian gumdiggers and their families, for instance, named English settlers *Maslars*, 'butter-eaters'. Pioneering bush-fellers and goldminers introduced many slang terms, and the rural domain was, and still is, so dominant in New Zealand that much of its slang and technical language passed into general national usage. It was in the rural sector that slang relating to the Irish has been most obvious.

Nineteenth-century New Zealand women were able to vote before women from other Western nations, and have been appointed to the highest offices in the land, including the positions of prime minister, governor-general, attorney-general, chief justice and speaker of the House. Despite that, much of the general slang in the nation is that initiated and used by males, the stereotype of which is a *hard case* 'fun-loving eccentric', a *real Kiwi bloke* or a *southern man* 'strong, silent type', who refers to his wife as *the handbrake* 'spoilsport'. Following the 1941 publication of Sidney J. Baker's *New Zealand Slang: A Dictionary of Colloquialisms*, amateur lexicographers began to gather words for short slang glossaries, many of which have supported the stereotype of the *kiwi bloke*, particularly since many slang terms developed during both the First and Second World Wars or came from the rural domain with a principally isolated male demographic.

The twenty-first century

Features of New Zealand slang are its national spread and its staying power – Antipodean slang survives. Apart from some restricted slang of minorities, certain demographic groups and marginal groups, new slang spreads quickly throughout a small nation of fewer than five million people. An example from 2011 is the slang that was applied to, and that which developed, around the devastating Canterbury earthquakes. Very soon the names coined for the most damaging major quake, *Old Bucky* and *grand mal*, were readily recognized and used so widely as to become national colloquialisms. At the same time, the city of Christchurch became nationally known as *Shaky City*. In the media, houses and other buildings were *munted*, a New Zealand slang term for ruined, and they were *buggered, puckerooed, rooted* and *stuffed*. An unexpected heavy and damaging snowstorm following the quake became known as *the icing on the quake*. Devastated historic buildings were described as *dungers*, a term usually reserved for aged vehicles. *Muntage* and *megamuntage*, used by local and national politicians to describe the damage, were used nationally, while farmers who moved to the city to clean up silt liquefaction and remove debris became the *Farmy Army*.

New Zealanders are by nature travellers prepared to take on long-distance travel. The initialism *OE* (overseas experience) and *the big OE* are part of the national slang in New Zealand, a product of its geographical isolation from the rest of the English-speaking world. The expression is in general use for an overseas holiday, whereas a working holiday or extended time out of the country is usually known as *the big OE*. *OEers* are described as *oe-ing*, being *on their OE* or *doing their OE*. At the same time, *Pom* and *homey/homy* are used for British immigrants; *whinging Pom, ten-pound Pom* and *ping-pong Pom* being familiar collocative terms.[1]

Despite geographical isolation, English-speaking New Zealanders have used global slang since settlement times. While Australian slang usage is most common, some slang from Britain and, to a lesser extent, the United States has always had currency. Adopted terms, e.g. *random* 'unpredictable' or *YOLO* 'you only live once', are used principally by young people, while the older age group will still use dated slang like *plonk* 'wine' and *couch potato* 'passive television watcher'. *Bro* is not used in New Zealand for a white, middle-class, male student or party-goer, but is a camaraderie term for friend or family member, particularly among Maori. Generally, hip-hop slang is not used in New Zealand.

The lexicographical labelling of slang terms in New Zealand English has not been consistent, as is the case with Australian English, where there is little distinction between formal and informal usage. In the *New Zealand Oxford Dictionary* 2004, the broad style label 'colloquial' included slang terms, while 'coarse colloquial', 'derogatory' and 'offensive' indicated levels of usage within the category. In the *New Zealand Oxford Thesaurus* 2005, terms such as *stuff* 'to damage' are labelled slang or derogatory. A style note reads that slang is used for a very informal usage or one which is restricted to a particular group, while derogatory is a usage that is intentionally insulting.

Morphology or forms of New Zealand slang

The morphology of New Zealand slang includes borrowing and blending with te reo Maori (Maori language), hybridizing using an analogous aspect from te reo Maori, abbreviations and shortened forms, hypocorisms, alliteration and rhyming slang.

Borrowing and blending with te reo Maori

It is most unlikely that terms in this group will be used outside of New Zealand, hence the claim for them as the most significant contributors to a national slang. In saying that, some terms are more transparent than others – *kete case*, for example, an alternative to *basket case* 'a person or object unable to function', *kete* 'basket', is relatively easily understood. Te reo Maori is taught in schools and the language is in common use in all media, while two television channels are dedicated to Maori usage. At least six in every thousand New Zealand English terms are Maori loanwords, but of these many are treated in a jocular or slang manner (Macalister 2005: 191). *Waka* 'canoe' is a common element in slang blends and compounds, examples including *waka-jumper* 'a politician who changes parties' and *wakaport* 'waterfront'. Another common usage is *half pai* 'incomplete' or 'half and half', from *pai* 'good'. *Puku* 'stomach' is another term used in New Zealand English slang, while a *pie cart* (a mobile café) is known as a *kai cart* from *kai* 'food'. *Jack Nohi* is the New Zealand English term for the globally used *nosey parker*, sometimes abbreviated to *nohi* 'nose'. Other examples of Maori-English blends and compounds include *hippietanga* 'hippie identity' and *Maussie*, 'a Maori resident in Australia' (in New Zealand an Australian is commonly known as an Aussie).

The hybridizing of a Maori term using an analogous aspect is common. A Maori tribal prefix, *Ngati*, 'tribe, clan', is used as a prefix indicating humorously or ironically a quasi-Maori tribe or entity, e.g. *Ngati DB* (Dominion Breweries) 'beer drinkers', *Ngati Drongo* 'incompetent people', *Ngati Naughty* 'lawbreakers' and *Ngati Nimby*, 'not in my back yard' for people objecting to potentially devaluing developments in their neighbourhood. *Tutae* 'excrement' is commonly used, particularly in the phrase *tutae happens*.

Poofanui is the name given to the prestigious beach town Pauanui, from *poof* 'a person with an overinflated sense of importance' (an additional sense in New Zealand English). Parodies of Maori place names are also common, such as *Whykickamoocow* for *Waikikamukau*. The reduction of polysyllabic Maori proper nouns to monosyllabic forms is another type – *Kune* (Ohakune), *Naki* or *The Naki* (Taranaki) and *Tiki* for Opotiki are in common usage. Traditionally a Maori protest march by foot to Parliament is a *hikoi*, and in 2009 motorcyclists protesting the rise in motorcycle licensing fees began the first of many *bikois* to Parliament. Other terms borrowed from Maori and used as slang with a change of word class include *hoha* 'fed up' and 'a person who is a nuisance', *taihoa* 'slow to act' and *puckeroo*, from *pakuru*, 'to break or be broken'. Such terms only have currency and effect in a New Zealand context, where at least a rudimentary knowledge of te reo Maori is helpful. Maori individuals also coin slang terms in English, an example being *howlybag* 'crybaby' or 'coward'.

Abbreviations, ellipses and shortened forms

Acronyms and initialisms are increasingly in circulation. The acronym form *SOOB* 'Small Owner Operated Brothel' arrived with the legalization of prostitution in 2003. *JAFA* is an acronym which stands for Just Another Fucking Aucklander, while the opposite *RONZ* represents Rest of New Zealand, both terms being coined in response to the rapid growth of Auckland, the nation's largest city. Other abbreviated usage includes *a into g* (*arse into gear*) 'to start action', the legendary *K Road*, (Karangahape Road, also parodied as *Gay Road*), *KF* 'paedophile' (from *kiddie fucker*) and *P*, 'pure form', a term for methamphetamine.

Hypocorisms and related forms

Known variously as clippies, pet-names and diminutive forms, hypocorisms in New Zealand are commonly of three forms, the most common being a monosyllabic base with -ie or -y added, as in *Gissy* (the city Gisborne). A second common form is a pet-name base preceded by the definite article (as in *The Beehive* for the House of Parliament or *The Cake Tin* for a sports stadium), while among young people, a more recent form is a monosyllabic or polysyllabic base with a sibilant ending, as in *Dunners* for the city Dunedin. Although an -ie or -y ending is most common, alternative or synonymous forms, such as *corrie*, *corro* and *corru* (for the ubiquitous building material corrugated iron) are sometimes used.

While hypocorisms have been a feature of New Zealand English since the 1830s, such lexical items are increasingly used and are increasingly diversified in the twenty-first century, being applied to well-known figures such as sportspeople and politicians, for places such as *Palmie* (Palmerston) or *Remmers* (Remuera), products such as *voddy* (vodka), *biggie* (big deal), and TV programmes, such as *Shorty*, *Landy* or *Streetie* (all hypocoristic forms for the soap *Shortland Street*). Some place names show a departure from the common forms: *Cardy Capital, Cardy Town*, 'the stereotype of grey cardigan worn by the capital city's bureaucracy'. *Wellies, Wello, Wellers* and *Wellytown* are all hypocorisms of the capital city, Wellington. In general, pun forms are not usual, the best-known possibly being *Taradise* (Taranaki + paradise) and *Nakiwood* (Taranaki + Hollywood) and *Waiberia* (Waiouru + Siberia). Blends include *Rotovegas* (Rotorua + Las Vegas) which relates to the flashy ribbon development of the town and its accommodation, while *Te Texas* (Te Teko + Texas) connotes the 'back country' or frontier aspects of the town.

In the public forum, no section of a newspaper is exempt from hypocorism: forms such as *steppie/steppy* 'stepmother/stepfather' are found in death notices, along with *streetie* 'street inhabitant' in obituaries. *Glassie* 'glass-washer', *hospo* 'worker in the hospitality industry' and *skiddy* 'sawmill skid worker' are examples from Situations Vacant columns in the *Dominion Post* and *New Zealand Herald* newspapers. One even finds, in the newspaper columns, a city mayor referring to his city as *Wangas* (Whanganui).

Hypocoristic business and brand names also feature widely. As elsewhere, people speak of a *Beamer* (BMW), a *Steiny* 'Steinlager beer' and *Vinnies* or *St Vinnies* 'St Vincent de Paul'. Terms for religious groups and sects include *benders* or *Doolans* (from *Mickey Doolan*) 'Catholic', *Pressies* 'Presbyterians', *Sallies* 'Salvation Army' and *Scarfies* 'members of the Exclusive Brethren' (from their distinctive head-coverings), along with *Happyclappies* ('members of charismatic denominations)'. However, the widespread use of hypocorism in the media is not a wholly popular trend:

> I am fed up with 'Palmie' for Palmerston North, 'chrissie' for Christmas and 'the heke' for Waiheke Island. Jim Mora [National Radio host] does not sound like us.
>
> *(New Zealand Listener 24 February 2007: 4)*

This is not a singular view. Other critics include Booker Prize-winning Keri Hulme, who referred to hypocorism as 'this godzone babytalk' (Hulme 1986: 31).

The nation-wide aspect of hypocoristic use is seen still further in the naming of residents such as *Far-downers*, with residents of Carterton being termed *Cartertonics*, while those from *Ashburton/Ashvegas* are known as *Ashvegans*. The term for university students, *scarfies*, is used nationally and now refers to all university students and not just those attending the University of Otago, where it originated.

Compounds are often used, for example *clan lab* 'clandestine laboratory', also known as *cookie kitchen*. Compounds where both parts are hypocoristic are also found, such as *walkie-chalkie* 'parking warden who marks car tyres with chalk' and *undie-5-hundie* (a 500m sprint street race in underwear). New compounds are also often formed from existing hypocorisms, as in *Westie*, which is derived from the notional West Aucklander. *Westie chic, westie chick, westieism, westiemobile* and *westieness* commonly feature in mass media.

Owners of second homes, holiday houses or weekend cottages (known as *baches* and *cribs*) are called *bachies* and *cribbies*, while polysemous hypocoristic forms are common, examples being *bluey* 'blanket roll', 'blue blanket', 'blue denim overall', 'beast with red or blue colouring', 'error', 'luggage or pack', 'public bar banning notice', 'traffic ticket', 'court summons' and 'red-haired male', and *flattie* 'small flat-bottomed boat', 'flat-mate' 'flat tyre', 'confusion' (as in 'flat spin'), 'low-heeled shoe' and 'flat-headed nail'.

Alliteration, onomatopoeia and sibilance

Slang terms are frequently alliterative, including such examples as *big bikkies* 'things of monetary value', *cow-cocky* 'dairy farmer', *cup-cake* 'stupid person', *grub-ground* 'vegetable garden', *hui-hopping* 'switching allegiance' and *tiki tour* 'slow drive'. While some slang arises from onomatopoeic origins, there is little evidence of this in New Zealand slang. *Biff* 'throw' and *hiff* 'throw' are among few examples. The number of slang synonyms for 'drunk' in New Zealand possibly reflects what is regarded as an ambivalent attitude to alcohol. Bardsley (2012) identified 69 slang synonyms for 'drunk', many with a tendency to sibilance: *fizzled, horsed, muzzied, pissed, plastered, rinsed, shickered, sloshed, soaked, sogged, soused, steamed, stewed, stunned* and *wozzy* being among these.

Rhyme, reduplication and other forms

Rhyme is hardly a feature of the New Zealand lexicon, being far less notable than in Australian English, with the exception of prison argot, although terms such as *op shop, wacky baccy, Rob's mob* (a political group) and *illegal tegel* 'protected indigenous bird illegally eaten' (from a poultry brand called *Tegel*) are found in general use. *Hoof and tooth* is a slang verb form for mobstocking, the management of pasture with temporary overstocking.

Semantic shift is often evident in New Zealand slang, a prime example being the Australasian *wowser*, a semantic gadfly. First used specifically in the prohibition context with the sense prohibitionist, it is now used for 'a narrow-minded person', following years of changes of sense which included a person who whines, a prude or spoilsport, a teetotaller, a highly religious person, a pious person and an obnoxious person.

The use of *rattle your dags* is changing. In times past, as an imperative, the term meant 'to hurry'. Generally, but more often in sport, it can now mean 'to upset', as illustrated here:

> this whole mining thing has gotten my goat. It's twisted my knickers. It's rattled me dags. It's put a hole in my pie.
>
> (Southland Times *27 March 2010: A1*)

Some domains of slang

Resistance to the use of slang still comes from the older age group, particularly retired school teachers. Known locally as *tongue troopers*, they fill the editorial pages of newspapers, lamenting the loss of the Queen's English. This is not recent; nineteenth-century newspaper archives provide plenty of evidence in such letters and columns. To contrast, third-year students surveyed at Victoria University of Wellington in 2012 use slang with enthusiasm. When they are successful at anything, they are *shot*. They get *horsed* when they drink too much, they find the thought of a *fox*, an attractive young woman, enthralling, and a studious person these days is a *strainer*. Elliptically, a foggiest idea simply becomes a *foggy*, as in 'I didn't have a foggy'.

In response to the question 'Why do you use slang?' in an assignment, my Linguistics 322 class contributed reasons not dissimilar to those listed by Partridge (1933). Students claim they use slang for 'ease of communication', 'to give me street cred', 'to be ironic', 'to be creative', 'to combine words and feelings' and 'to exaggerate feelings', or simply 'it is more appropriate than Standard English in socially relaxed situations.'

Slang also belongs in the domain of sport. Rugby, a significant sport in New Zealand, has its own distinctive slang, particularly for play that is unsporting or illegal. *Coathanger, clothesline* and *Ponsonby handshake* are all terms for dangerous high tackles or deliberate aims at players' faces, while a *dropkick* is 'a stupid person'. New Zealand *trampers* 'hikers' also have their own specialist slang. A *hisser* or a *screamer* is a fast tramper and one who tallies visits to as many of the 1500 tramping huts in the country as possible is involved in *hut-bagging. Spud dust* 'freeze-dried potato' and *scroggin* are what *rock-hoppers* 'trampers' keep in their *kidney-rotters* 'packs' for when there is a *scrog stop* 'a rest for refreshments'.

Historically, New Zealand's rural domain is particularly rich in slang. Hill-country sheep farming was the enterprise of many pioneers, and two Scots shepherds arriving at a large station in 1875 described the choice of using esoteric terms or risking ostracism:

> These queer words and phrases were in common use [on the station] and we had to acquire this jargon or 'colonial slang' or be thought odd.
>
> *(Beattie 1918: 14)*

In a study of rural lexis, Bardsley (2009) found 60 slang terms for sheep and 46 for sheepdogs. In addition, farm workers and their methods attract a range of colourful slang names: musterers are known as *coatflappers, dogwallopers, gullyrakers, hillmen, sandyhookers, muttonpunchers, scree-scramblers* and *tussock-jumpers*. Humorous idiomatic expressions in relation to drought and general weather conditions are characteristic: 'Wind was so strong that it blew everything off the place except the mortgage', 'Place is so dry that even the rabbits have to take a cut lunch', 'There's nothing for the sheep to eat except stones and scenery' (Bardsley 2009: 63).

Homegrown names for cannabis are numerous, the more common including *bush dak, electric puha* (from the Maori name for 'an edible sow thistle'), *Maori cabbage* and, when contained, *baggie* 'a specific amount in a plastic bag' and *tinny* 'cannabis wrapped in foil'. *Tinny house* 'a source of cannabis' and *tinny householder* 'a supplier of cannabis' are used in the media and generally beyond the criminal world.

Among other studies of marginals and minorities is a study of *bogspeak*, the lexis associated with male prostitutes (*bog cruisers*) and male prostitution by practitioner and researcher Welby Ings (2008). *Bogs* 'toilets' are frequented by *bog queens*, males who cruise them for sex. *Bog cruisers* involved in the *bog trade* often leave a *bog bio* or *menu*, a personal profile left on a toilet wall, indicating age, size and race. Drag queens, particularly Maori, are known as *hinetau*.

In addition to endorsing or enhancing solidarity, criminal slang is significant as an anti-language or a code to deter detection, particularly among the incarcerated. Looser's 2001 PhD study of *boobslang* 'prison argot' examined slang in 18 New Zealand prisons between 1996 and 2000. The abundance of racist terms used in prison environments is perhaps unremarkable: along with the more general *coconut*

'Pacific Island person', Looser collected numerous examples in both women's and men's prisons, including *jungle bunny, mongie, ropehead* and *soot farmer*.

Notable in prison use are animal terms, particularly those used dysphemistically, e.g. a *scab* 'parasite' or 'pimp' is termed a *fly*, a *gannet*, a *hyena*, a *leech*, a *magpie*, a *seagull*, a *piranha* or a *vulture*. (Outside prison, slang involving animal terms is also found: *buck rat, chook, cow* or *fair cow, fruit fly, kuri* (Maori dog), *maggot, morepork* and *rooster* are terms for angry, foolish or unreliable individuals or situations.) Maori terms are used as codified prison slang: among examples are *wharekuri* 'dog house', a cell belonging to a Mongrel Mob member, while *kupenga* 'net' and *hinaki* 'eel trap' are terms for punishment cells.

Situations about which inmates feel strongly are also highly lexicalized, the solitary confinement cell, the paedophile and the homosexual being significant contexts or areas of superlexicalization. The solitary confinement cell is known as *Bahamas, Barbados, basement, birdcage, block, Bronx, chateau, Club Med, den, digger, dog box, dog pound, dollar, downunder, dungeon, go-slow, him-and-her, hinaki* 'eel trap', *hole, ice-cream parlour, isolation cell, kupenga* 'net', *lone hand, lost-and-found, pit, pokey* or *porky, pound, rest home, sand bin, segs* 'segregation', *septic tank, Siberia, slammer, time out place* and *whorehouse*.

National slang

The slang of New Zealand English suggests that the claim for the existence of national slang within a modern global context remains relevant. It is noteworthy that the majority of the citations here are taken from twenty-first-century media sources, indicating that much slang is a public feature of this variety of English and not, as it once was, confined to personal or small group situations. Furthermore, death notices among present-day newspapers contain a wide range of slang and informal comments, some addressed to the deceased, such as 'You were a diamond in the rough. A true mate and a top *bloke*' (*Press* 5 January 2006: D9). Others, such as 'Roger will be sadly missed by his Whanau and all his shearing mates*, cockies, rousys, gangers* and all who knew him', 'Love from your *nephie*', '*Ratbag* cousin of ...' and 'a really great old *bugger*' are found in the pages of death notices.

Terms of wide usage and long standing could well be regarded as a distinctive cultural or national slang: *box of birds, box of fluffy ducks, up the booaye, curly/curly one, gummies, smoko* and *swanny* are examples. The term *curly/curly one* (difficult/a difficult situation, a quandary) was highlighted when a prominent Olympic sports star was asked a significantly embarrassing question about alleged illegal activity – the use of 'That's a curly one' as the reply became one of those terms that are captured by the moment in that it has reminded citizens of New Zealand of this scandal ever since. It's a term that is used in a range of media contexts. For example:

> This wasn't in the programme or on the plans. You've thrown us a curly one that we will all have to cope with.
>
> *(Family death notice:* Dominion Post *22 May 2006: D7)*

What connects the Colin McCahon painting Small Brown Hill and a service treating injured pets with oxygen therapy? OK, it's a curly one, so here's the answer – it's Christchurch-based investment banker Kenji Steven.

(*Business:* Sunday Star-Times *5 June 2011: A11*)

Fuel prices had increased in New Zealand and the exchange rate was a curly one.

(*Tourism:* Southland Times *21 April 2011: A3*)

It's a real curly one for Mayor Aldo Miccio.

(*Politics:* Nelson Mail *19 October 2010: A9*)

And asking someone else – be they a loved one or a medical professional – to do it for you seems a bit of a cop-out. It's a curly one and as the population ages, the issue of euthanasia will be one we all have to come to terms with.

(*Ethics:* Herald on Sunday *1 August 2010: A26*)

There has been a softening of attitudes to obscenities and swearing in public, and the New Zealand Broadcasting Standards Authority and Advertising Standards Authority have allowed *bugger*, *sheep shagger* and *Pommy git* to be used in newspapers and in advertising. A handyman advertising in the *Kapiti Observer* wrote that he was available for 'making things work again or general *unbuggering*' (*Kapiti Observer* 30 April 2009: 4).

Many terms such as *boonga*, *coconut*, *fob* 'fresh off the boat', *fobby*, *honky*, *hori*, *mallowpuff Maori*, *plastic hori*, *raro* and *spud* or *riwai* 'potato, brown on the skin only' are acceptable in use by Maori or Pasifika, but not by European. *Chiwi*, a blend of Chinese and Kiwi 'New Zealander' is not generally considered derogatory, while *couch kumara* 'Maori couch potato' is considered racist.

Newcomers to New Zealand are flummoxed by the opaque nature of much slang etymology, along with the polysemous nature of some terms. The use of *crook* is an example, a term used in both New Zealand and Australian English with several distinctive senses. While many slang terms are shared with Australian English, they are often in the form of a phonetic variant, such as *wop wops* and *Woopwoops*, or a semantic variant, as in *tussockjumper* or *gullyraker*. Sausages are *snarlers* in New Zealand and *snags* in Australia. New Zealanders adopt and adapt global concepts such as *apples* 'indigenous people who adopt the dominant culture' and *tall poppy* 'a high-profile person', the local variants for the latter being *tall ponga*, *high-heeler*, *stilt-person* and *Ngati Aorere* (cloud-piercer).

But such terms, whether national or shared, coinages or semantic shifts, function to coruscate the Antipodean Godzone means of communication.

Note

1 *Pom* is an elliptical form of pomegranate, thought to be from jimmygrant or immigrant: *whinging Pom* was the name given to a British immigrant in the 1950s who expressed

discontent in New Zealand; *ten-pound Pom* is the term for a British immigrant who paid £10 for a passage to New Zealand; *ping-pong Pom* is the term given a British immigrant who returns to Britain, is dissatisfied and returns to live in New Zealand. Writer Fay Weldon, who lived in New Zealand as a child, wrote 'Home was England. We came from England which was why we were called homies' (Weldon 2002: 37).

9

SCOTTISH SLANG

Maggie Scott

Introduction

As Görlach has observed, 'There is no dictionary or comprehensive monograph devoted to Scottish slang' (2002: 119). This lacuna can be partially explained by the history of attitudes to the two language varieties known as Scots and Scottish English, neither of which is fully codified. In popular discourse, the term *slang* is often pejorative. It is associated with lexis that exists primarily in informal, verbal contexts. Much Scottish vocabulary functions in exactly this way. The confusion that enables Scottish lexis to be dismissed as slang is understandable, yet it can pose a cultural threat. Those who seek to improve perceptions of regional language varieties often strive to avoid the negative implications of the *slang* label. Furthermore, the identification of Scottish slang is complicated by the pragmatics of the Scots–Scottish English continuum. In different situations, the relative status of Scots and Scottish English differs; many speakers will code-switch between the two. However, in a formal context, the use of Scots may be viewed as a highly informal deviation from the 'respectable' communicative norm, Scottish English. To an extent, then, Scots words and phrases can perform similar pragmatic functions as slang, in a formal, Scottish English context. More clearly demarcated is Scottish rhyming slang, often separable from other forms of rhyming slang by its distinctive pronunciations. This chapter seeks to demonstrate that Scottish slang, a neglected dimension of the lexicon, deserves further investigation and raises questions relevant to wider issues of cultural taxonomy and perception.

The linguistic background

Modern Scotland is broadly recognized as having three main linguistic identities (Murdoch 1996: 2; McLeod and Smith 2007: 21). One of these is a Celtic language, Scottish Gaelic, while the other two are Scots and Scottish English, two closely related varieties with an intertwined and complex political history (see further e.g. Watson and Macleod 2010; Corbett, McClure and Stuart-Smith 2003; Jones 1997; Bergs 2005; Douglas 2009). Scots and English have evolved, in parallel, from the collection of Germanic dialects spoken by Anglo-Saxon invaders and settlers who crossed over from the continent during the fifth and sixth centuries. By the fifteenth century, emergent standard forms of Scots and English are traceable from the written record, and the two were distinguished as separate languages throughout the sixteenth century, when the Scottish court was speaking Scots. There were many reasons why Scottish English eventually became the generally accepted standard for formal communication in Scotland, including the effects of the publication of many Reformation texts in English, and the movement of the Scottish court to London in 1603 when James VI of Scotland succeeded to the throne of England and Wales. The Union of Parliaments in 1707 also removed a significant Scottish forum, and it is worth noting that since the Scottish Parliament was restored in 1999 – albeit with significantly restricted powers – this national forum has been re-established; this point is discussed below. Williamson (2012: 14) writes that the earliest examples of 'lexicographical activity' in Scots can be found in medieval Latin glosses. Scots never died out as a vernacular and maintained a literary presence in various guises, but it was side-lined and stigmatized as English became standardized; and the eighteenth century bears witness to strongly polarized views on language politics (Jones 1995). This history has not been taught in any systematic way in Scottish schools, and Scots has often been dismissed as 'slang' or 'bad English' by teachers who were not trained to view it in any other way. It is only very recently that Scots has been formally recognized at national educational policy level, and part of the credit for this is due to Matthew Fitt, whose work in Scottish schools has demonstrated that children who are allowed to experiment creatively with Scots often improve their language skills and overall confidence (*Cuddy Brae: Language at Letham, the Scots Language in a Scottish Primary School* 2007). The development of the new 'Curriculum for Excellence' (Scottish Government 2012) has provided an opportunity for a re-assessment of language teaching, and 'Building the Curriculum 1' states that 'Scotland has a rich diversity of language, including Scots' (Scottish Government 2006). There are still problems with the assumed working-class and subaltern status of Scots, and the categorization of Scots under the subject area 'Literacy and English' is problematic (Scots Language Centre 2009). Scots has no standard form, and is often spelled as it is pronounced, varying regionally. Many Scots words have evolved in tandem with their English cognates, differing only phonologically through recurrent features such as l-vocalization (e.g. *fa* 'fall', *caw* 'call') and v-deletion (*siller* 'silver', *hae* 'have', *gie* 'give'). There is no general agreement on whether Scots is a language or a dialect, although there is a growing consensus that 'whether one speaks Scots or English seems to be a matter of opinion, often with a political significance' (McLeod and Smith 2007: 22).

The dominant formal language variety in Scotland is Scottish Standard English (SSE), and although not fully codified it has been extensively studied and documented

(Milroy and Milroy 1993; Corbett and Stuart-Smith 2012). SSE grammar typically includes, for example, 'need + past participle' constructions: 'the car needs washed', 'the dog wants fed'; inclusion of the definite article where it would not occur in Standard English: 'he's got the cold', 'she's at the school' (after Corbett 1997: 17). SSE vocabulary includes terms such as *ashet* 'oval serving dish', *burn* 'stream', *provost* 'mayor', *outwith* 'outside, beyond', *swither* 'to be undecided, to waver', and *loch* 'lake'. Many of these lexical items can occur at any point on the cline from Scots to SSE, for example:

(Scots) 'Ah'm swltherin, ah cannae mind which ashet she wantit', or
(SSE) 'I'm swithering, I can't remember which ashet she wanted', which we might render as:
(English English) 'I'm undecided, I can't remember which serving dish she wanted'.

Distinctive aspects of Scots grammar include multiple modals – 'ye'll no can be able to'; negation: *cannae* 'can't', *dinnae* 'don't'; past tense forms: *tellt* 'told' – and may appear within a Scots context or in a predominantly SSE informal context, e.g. (Scots) 'Ah cannae caw the haunle' or (SSE) 'I cannae turn the handle'. SSE vocabulary includes a wide range of terms, including slang, also found in other varieties of English. Mainstream Scottish newspapers are predominantly written in Scottish English, often making deliberate use of Scots words and expressions to emphasize their Scottish cultural identity (Douglas 2009).

The polarization of 'working-class Broad Scots' and 'middle-class SSE' is a commonplace generalization that reinforces the view that Scots and its speakers are socially subordinate. One of the interesting arenas where this dual linguistic identity can now be observed is the chamber of the Scottish Parliament. While it is beyond the scope of this paper to explore this topic fully, a selection of examples of Scots from the first session of the modern Parliament (1999–2003) can be found in Fitt and Robertson (2003: 263–9). Sometimes these are isolated words or phrases, as in Christine Grahame's remark: 'the thought of *clyping* ["informing on someone"] never came into my head', or Johan Lamont's description of 'getting into a *guddle* ["mess"]' (emphasis mine; Fitt and Robinson 2003: 266, 267). Scots is often used to underscore a political point, as demonstrated by the following observations on the Culture Bill by Karen Gillon, then Member of the Scottish Parliament (MSP) for Clydeside (14 November 2002):

> It is guid to hae a bit blether aboot culture on a day like the day, is it not? It has been a wee bit o a rammy and some o ye hae been mince. Mike Russell and John Farquhar Munro are gey seeck because the heidie said nae to their bill. Rhona Brankin is a bit scunnert and Linda Fabiani had a guid moan.
>
> [Standard English (my translation): It is good to have a little chat about culture on a day like today, is it not? It has been a little bit of a fight and some of you have been rubbish. Mike Russell and John Farquhar Munro are

very displeased because the First Minister said no to their bill. Rhona Brankin is a bit fed up and Linda Fabiani had a good moan.]

(Fitt and Robertson 2003: 269)

These examples are often politically loaded, but they nevertheless attest to the use of Scots in a formal, national context; as MSPs exercise their Scots voices it may become more apparent that Scots has been unfairly stereotyped as the language of the working class.

Slang, Scots and non-standard language

The items of Scottish and British lexis discussed in this and subsequent sections are largely drawn from the major historical dictionaries of Scots and English, unless otherwise stated. I contributed to the *New Supplement* (Macleod 2005; hereafter SNDS2) to the *Scottish National Dictionary* (Grant et al. 1931–76; hereafter SND) while employed as an editor for Scottish Language Dictionaries in Edinburgh (2003–8). This type of evidence-based dictionary work encompasses a wide range of genres and sources, some personal and anecdotal, drawn from local informants, and some widely attested in newspaper databases or in online corpora such as the Scottish Corpus of Texts and Speech. Lexicographers purposely cast their nets widely, and the data they collect is diverse; this is particularly beneficial when capturing evidence for the more elusive, spoken varieties of language.

Scotland shares a wide range of lexis – including slang – with the rest of Britain, including words such as *gig* 'live performance', *jammy* 'lucky', *lard-arse* 'an over-weight person', and expressions such as *put the kibosh on* 'to end, spoil', *leg it* 'run away', and *monkey about* 'to interfere (with)'. Similarly, the ever-evolving, globally influential slang, from *hip* to *cool* to *wicked* to *phat*, mainly derived from American popular culture, is also found in Scotland. Scottish people can be seen wearing *hoodies* 'hooded tops', they might describe an unlikely story as *bullshit* or *horseshit*, or use the word *gay* in the pejorative sense 'weak, uninspiring'.

If a non-standard term has been used by several generations, it is more likely to be classified as local than slang. One consequence of this is that local lexical innovations are typically dismissed as slang, their longevity as yet unknown (Beal 2010: 69). Furthermore, within localized non-standard languages, there can still be different levels of formality. Extant taxonomies tend to use 'opposing' labels: 'What one lexicographer labels as slang, another will consider colloquial language, jargon, or dialect' (Coleman 2009b: 314). Recognizing that there are both local varieties and local slangs may be the most constructive way forward for those language varieties, and it is possible that by embracing slang as a dynamic, creative, and exciting sub-set of these varieties, some of the negative stigma of *slang* can be ameliorated.

Besides the issue of longevity, a further complication arises with semantic change. The Scots word *ned* has been recorded since the early twentieth century as 'A lout, a drunken brawling fellow, a tough' (SNDS s.v. ned *n.*). OED gives the meaning: 'A stupid or worthless person … a hooligan, thug, yob, or petty criminal' (s.v. ned *n.*²)'. When discussing lexis in seminars at Glasgow University from the 1990s to 2000s, middle-class students would typically provide detailed descriptions of the dress and habits of an apparently identifiable underclass – from low socio-economic backgrounds, often with drug habits and criminal records, typically wearing shell suits and excessive amounts of jewellery. On one level, *ned* is a Scots term because it has been in use for over a century, but on another, it is a slang term whose meaning shifts with each generation. Comparable here is *schemie*, defined in SNDS2 as 'a derogatory term for a person from a housing scheme, and by extension for a person who evidences anti-social characteristics commonly associated with poverty and deprivation'. One Edinburgh informant's definition was 'a person who behaves, dresses etc. as if coming from a housing scheme (e.g. wearing wide-legged, light-blue jeans, shell suits, heavy make-up, jewellery etc.)' (SNDS2 s.v. schame *n.*, *v.* 2. (2)). The pan-British slang term *chav* occupies a similar semantic range as *ned* and *schemie*. As Coleman notes, 'each generation has its own slang of approval and disapproval' (2004a: 4), and comparisons of national and regional slangs can shed light on wider trends. Further class-based Scots slang includes *cooncil telly* 'terrestrial television', *cooncil curtains* 'boarded-up windows', and *cooncil juice* (*council juice*) 'tap water', with its English slang parallel *corporation pop* (Dalzell and Victor 2006: s.v.).

Slang and The Scottish National Dictionary

Scots and Scottish English have been extensively documented in SND and SNDS, and in *A Dictionary of the Older Scottish Tongue* (Craigie et al. 1931–2002; hereafter DOST), all of which became available online as the 'Dictionary of the Scots Language' in 2004. The content of these collective works has been largely dictated by policies instigated in the early to mid twentieth century, influenced by contemporary ideologies. The label 'slang' is sparingly used in SND, as discussed below, but as the compilers did not focus on urban language, much of this was intentionally excluded (Scott 2008: 188–9). When the dictionary was originally planned, it was motivated 'partly [by] a desire to capture a dying language before it disappeared' (Macleod 2012a: 145). This focus on traditional words and phrases, typical of early- to mid-twentieth-century dialectology, has tended to obscure innovations in Scots and Scottish English lexis, and one of the notable areas of addition and expansion provided in SNDS2 is Scottish urban vocabulary. Scots lexis (including slang) is also found in *Urban Dictionary*, variously classified.

Slang usages are exceedingly rare in DOST, although there is an isolated example of the term *rino*, of unclear meaning, perhaps a parallel to English slang *rhino* 'money' (s.v. rino *n.*). SND uses some form of 'slang' as a label for only 181 words, a very small fraction of the lexis it covers in its ten volumes and two supplements. Out of this total, only 69 words are identified as 'slang' without further qualification; there are several other sub-categories, including *army slang*, *thieves' slang*, *school slang*, *football slang* (once), *printers' slang* (once), *engineers' slang* (once), and *urban slang* (once). *Rhyming slang* forms a significant part of the total, with 28 examples. Rather disproportionately, 35 items of 'Heriot's School [or Hospital] Slang', have been included from several nineteenth-century sources, including Jamieson Baillie's *Walter Crighton, or, Reminiscences of George Heriot's Hospital* (1898) and William Steven's *History of George Heriot's Hospital* (Bedford 1859).

The relationship between terms that occur in both Scots and English is often noted in SND. If a term is clearly slang in one context but not the other, this is usually indicated. For example, *big* 'elated, swollen-headed, consequential' is clearly labelled as 'Gen[eral] Sc[ots]' but '[r]egarded as colloq. or slang in St[andard] Eng[lish]' (SND s.v. big *adj.* 1). The verb *nick* 'catch, seize' is described as '[a]lso in Eng[lish] slang or colloq[uial] usage', indicating that the word is not slang in Scotland (SND s.v. nick *n.*[1], *v.* II. 4).

Where usage is similar, this is often noted without clearly labelling the Scottish term 'slang', e.g. *tile* '[a]s in Eng[lish] slang, a hat; in Scot[land] restricted to mean a man's tall silk top-hat' (SND s.v. tile *n.*, *v.* I. 1). *Raddle* 'to stupefy' is '[a]ppar[ently] of slang orig[in], obs[olete] in Eng[lish] (or England)]' (SND s.v. raddle *v.*), suggesting that the word existed in pan-British slang before being more widely used in Scots and dying out in (presumably) the English of England. SND also draws attention to English parallels and cognates. For example, Scots *snipe* 'a tailor' is compared with 'Eng[lish] slang' *snip* in the same sense (s.v. snipe *n.*[2], *v.*[2] I. 4), and *lowie* 'money, cash', of Romani origin, is '[a]lso in Eng. slang as *lour, lower*' (SND s.v. lowie *n.*). Words borrowed from general Scots usage into English slang are also noted, for example *pin* 'a peg used to control or regulate … in reference to drinking, later adopted in colloq. or slang Eng.', typically used in phrases: *to keep in the pin, to let out the pin* (SND s.v. pin *n.*[1], *v.*[1], I. 2).

Rhyming slang

Scottish rhyming slang is often distinctive because of its phonology: 'Expressions such as *corn beef* for "deef" ['deaf'] or *Mick Jagger* for "lager" can be useful to the lexicographer in that the rhymes would not work in English and they are thus confirmed as Scots rather than more widely used slang' (Macleod 2012b: 187). Lillo is slightly more circumspect, observing that Scottish rhymes that would fail in Received Pronunciation may still work in other varieties of English English: '*Denis Laws* "baws" ["balls"] and *Sam Snead* "deed" ["dead"] … would also work perfectly well in Cockney and Geordie, respectively' (Lillo 2012: 72). He also notes that Scottish cultural references may be used as the basis of non-Scottish rhyming slangs, giving as an example '*Atholl brose*, one of the most traditional of all Scottish desserts', which is Cockney rhyming slang for 'nose' (Lillo 2012: 72). Lillo's appendix of examples is useful but not exhaustive; terms found in journalistic settings are particularly likely to be hapax legomena or idiolect, so although they reflect a tendency to invent rhyming slang, they do not necessarily indicate that the terms are themselves in general currency. Instances include: *Alan Hutton* 'mutton' evidenced by a quotation in the *Daily Record* from 2007: 'Check the state of that auld yin! Talk about Alan Hutton dressed as lamb?' (Lillo 2012: 79) and *Eglinton (Toll)* 'hole, i.e. anus' used as a synecdoche for 'backside', evidenced by a quotation in *The Times* from 2004: 'Are you gauny get aff yer Eglinton an buy me a hauf and hauf?' (Lillo 2012: 82–3). Conversely, it is very difficult to capture *all* examples. Notable absentees for some might include *winners (and losers)*, rhyming with Scots *troosers*, 'trousers' and *persians*, from *persian rug*, rhyming with Scots *dug*, 'dog', typically used in reference to greyhound racing,[1] and *scooby doo* 'clue' (often shortened, e.g. 'ah havnae a scooby whit ye mean').

Scottish slang in English dictionaries

One of the people to have extensively contributed to the documentation of Scottish lexis is Michael Munro, whose glossaries of expressions used in Glasgow (though not always exclusively) have proven exceedingly popular (1985, 1988, 1996). These works have also been used as evidence by many editors and compilers of dictionaries of English slang. By way of example, within the section of words beginning with 'A' in the *Concise* edition of Dalzell and Victor (2008b), nine words or phrases are noted as used in 'Scotland', including:

airie noun an aeroplane. In Glasgow, a shortening of the local pronunciation 'airieplane' UK: SCOTLAND, 1985.
make an arse of to make a mess of something; to botch something UK: SCOTLAND, 1996.
Arthur Lowe; Arthur noun. Glasgow rhyming slang, formed from the name of the English actor, 1915–82, who is fondly remembered for Dad's Army, 1968–77 UK: SCOTLAND, 1988.

(Dalzell and Victor 2008b: s.v.)

Although this is not made clear by the authors, the dates 1985, 1988, and 1996 match the dates of Munro's publications, and a quick search of his glossaries reveals entries for all of these terms at the corresponding dates. However, Munro does not consider all these words to be slang; only *Arthur Lowe* is classified by Munro as 'slang' (specifically rhyming slang). Munro does use 'slang' elsewhere (e.g. *kegs* 'a slang term for men's underwear': 1996; 89), but his use of the label has not been followed by Dalzell and Victor, who take an inclusive approach to what is 'slang or unconventional'. This sits rather uneasily alongside Munro's stated objective: 'to record in print an impression of the dialect of Scots spoken in and around the city of Glasgow [in support of] the idea that Glasgow language is a valid and creative dialect of Scots' (Munro 1996: v).

Lexicographers traditionally draw from each other's findings, especially when researching elusive, rare words. Besides various editions of Eric Partridge's *Dictionary of Slang and Unconventional English*, a handful of English slang and cant dictionaries are referenced as sources in SND: Brandon (1839), Hotten (1860), Barrère and Leland (1889–90), Farmer and Henley (1890–1904), Cary (1916), and Partridge (1950).

A small number of words and senses in SND appear to have been included on the basis of the evidence of English slang dictionaries. A 1736 quotation from Cary

(1916) is the only source cited for *jog* 'to have sexual intercourse with' (SND s.v. jog *v.*, *n.* I. 2), and Hotten's dictionary provides the only citation for *Gourock ham* 'a salt herring' (1860). The phrase *to have been talking to Jamie Moore* 'to be drunk' is supported only by Farmer and Henley (1896; SND s.v. jamie *prop. n.* 3) as is the obsolete term *dirt-bailie*, rather quaintly defined as 'an inspector of nuisances' (1891; SND s.v. dirt *n.* I. 4. (1)). Similarly, Partridge is the only cited source for the following:

gripping 'cramping' (SND s.v. grip v., n. I. 3 (3); Glasgow, 1934 in Partridge)
Jenny Wullock 'a hermaphrodite, a sexually-deformed male' (SND s.v. Jennie *prop. n.*, *v.* I. 2; Glasgow, 1934 in Partridge)
knit it! 'stop!; shut up!' (SND s.v. knit *v.* 1. (2) (b); Glasgow, 1934 in Partridge)
Pig and Whistle Light Infantry 'a jocular name for the Highland Light Infantry' (SND s.v. pig $n.^1$, $v.^2$ I. 1 (9) (ii); 1949 in Partridge)
quickie 'the act of backing a horse after the result of a race is known' (SND s.v. quick *adj.*, *adv.*, *n.* II. 2; Glasgow 1934 in Partridge)
roast 'pester, annoy' (SND s.v. roast *v.*, *n.* I. 2; Glasgow, 1949 in Partridge)
skittling 'the feminine practice of washing stockings, handkerchiefs and "smalls" in the bedroom or bathroom wash-basin in hotels' (SND s.v. skiddle $v.^1$, *n.* I. 1; 1920 in Partridge)
snib 'to coit with' (SND s.v. snib *v.*, *n.* I. 3 (3); Scottish, *c.*1810 in Partridge)
tosser 'a coin used in the game of pitch-and-toss' (SND s.v. toss $v.^1$, $n.^1$ I. (1); Glasgow, 1934 in Partridge)

None of these words is 'actively' supported by further evidence in SND, yet neither are they identified as having only one 'witness'. Editors may have discussed these with native speakers (themselves included) to establish the terms' currency, or they may have preferred to hedge their bets rather than suggest (erroneously) that such terms were exceptionally rare.

The longevity of certain terms has caused dictionary editors to reposition them as mainstream Scots rather than slang. *Cludgie* 'toilet' is 'slang' in SNDS and only supported by information gathered from local informants in 1975. Evidence in SNDS2 extends its usage to literary and media sources dating from 1980–2000 (s.v. cludgie *n.*). According to Dalzell and Victor, *cludgie* is 'Scottish dialect, now in wider use' (2005 s.v. cludgie *n.*). That said, *cludgie* remains informal, and a Scots speaker using it as an everyday term is still unlikely to employ it in a formal, SSE-dominant context. It is also necessary to critically evaluate what is meant by a 'formal context', since this is the amorphous benchmark against which language is being judged. This itself is not static. If Scots were to become more acceptable as a parliamentary medium, for example, perceptions of 'appropriate' formal language may require revision.

Conclusion

The term *slang* remains difficult because it has too often been employed as a convenient weapon in rhetorical battles about language legitimacy. Slang has been '[r]eviled and proscribed by pedants and purists' (Green 1998: introduction). The negative uses of *slang* often reflect what Crowley describes as 'a moral investment in the [Standard] language' (1989: 253). For those who make this investment, any deviation from the standard represents a threat to the linguistic hegemony to which they subscribe. Slang words may be used in deliberate opposition to standard (or more respectable) terms, but if Standard English (or SSE) is regarded as the respectable 'norm', Scots clearly stands in opposition to it. Disruption of the usual linguistic hierarchy may well be part of the speaker's objective when they choose to use Scots. That said, every context is different, and among Scots speakers, the use of Standard English can also be humorous, rude, or disruptive, depending on the circumstances.

Lexicographers need to take particular care to be aware of the ontological perspectives they impose or challenge when analysing language. On a pragmatic level, the choice to use Scots may be motivated by a desire to address a particular audience, to demonstrate social or cultural allegiance, or foreground the national or local. The labelling of words as 'slang', whatever the intention, is often dismissive, and 'slang' can be especially discomfiting for those who have fought long and hard to secure respect for non-standard language varieties. As Coleman has observed, 'Dictionaries of dialect, particularly the dialects of America, Ireland, and Scotland, are often marketed as glossaries of regional slang' (2009b: 314). The categorization of Scots and Scottish English lexis is still very much open to this form of mis-interpretation. Nevertheless, as suggested here, a more open recognition of the existence of Scots slang may alternatively signal an evolution in the status of Scots itself – we can choose to recognize Scots slang as evidence of the language's vitality and on-going evolution.

Note

1 I am grateful to Dr Ward Scott for corroborating the use of these terms among his peer group in his native variety of Ayrshire Scots since at least the 1950s. In English English, *persian rugs* is rhyming slang for 'drugs' (Dalzell and Victor 2006 s.v.); in Australian English it is rhyming slang for 'bugs' (Green 2010 s.v.).

10

JAMAICAN SLANG

Joseph T. Farquharson and Byron Jones

Jamaicans are so creative that we coin words, phrases and slangs, which, to the non-Jamaican, sounds like gibberish, but to a 'yardman' we know weh dem a deal wid!

(Miss Kitty 2010)

Introduction

This chapter presents a brief introduction and overview of Jamaican slang. As far as we are aware, it is the first academic study of this aspect of the Jamaican lexicon, and probably represents just the tip of the iceberg. Jamaica is a small but well-known island state in the western Caribbean lying to the south-east of Cuba and south-west of Haiti. The island was a British possession from 1655, when it was taken from the Spanish, until 1962, when it gained political independence from Britain. While English is the official language of Jamaica, most Jamaicans also speak Jamaican Creole (hereafter JC; see Lewis 2013), an English-based Creole which developed in the late seventeenth century out of the contact between speakers of numerous Niger-Congo languages who were transported to Jamaica to work as slaves on plantations and speakers of several dialects of British English.

Jamaica is the most populous of the Caribbean countries that have English as an official language. English, which is used for official business, exists alongside JC, which dominates non-formal or familiar domains of interaction (Devonish 2003: 157–77). The linguistic landscape has been described as a (Creole) continuum (DeCamp 1971) with the acrolect, Standard English, at one end, various intermediate or mesolectal varieties, which are the result of short- and long-term code-mixing between English and Creole, and the basilect, a variety of Creole that is maximally distinct from Standard English, at the other extreme.

We are aware of no study which investigates the speech practices of mono-lingual speakers of Jamaican English, but we suspect that this linguistic minority is more likely to borrow slang words from JC or American English than create its own. In the context of the present volume, Jamaica is interesting because slang is mostly generated within Jamaican Creole, not Jamaican English. Seeing that JC is not a standardized language, and no formal register has been (officially) designated, the term slang is often used loosely in books and on the web to cover words not only from non-standard(ized) varieties of Jamaican English, but all words from JC. This is problematic seeing that JC is really a separate language which, like any other language, contains variation based on geography, age, gender, etc. It does have slang vocabulary, but its entire lexis is not slang.

The only decent criterion we can offer as a way of delimiting Jamaican slang is one that is based on age and restricted usage. Therefore, we take as slang, words that we would not expect to be known to or commonly used by people over 45. They represent the (pseudo-)secret language of young people and deal chiefly with sub-cultures created around fashion, music, partying and other forms of entertainment.

Most academic studies on the lexicon of Jamaican have focused on the language of older people, and so an area such as slang, which finds its highest usage among the young, has been overlooked. The major lexicographic works which treat Jamaican varieties either do not use the word 'slang' as a label (Allsopp 1996, 2010) or seem to have included it as an afterthought (Cassidy and Le Page 1967, 1980; hereafter DJE). The *Dictionary of Jamaican English* (DJE) is a dictionary on historical principles which documents the vocabulary of Jamaican English and Jamaican Creole from the 1650s to the early 1960s. While the editors make distinctions between dialectal (i.e. Jamaican Creole) and non-dialectal (i.e. Jamaican English) words, and point out vulgar, jocular and erroneous usage, slang is mentioned only rarely. For example, *breeze* '(1) air, hence freedom; (2) small change' is one of the few entries marked as slang in the DJE, but the editors do not mention this term in the dictionary's front matter. Likewise, Allsopp's (1996) dictionary, which covers the lexis of the English-official countries of the Caribbean, marks words as either formal, informal, anti-formal, erroneous/disapproved, Creole, jocular, derogatory or vulgar, but does not attempt to identify slang terms.

At least for contemporary slang, it is more useful to survey the many internet glossaries of Patois (the popular name for JC) and print dictionaries/glossaries prepared by non-specialists. The internet glossaries (e.g. Pawka 1992–2008) tend to be linked to websites that deal with either reggae or dancehall music, while the booklets generally focus on the vocabulary of dancehall (e.g. Francis-Jackson 2002; Williams 2003). A few Jamaican slang terms can also be found on *Urban Dictionary*. The reader should note, however, that the information found in these sources contains many of the common failings of works prepared by non-specialists and therefore they have to be approached with caution. In our opinion, the best work by an amateur lexicographer to appear so far is Reynolds (2006), but one has to extract the slang entries from among the non-slang ones without editorial assistance. Outside of these more convenient sources, one can scour social networking sites such as Facebook, Twitter, Hi5 and Myspace to find examples of Jamaican slang in use. The data for this chapter were drawn from Jones's work on the linguistics of

Jamaican popular music (in progress) and Farquharson's work on the *Jamaican National Dictionary* (JND, in progress), which is a web-based, multimedia dictionary of JC and Jamaican English that is now in preparation. These sources were supplemented by our native-speaker knowledge of JC, our own use of Jamaican slang and our interactions with friends via social networking sites such as Facebook.

Terms of address

Terms of address represent one of the most popular semantic domains in which slang items are found in Jamaica. The proliferation of terms in this domain finds a ready explanation in the search of young people for identity and self-definition, and the creation of bonds among youth, especially young men. Here, we deal with a few of the more significant aspects of this class of words. First, there are far more terms of address for young men than for young women. Second, while men regularly choose from among terms of address, first names and aliases in interactions with other males, females generally use only first names or aliases.

Of particular note is the co-optation of kinship terms that normally designate consanguine relationships to refer to friends or acquaintances, e.g. *faada*, *madda*, *dawta* 'a young woman' (<English *daughter*), *uncle*. For example, *madda* (<English *mother*) and *fadda* (<English *father*) can be used to address friends and acquaintances, but can also be used as titles of respect for complete strangers. Whereas using *fadda* is always interpreted as a sign of respect no matter if the addressee is old or young, *madda* tends to be restricted to a woman of the same generation as one's mother, a pregnant woman or a woman who is accompanied by a child at the moment of speaking. Using *madda* to refer to a young woman (who is not a mother) may be interpreted as an insult.

Within this group, we also have examples of mainstream words which were probably on the brink of extinction that have made a comeback in slang usage. This can be illustrated with the word *mumma* 'grand(mother)', which was generally associated with conservative (i.e. rural) varieties of Jamaican and carried a connotation of 'old, aged'. It is now being used among young females (and by some males) as a term of respect to refer to a woman who is recognized as a leader in her profession/undertakings. It is also used among females who belong to the same age group or have the same social status as a way of complimenting each other with regard to things such as clothing, make-up and accessories.

We can trace some of the terms of address used among men back to the 1960s and 1970s, and the concepts that they reference link them either to Rastafari (-anism) or the Black Power movement of that era. Some of these terms are *blood*, from the concept of blood relations, *fyah* (<English *fire*), *bredren* (<English *brethren*), *nyah* [naɪja], *iyah* [aɪja] and *idren* [aɪdʒɹɪn]. The word *nyah* was created by back clipping the name *Nyahbinghi*, which is one of the sub-groups of the Rastafarian movement. The term *iyah* is derived from *nyah* using Iyaric, a common feature in Rastafarian speech, where the first phoneme or syllable of a word is replaced by *I* [aɪ]. This feature is also responsible for *idren*, which is derived from JC *bredren* by

replacing the first syllable with /aɪ/. Many of these words are no longer common but are still known and used. These have been joined along the way by other terms such as *bonified* (<*bona fide*), *star, fam(b)ily, boss(ie), boss-man, daddy/dawdie, chief, elder, don, thugs, rude bwoy, chargie* (<*charge* + hypocoristic suffix -*ie*), *linkie, parie* (<English *spar*, as in boxing), *pawdie* (<JC *padner* 'partner'), *shotta* (<JC *shot* 'to shoot' + -*a* agentive suffix), among others. The word *dawdie* is used as a general term of address among young males, whereas *daddy* is used to show respect to men of any age. So far, the only neutral expression we have come across for addressing young females is *my girl*.

There is a regular pattern where several of these address terms are combined with one of the versions of the first-person singular possessive determiner (*mi* or *my*) to create more complex forms. The form *mi* is associated with basilectal Jamaican Creole, while *my* is used in several mesolectal varieties. Some of the more popular examples are *mi boss, mi don, mi dupes* (etymology uncertain, but compare the third syllable of English *super-duper*), *mi thugs, my girl, my lord* and *my yute. Yute* is the JC word for 'young man', which in turn is from English *youth* with the same meaning. All of these '*mi/my* X' expressions are equivalent to the *my dude* attention-getter of American slang and are also used in salutations (e.g. *Zeen mi thugs?* 'Everything cool, dude?'). An interesting feature of these terms is that the form of the determiner does not appear to be interchangeable. Hence, constructions such as **my thugs* and **mi lord* are evaluated as unnatural, if not ungrammatical by speakers.

Approval and disapproval

The Jamaican slang repertoire contains quite a few items that are used for approval and disapproval. This is understandable, seeing that slang creation and use are probably highest among adolescents, who are at that stage of life when peer acceptance and group membership are of paramount importance. Identification with or membership in a cool group is highly desirable and so 'cool' youth develop language to set themselves off from everyone else. This desire manifests itself in vocabulary that is used to signal approval and disapproval. Some of the expressions used to signal approval are *bad, ill, loud, mad, mek it* (<*make it*), *sell off, shat* (<JC *shat* 'to shoot'), *shell off, shell dung, shell weh, shock out, sick, slap weh* (<slap away), *tek life* (<take life), *terrible* [tɜɹɪbl], *tun up* (<*turn up* 'to increase, e.g. heat, volume), *vile* and *wicked* (see below). All of these expressions can replace *sell off* in the first example below, but note that *shat* and *tek life* are generally used with the preverbal progressive marker *a*, as in the second example.

> *Dah song deh **sell off**.*
> [demonstrative] song [distal marker] sell off.
> 'That's a really great/cool song.'
> *A skinny jeans a beat.*
> [focus marker] skinny jeans [progressive marker] beat
> 'Skinny jeans are in (style now).'

To the list of expressions that normally co-occur with the progressive marker can be added the now current verb *beat* and its older counterparts *dweet* (<do it), *lick* and *carry de swing*, which all mean 'to be in style, to be the latest craze'.

Also worthy of note is the word *occur* [akɜɹ] and its synonym *apm* 'happen' which mean to look/be/feel good. These two verbs are interesting because they are rare in basilectal JC, where *take place* [tɛk plɪɛs] is the more common way of talking about the unfolding of an event. The slang use of *apm* and *occur* was probably influenced by the US expression *to be happening* which means 'to be a hit or sensation'. It is likely that this was taken over into JC and used along with the preverbal progressive marker *a* to denote the same concept. For example:

> *My girl, yuh a apm*
> [first-person singular possessive] girl [second-person singular] [progressive]
>   happen
> 'Hey baby, you're sexy (as hell)'

Afterwards, *occur* was introduced as a jocular alternative in JC, playing on the synonymy in English between the verbs *happen* and *occur*.

The final thing we would like to mention in this section is the use of sound symbolic elements to express approval. In this category we find expressions such as *b(r)ap b(r)ap!* and *bullet (bullet)!*, which both reference the discharging of a firearm and are essentially the linguistic version of a gun salute. While there are dedicated expressions for disapproval such as *luu* (of uncertain etymology), terms for disapproval are regularly generated by placing the negator *no* before some of the verbs used for approval. For example:

> *Dat no mek it.*
> That [negator] make [third-person singular neuter]
> 'That's not cool/hip' or 'That won't do.'

Sex and sexuality

The areas of sex and sexuality account for a good portion of existing slang words. In this domain, the male-centred nature of slang is very visible. To illustrate, we can use a set of derivatives and compounds which contain *gyal* 'girl' as their initial element. A man who is used by women is called a *gyal clown*, because he has not developed the skills of his more revered counterpart, the *gallis* [gjalɪs] 'a man who has multiple women', who regularly visits *gyal bush* 'a place for picking up women' and so *gyal out him life*, i.e. passes his time chasing women. Most of the slang terms used for men who have multiple women are approving terms: *girls-man, gallis, stulla* [stʊla] (of unknown origin), but there is still no approving term for women who have multiple sex partners except for *stullesha*, the female version of *stulla*, but the root speaks more about sexual stamina than about promiscuity. Negative terms for promiscuous females abound, such as *mattress, sketel* (etymology unknown) and *ho*.

In the bedroom, there are terms referring to sexual prowess such as *stullesha* and *stulla*. The latter stepped in to replace the older *bedroom bully* or *agony daddy*; however, it appears that *bedroom bully* is on the rebound. General terms for sexual intercourse are suggestive of a preference for rough sex: *dagger* (verb), *kick weh* [*weh* <English *away*], *kill suppen* [<*something*], *run in pon*, *slam*, *slap*, *sort out* and *stab up de meat*. Sexual intercourse is sometimes done with the man wearing *rubbers* or *boots* 'a condom', and the participants going through several sex positions such as *backshot*, *backers* 'doggie style', *headtop*, etc. *Headtop* is a sex position in which the woman is perched on the crown of her head, using one or more points for leverage (e.g. partner, wall), while the man penetrates her from above. The term *battery dolly* is used either for a girl who participates consensually in gang-bangs (i.e. group sex) or who has been gang-raped. The initial element of the compound (*battery*) also occurs as a verb denoting the collective action of the males on the female in a gang-bang. The terms *done* and *done out* are used either attributively or predicatively to refer to the state of being spent due to over-indulgence in sex. There does not appear to be a lot of terms for (male) masturbation, but *back (yuh) fist* readily comes to mind alongside others like *beat off* and *jack off* that are probably imported.

Here we turn our attention briefly to taboo, another fertile area for slang terms. Given that language is employed as a strategy to police sex and sexuality, things considered taboo, such as oral sex, anal sex and homosexuality, commonly receive labels so they can be proscribed. In essence, labelling or name-calling is used to enforce hetero-normative behaviour. To aid in the public performance of denouncing oral sex, we have recorded *bow* for the act of oral sex, and derivatives, such as *bow-cat*, *bowers*, *nyam-well* (<Jamaican *nyam* 'to eat, especially voraciously', ultimately from Wolof *ñam* 'to taste; food') and *suck-well*, which when applied to men refer to one who performs cunnilingus, and when applied to women mean 'fellator'.

Considering that Jamaica has been described as a virulently homophobic society (cf. Gutzmore 2004), it is not surprising to find a plethora of names for gay men. Here we list a few of those supplied by Farquharson (2005: 117–18): *batty-bwoy*, *batty-man*, *booga-man*, *chichi-man*, *fish*, *funny-man*, *poonga-man*, *beeps* and *beeps-man*. Patrick (1995: 234) says that the final two were common in the 1970s. These labels and word-plays help to police (male) homosexuality, which is still viewed by many Jamaicans as a morally/socially transgressive act. Many who continue to oppose homosexuality base their objection on the authority of Jamaican law, which still treats buggery (i.e. anal sex) as an offence, and on the Bible. Unfortunately, we do not know what terms male and female homosexuals use to refer to each other.

Many young Jamaican males, in conversation, will try to avoid any words or expressions associated with homosexuals or homosexuality. For example, since about the beginning of the last decade, the word *fish* has been added to the long list of designations for gay men. This means that some young men when in the company of their peers will not order fish in the market or at a local eatery but will ask instead for *swim-around*. The word *men*, from the plural of English *man*, is Jamaican slang which arose in the 1990s to refer to a male homosexual, and words or parts of words that contain phonetic strings which are close to *man* or *men* are also avoided. Therefore, place names such as *Manchester, Mandeville* and *Montego Bay* have their first syllable replaced by *gyal* 'girl', producing *Gyalchester, Gyaldeville* and *Gyaltego Bay*. Males go to or workout at *kim* instead of the *gym* because the latter is homophonous with the male name *Jim*. Likewise, in testing the volume and sound quality of a microphone, some men have stopped using the once popular *mic check* because the initial element is homophonous with the male name *Mike*. For *mic* they substitute *Michelle*.

In that same vein, the expression *play numba two* means to have anal sex; hence, some young people avoid the use of the number *two* in conversation. In counting, they will either say *one, few, three* or will skip *two* altogether. Also, *forward* is used by some youth instead of *come* because the latter can also mean 'to ejaculate'. Therefore, a response such as 'I'm coming' or 'I'll soon be there' would be rendered as *Mi soon forward*. The use of *forward* to replace *come* has been around at least since the 1970s, and it is not entirely clear whether the modern trend is new or a continuation of the earlier practice.

Salutations

One finds quite a few salutations among the Jamaican slang lexis. A few of these have apparently been influenced by the language of Rastafari(ans) and other religious groups, e.g. *bless* (<English *blest*), *yes (mi) lion/elder, yes I*. Some, such as *hail, wha(t) a gwaan?* 'what's going on?', *whaddup?*, are restricted to greeting function, while others, such as *do so, easy, ina di likl more/laters/morrows/lights, bung bang, linkage, movements, mi a cut* 'I [progressive marker] cut', *nuh seh nutten* '[negator] say nothing' and *nuh watch nuh face* '[negator] don't watch [negator] face', are used to take leave of company. We may also recognize a sub-class which comprises expressions that can be used both as forms of greeting and leave-taking, e.g. *bless, zeen* (probably <*seen*).

Foreign words

While young Jamaicans create slang items at a staggering rate, they still borrow a few items from abroad. Despite the country's historical links with the United Kingdom, and the presence of large Jamaican communities in many British cities, over the past two decades, the UK has not figured much as a source of borrowed slang. In fact, the few British items that have entered during this period, e.g. the tag question *innit*, tend to be restricted to people who have lived in/travelled to the UK, or their close associates. Today, when young Jamaicans look outside Jamaica for slang terms they mostly look to North America, especially the USA.

The major channels for the importation of US slang have been music and entertainment facilitated by cable television (especially BET and MTV and pro-grammes such as *106 & Park, TMZ Live* and *Jersey Shore*), internet sites and forums, and rap and hip-hop music. Many of the borrowed words and expressions fill no obvious gap in the lexicon of Jamaican youngsters but mark users as cool, up-to-date and exposed (to 'international' culture). Although the words tend not to fill any lexical gaps, their use provides a useful method of avoiding vulgar or taboo subjects. Therefore, a foreign expression will often be used instead of a Jamaican one in more formal contexts because the Jamaican one is considered too vulgar for polite conversation/writing. This is probably what led Jamaican athlete Asafa Powell to choose US *booty shorts* over Jamaican *puni printer* or *pumpum shorts* in the following extract:

> 'We are currently focusing on T-shirts now, but the ladies wanted to be included and wanted something a bit sexier so we went with the booty shorts,' he chuckled.
>
> *(Grandison 2012)*

The words *puni* and *pumpum* are African-derived words for the vagina in Jamaican Creole. These words are rarely, if ever, printed by national dailies such as the *Jamaica Observer* from which this quotation was taken.

We have already shown that there are many terms of address in Jamaican slang. Terms of address are also one of the chief domains into which Jamaicans borrow slang. Like native slang, there is an over-representation of terms referring to males: *bro, dawg, dude, homie* and *punk*. So far, the only address term we have identified for females is *mami* 'close female friend; sexy female'. Note, however, that *mami* and its male counterpart *papi* are mostly used by middle-class youth. One significant thing about the words in this group is that they generally retain their source phonology, or most users will at least attempt to approximate the American pronunciation of the words.

Another popular domain contains lexical items related to a flashy lifestyle or life in the fast lane, e.g. *bling-bling* 'cheap, showy jewellery', *rave* 'a party; to party', *floss* 'to flaunt one's wealth, e.g. through the display of cars, jewellery, clothing, etc.' and *swag* 'keen fashion sense'. The latter also has derivatives *swaggerific, swaggerlicious* and *swaggerdocious*, which might be loanwords or the result of parallel innovation. The last set of common borrowings we will present here are terms of approbation. This category mostly comprises words that denote negative things in mainstream language but which undergo amelioration when they are incorporated into the slang repertoire. The main examples are *crazy, mad, ill, sick* and *wicked*. Although we present these words as being loanwords, we are open to the possibility that some of them might be local creations, or may be the result of polygenesis. The use of the word *phat* 'of women: sexually appealing' is common, and one also finds the discourse marker/attention grabber *yo*.

Jamaican slang abroad

Jamaica's small size, in terms of land mass, belies the significant cultural impact it has on the rest of the world. This impact is primarily due to Rastafari(-anism), reggae/dancehall music and sports (especially athletics). While Jamaica does exert direct influence on other cultures via traditional and new media, the country owes some of its popularity to large Jamaican diaspora communities in the big cities of Canada, the United Kingdom and the United States, which have acted as dispersal points for things Jamaican. Currently, dancehall music is the major channel through which Jamaican language and culture is disseminated to the (younger members of the) global community. This state of affairs seems to mirror the magnetic effect that reggae had on youth worldwide in the 1970s. The main language of dancehall music is not English; it is Jamaican Creole, the language that is the L1 of the creators of Jamaican slang. Some of the other chapters in the current volume make mention of Jamaica's contributions to New York street talk (Kripke, Chapter 2), Multicultural London English (Green, Chapter 5) and the cant of the British criminal classes (Thorne, Chapter 6).

Although we do not yet possess empirical evidence to back up the claim, it appears to us that as far as slang is concerned, JC acts more often as donor language than as a recipient language. We find it necessary to distinguish two types of borrowing relationships in this regard. The first type involves the adoption of mainstream Jamaican Creole words into the slang of other countries and can be illustrated by Jamaican words such as *bombo-klaat*, which is a swear word, and *ganja* 'marijuana'. The compound *bombo-klaat*, which is now used as an interjection expressing frustration or anger, is no longer used with its original sense 'sanitary towel' as far as we know. The first element is from one or more Atlantic-Congo languages (e.g. Temne *a-bombo* 'vagina' or Kimbundu *mbumbu* 'vulva'), while the second element is from English *cloth*. These words have been adopted into the speech of youngsters in Africa, Europe and North America as slang, but they have been in use by a wide cross-section of the Jamaican population probably as far back as the nineteenth century. The second type involves Jamaican slang words being borrowed into the slang repertoire of other countries. This can be illustrated by *gallis* 'a lady's man' in Trinidadian slang and *chichi-man* 'male homosexual' in Belizean slang, and both *screw* 'to scowl' and the term of address *star*, used by (urban) British youth.

Sanders (2005: 22), in his ethnographic study of youth crime and culture in inner-city London, found that the speech of his informants had been influenced by Jamaican Creole. He lists the following as slang words derived from JC but does not provide glosses. The definitions given here are for their Jamaican usage: *rude boy* 'thug; term of address', *star* 'term of address for men', *batty man* 'male homosexual', *breaddren* [bɹɛdʒɹn] '(close) male friend' (<English *brethren*), *lick* 'to hit', *screwing* 'scowling', *feisty* [fɪɛstɪ] 'rude, forward' and *safe* (used as a greeting). Partridge (1984: 57) lists *batty-man* 'a male homosexual' and labels it as 'a South London expression, of West Indian origin', while Dalzell and Victor (2008) record *ganja*, *marijuana*, *sensi*, *spliff*, *chalice*, *chillum* and *koutchie* (the last three are pipes used for the smoking of marijuana), *herbsman* 'a marijuana smoker'.

Jamaican slang words are regularly borrowed by Jamaica's English-official Caribbean neighbours. For example, Ali and Persad (2011), in an investigation of anti-language (including slang) used in a low-income community in Trinidad and Tobago, found that there was substantial borrowing from Jamaica. Our own survey of the 141 words and phrases they list in their glossary has produced approximately 35 items

(25 per cent) that are certainly of Jamaican origin or whose Jamaican provenance is highly probable. A survey of Ho's (2011) glossary, which contains about 13 double-columned pages of Trinidadian slang, produces similar results. Each page contains an average of 17 entries, about 4 of which are either from Jamaica or have been influenced by Jamaica. The majority of the Jamaican-derived terms relate to sex, partying, activities outside of the law and terms of address. According to Blench (2013), we find the following Jamaican terms in Belize: *bash, bashment* 'party, celebration', *batty boy, batty man, chichi man* 'male homosexual', *dutty wine* 'a … dance involving simultaneous and coordinated movements of the hips, knees and head', *Joe grind* 'a man who has an affair with another man's woman', *Yard* 'Jamaica' and *ganja* 'marijuana', which probably entered the lexicon of Belizeans through interaction with Jamaicans.

There is need for an investigation of the impact of Jamaican slang on the linguistic varieties spoken in Spanish-speaking Caribbean countries such as the Dominican Republic and Puerto Rico, French- and French-Creole-speaking countries such as Guadeloupe, Haiti and Martinique, and Dutch-official countries such as Suriname and the ABC islands.

Conclusion

Given the international reputation of Jamaica in music and sports, and the desire of many persons around the globe to learn to speak like Jamaicans, there is urgent need for lexicographic work on this aspect of the language of Jamaicans. This chapter has taken the first steps towards identifying and treating slang terms used by Jamaicans. As suggested in the introduction, we suspect that we have only scratched the surface. However, we hope that we have managed to awaken interest in an area that is still wide open for research.

11

INDIAN ENGLISH SLANG

James Lambert

Indian English slang – that is, the slang used in the English of the subcontinent – is an exciting field of research because to date so little work has been done. There are no scholarly works devoted wholly to Indian English slang in the current literature, nor has the topic attracted the attention of professional lexicography, and thus it represents a significant *terra nullius*. This chapter offers a brief overview of current Indian English slang and highlights along the way some of the special difficulties faced by slang researchers and lexicographers when dealing with this lexis. The items of Indian English slang presented here are based on a citation database of over 15,000 records of Indian English extracted from a variety of printed sources. Supporting evidence for this material came from a 25.4 million word corpus of the *Times of India* data (2001–03), current glossaries and lexicons of Indian English (actually of limited assistance, as noted below) and internet sources written in Indian English, including newspapers, chatrooms, blogs and relevant Google Books (on the validity and issues involved with using the internet as a corpus see Taylor 2012: 13–18; Kilgarriff and Grefenstette 2003). The chapter consists of a brief background of Indian English and a review of the currently available lexico-graphical works, followed by samples of the slang lexis of Indian English examined in three sections: (1) borrowed slang, (2) neologisms and (3) direct loans from Indian languages.

English has had a continuous presence in India since Elizabeth I granted the East India Company charter in 1600, a period of over four centuries. As slang and standard language are opposite sides of the same coin, the existence of Indian English slang implies that there is a standard Indian English. However, this is far from an agreed position. Graddol observes that proficiency in English is 'distributed very unevenly across the various socio-economic groups' (2010: 66), leading some researchers, such as Kachru (1986: 31) and Schneider (2007: 172), to employ the plural term *Indian Englishes*. This variation is influenced by a multitude of factors, such as region, mother tongue, education, economics and history. Some scholars (e.g. Mahboob and Ahmar 2004; Sailaja 2009) differentiate Standard Indian English from Vernacular Indian English, but this distinction has not gained universal acceptance. Schneider notes that within India an endonormative attitude 'is far from being generally accepted' (2007: 171), and guides on how to correct Indian English to British English standards, such as Smith-Pearse (2000) and Yadurajan (2001), still find a ready market. Nevertheless, English in India still has formal and informal registers, irrespective of whether one takes an endo- or exonormative perspective.

Copious scholarly effort has been directed towards Indian English (for bibliographies see Ramaiah 1988 and Sailaja 2009: 120–32), but not specifically the slang lexis of Indian English. A Google search for 'Indian English slang' primarily finds glossaries of common Indian English words, such as *ayurveda, caste, chai, memsahib* and *vindaloo*, and little slang, if any. An exception to this is the *Double-Tongued Dictionary* (Barrett 2004–), which includes some Indian English slang along with citational evidence. An Amazon search for 'Indian English slang' only offers reprints of Barrère and Leland's *Dictionary of Slang* (1889–90) and Yule and Burnell's *Hobson-Jobson* (1903), both over a century out of date. The Indian edition of the *Oxford Advanced Learner's Dictionary of Current English* contains a glossary of Indian English (Sengupta 1996) which labels 127 terms 'informal' and 26 'slang', a modest selection. Moreover, the labelling is not consistently applied, with words like *topper* 'the student with the highest grade' and *sabjiwala* 'a vegetable seller' labelled informal, while *yaar* 'a friendly term of address' is left unlabelled and therefore marked as standard. Actually, the opposite labelling would be more accurate. Other contemporary lexicons of Indian English, such as Hawkins (1984), Muthiah (1991), Hankin (2003) and Lonely Planet's *Indian English* (2008), contain even smaller proportions of slang than Sengupta, while Mahal (2006) is largely concerned with British Indian English, not that of the subcontinent. An MA thesis by Richter (2006) examines in-group slang specific to students at the Indian Institute of Technology in Madras in terms of sociolinguistics, lexis and etymology, and has a glossary of 144 terms. Unfortunately, the text does not differentiate words restricted to IIT Madras from those, such as *poondy* 'pornography' and *phirangi* 'foreigner', that are part of wider Indian English slang. Taken together, these texts give a very piecemeal and incomplete record of Indian English slang, but, beyond these, little else is to be found.

Identifying Indian English slang requires a good familiarity with the variety as not everything that is considered slang in other Englishes is necessarily so in Indian English. Examples include *nab* 'to apprehend a criminal' and *hooch* 'illegal liquor.' While these are slang terms in Anglo-American English, in Indian English these words are unmarked and form part of the formal lexis of the language, being used in newspapers, police media announcements, parliamentary discussions, etc. Similarly, the terms *crorepati* 'a millionaire', to *eve-tease* 'to sexually harass women', *goon* and *goonda* 'a hired thug', *lathicharge* 'a charge by police wielding lathis (long, iron-ferruled bamboo bludgeons)', *metro* 'a city' and *medico* 'a doctor', are all formal Indian English: they do not make the context informal in any way.

Borrowed slang

As all varieties of English, Indian English uses a number of slang expressions borrowed from other varieties of English. Such borrowing is both historical and ongoing. Some terms come from British English, such as *cabbie* 'a cab driver', *fresher* 'a first-year university student' and *lolly* 'money'. Others are American in origin, such as *chill out* 'to relax' and *dork* 'an uncool person', whereas *Aussie* 'an Australian' and *journo* 'a journalist' are originally and chiefly Australian. However, it is not usually possible to detect a direct source for specific loans. Such Indian English slang terms as *dough* 'money', *dig* 'to enjoy', *idiot box* 'a TV', *puke* 'to vomit', *smooch* 'to kiss', *techie* 'a technician' and *weirdo* 'a weird person' are equally prevalent in most other major varieties of English. Some slang terms are more common in one variety of English than others: *hooker* 'a prostitute' is originally and chiefly American English, as is *nix* 'nothing' and *no-brainer* 'something requiring little thinking'. Yet they are also used in British English, and the possibility that Indian English got them from British rather than American English cannot be discounted. Finally, the intransitive use of *crap* meaning 'to lie, to bullshit' – 'Basically, I crapped, saying the same thing to all of them' (Sharma 2010: 184) – common in Australian English, but not other Englishes, may be an Indian innovation rather than evidence of Australian influence, though we cannot know for sure.

Some Indian English slang terms, while having the same denotation, have different connotations than the same term in other varieties. The term *dusky* 'having dark skin tones' has a long history in English, dating back to the 1820s. The *Oxford English Dictionary* (OED) says '[i]n the 19th c. (often in *dusky race*, *tribe*) a poetic if somewhat depreciatory commonplace, now chiefly *arch.*' In other varieties of English this term lies anywhere between pejorative to offensively racist, but in India it is not used pejoratively or offensively, and is not at all archaic, as witness this lipstick advice from the Indian version of the woman's magazine *Cosmopolitan* (August 2001: 42): 'Dusky babes should opt for reds with orange tones and fair femmes should try blue-toned reds.' Advice couched in these words would be impossible to give in the UK.

Occasionally, there are grammatical differences between similar expressions in Indian and other English slang varieties. Take this example: 'Abbas Akhtarkhavar, an undertaker, testifies that when it comes to a death, the family pulls out all stops, caring a toss about the environment' (*Times of India*, 5 April 2010). Here the usual *not care a toss* is stated in the positive, but the sense does not change. A *toss* is a small, unimportant amount, thus to *care a toss* is to care very little, whereas to *not care a toss* is to care even less than very little. This might seem as though the negative construction is stronger, but functionally they do not differ in impact. Further, both positive and negative constructions exist side by side in Indian English. This dual character also applies to the expression (*not*) *give two hoots*.

Thus Indian English has its own unique set of slang terms that overlaps, in differing ways, with the slang of other varieties of English. This is true of every variety's slang and is an area of slang research that requires more work. With the exception of British and American slang, slang dictionaries largely concentrate on only those terms that are specifically homegrown. Thus while *buck* 'dollar' and *dude* 'man' are current, and have long histories, in Australian English, they are not usually found in dictionaries of Australian slang. Similarly, both terms are also used in Indian English slang (though *buck* does double duty for both 'dollar' and 'rupee'), and thus should be part of any slang dictionary that covers the variety.

Neologisms

As other varieties of English, Indian English has created its own slang terms. Examples include *chocolate boy* 'a man who is extremely handsome in a non-macho way', *glam-brigade* 'the glitterati', *Patel shot* 'a photo of a tourist posing in front of a tourist attraction' and *reel life* 'the life of movie stars, as opposed to the real life of ordinary folk'. Note that, as with *dusky*, in *chocolate boy*, dark skin colour is referred to in a positive way. Abbreviation is another source of slang innovation, with examples such as *ethnu* 'ethnic', *funda* 'a fundamental belief or idea', *senti* 'sentimental' and *convenio* (*store*) 'a convenience store', a brand name that underwent genericization. The shortening *southie* is used in US English to refer to a southerner, but in India it specifically means 'a person from India's Dravidian south, as opposed to someone from the northern Hindi belt', hence, it has quite a different meaning and cultural and racial overtones.

Loan translations, or calques, provide another source of homegrown Indian English slang. Alongside the term *motherfucker*, Indian English also has *fatherfucker*, *brotherfucker*, *sisterfucker* and *daughterfucker* (and the associated terms *fatherfucking*, *sisterfucking*, etc.). These are literal translations of expressions in northern Indian languages (Hindi, Punjabi, Gujarati, Bihari, etc.). They are of great antiquity, dating from the seventeenth century, and thus older by more than two centuries than the earliest evidence for American English *motherfucker*. The expression *motherfucker* in Indian English is partially a loan translation and partially borrowed from English slang, its ubiquity and prominence in the latter being undeniable. With regard to the term *motherfucker*, Hughes claims that 'the incestuous relationship is always referred to from an "Oedipal" rather than an "Electral" point of view, *father-fucker* not being a term used in any culture' (1998: 32). Clearly, the evidence of Indian English slang defeats such a claim. However, examples of *father-fucker* from Australia (Weller 1981: 38) and America (Mann 1975: 193) do occur, as do *sister-*, *brother-* and *daughter-fucker* (see *Urban Dictionary*). The difference is that in other varieties of English these terms are extremely uncommon, having no real currency in day-to-day slang, whereas in Indian English slang the entire suite of terms is more commonly used. The most common of these is *sisterfucker*, which sometimes appears in literary texts in the bowdlerized form *sister-sleeper* (e.g. Rushdie 1982: 382).

Blends based on the words *Hollywood* and *English* are a productive source of neologism. Blending Bombay and Hollywood gives *Bollywood* 'the Indian film industry based in Bombay', a term now well known outside of India. However, other *-ollywoods* exist in India. The term *Mollywood* was originally used to refer to the Tamil film industry based in *M*adras (i.e. Chennai, Tamil Nadu), but now more commonly refers to the *M*alayalam film industry. The Tamil film industry is usually known as *Kollywood*, from *K*odambakkam, a residential suburb of Chennai central to the film industry. The Pakistani film industry based in *L*ahore has become *Lollywood*. *Tollywood* is both the name for the *T*elegu film industry of Andhra Pradesh and for the Bengali film industry centred in *T*ollygunge, Kolkata.

The portmanteau word *Hinglish* 'any mixture of the Hindi and English languages' frequently appears in media articles on Indian English, both in India and outside. Within India, however, other regional forms exist, all denoting a mixing of English with indigenous languages. *Bonglish* (derived from the slang term *Bong* 'a Bengali') or *Benglish* refers to 'a mixture of Bengali and English', *Gunglish* or *Gujlish* 'Gujarati + English', *Kanglish* 'Kannada + English', *Manglish* 'Malayalam + English', *Marlish* 'Marathi + English', *Punglish* or *Punjlish* 'Punjabi + English', *Sindlish* 'Sindhi + English', *Tamlish* or *Tanglish* 'Tamil + English' and *Urdish* 'Urdu + English'. These terms are found in texts on regional variation of Indian English, usually in complaint-tradition discussions of falling standards and language purity. They are used loosely to refer to various levels of language contact, including code-mixing, regional accent, borrowings and loan translations.

One final common method of creating new slang in Indian English consists of reduplication with modulation of the initial consonant, as with English *super-duper*. This feature of Indian English was commented on by Yule and Burnell (1886: 397, 481), and is still prevalent today:

> The tension-venshun that analysts and commentators are suffering on account of the outcome of the forthcoming Gujarat polls has a significance as semantic as it is political. For no matter whichever netas-shetas rule the roast [*sic*], despite all their talk-shalk, their lafda–gafdas will be much the same.
>
> *(Times of India, 18 December 2002)*

As in this passage, reduplication can be applied to both English words (*tension* and *talk*) and borrowings (*neta* 'politician' from Hindi नेता *netā*, and *lafda* 'dispute, fight' from Mumbai Hindi लफड़ा *lafḍā*). These can be formed *ad lib*, but a number, such as *love-shove* 'love' and *gup-shup* 'gossip' (from Hindi गप *gap*), have become regular features of Indian English.

Direct loans from Indian languages

Direct loans from Indian languages, particularly Hindi, are a significant part of the Indian English slang story. Hindi is the official national language, has the greatest numerical strength of all native languages and is taught to millions of citizens for whom it is not their mother tongue nor even the official language of their state (Mehrota 1998: 1). The popularity of Bollywood films and songs adds to its ubiquity. Thus, many borrowings are from Hindi, but certainly not all. One set of loanwords are the counterparts of the *motherfucker, sisterfucker* set described above. The terms in Hindi are:

Devanagari	Transliteration	Meaning
भाईचोद	*bhāīcod*	'brotherfucker'
बेटीचोद	*beṭīcod*	'sisterfucker'
बहिंचोद	*bahīncod*	'daughterfucker'
बाबाचोद	*bābācod*	'fatherfucker'
मादरचोद	*mādarcod*	'motherfucker'
माचोद	*mācod*	'motherfucker'

These terms and their cognates frequently have the reduced force that *motherfucker* has in English. The Indian terms are used in 'ordinary conversations' (Kumar 1997: 143; Chowdhry 2007: 113), used jocularly (Edwardes 1966: 295; Iyer 2007: 30), used for inanimate objects (Hankin 2003: 30) and are even addressed to children (Brard 2007: 87, 235). They are also used in forceful invective and as adjuncts and instigators of fighting (Pettigrew 1995: 16; Roberts 2003: 331; Chowdhry 2007: 113; Inder 2008: 33). This is identical to the dual role that many strong swear words play in English. The commonest terms are *betichod* and *bahinchod*, which were conspicuous enough in Anglo-Indian speech to be given an entry in *Hobson-Jobson*:

> **Banchoot, Beteechoot**, ss. Terms of abuse, which we should hesitate to print if their odious meaning were not obscure 'to the general.' If it were known to the Englishmen who sometimes use the words, we believe there are few who would not shrink from such brutality.
>
> *(Yule and Burnell 1886: 42)*

Banchoot has been in use in Indian English from as early as 1796 (Gilchrist 1796: 52). In modern Indian English slang, ignorance of 'their odious meaning' is not a question. The Hindi transliterations used here follow the transcription system in McGregor (1993) (though none of the terms are to be found in that work), yet there is no one system in universal use. The lack of a widely used standardized transcription system for Indian scripts makes for vastly varied orthographical forms. I have uncovered 38 modern forms of *bahinchod*, some of them recorded by the informants as being the Bengali, Hindi, Urdu, Gujarati or Punjabi forms. Examples include *baanchod, banchot, bainchoad, bhaynchod, benchaud, benchode, bhenchhod, pahnchod, panchodh* and *banjord*. Such spellings offer little concrete indication of pronunciation. The forms indicate that the final consonant could be unvoiced unaspirated (*t*), voiced unaspirated (*d*) and voiced aspirated (*dh*), but there is no indication of whether they are dental or retroflex, and the actual vowels of *chod, choad, chode* and *chaud* remain a mystery (/o/, /əʊ/, /ɔ/ and /aʊ/ are all possible). A good street knowledge of the source languages is needed as dictionaries of Indian languages tend to omit such coarse slang terms. The situation is extremely complex and how to cope with this is a major difficulty facing any slang lexicographer who wishes to take on Indian English slang in any serious manner.

One of the characteristics of borrowed lexis is the transference of some morphological and grammatical information into Indian English slang from the source languages. The noun *gora* 'a pale-skinned foreigner' (from Hindi गोरा *gorā*) is transformed into an adjective by changing the terminal *-a* to an *-i*, giving *gori* 'relating to pale-skinned foreigners' (Hindi गोरी *gorī*). A similar situation occurs with the noun *angrez* 'the English' and the adjective *angrezi* 'English' (Hindi अँग्रेज़ *angrez* and अँग्रेज़ी *angrezī*). The lack of capitals for *angrez(i)* is consistent with the fact that Indian scripts do not have capital letters. Gender distinction is embodied in the terms *chamcha* 'a male flatterer or toady' and *chamchi* 'a female flatterer or toady' (Hindi चंचा *camcā* and चंची *camcī*, literally, spoon).

In standard Hindi the words *garam* 'hot' (गरम *garm*) and *thanda* 'cool' (ठंढा *ṭhanḍā*) are opposites, but their Indian English slang senses are semantically closer, with *garam* meaning 'good-looking, sexy, exciting, cool' and *thanda* meaning 'cool' in the slang sense. Yet Indian English slang also uses the English words *hot* and *cool* in the same slang senses as other varieties of English, and thus the question arises whether *garam* and *thanda* are examples of Hindi loan translations from English or whether the senses arose natively in Hindi. Perhaps the flow of senses in the Indian English context was two-way.

In terms of orthography, borrowings from native languages present challenges especially in the vowels. The term *yaar* 'friend, mate' (from Hindi यार *yār*) is commonly spelt with doubled '*a*' to represent the Hindi long vowel, utilizing a transliteration system developed by the Sanskritist William Jones in 1801. The popularity of this system owes something to the fact that it does not utilize diacritics, as opposed to the one used by McGregor (1993) with macrons indicating long vowels: *yār*. However, such transliteration is only patchily employed. For instance, the word *masala* 'spicy, exciting, thrilling' (from Hindi मसाला *masālā*) is never spelt *masaalaa. Similarly, its opposite, *pheeka* 'bland, dull, lacking in spice' (from Hindi फीका *phīkā*), has double '*e*' for the first long vowel, but not for the long '*a*', that is, it is never spelt *pheekaa.

Among the borrowings we find examples of terms that seem to be able to swap between being used as slang and being used as unmarked, everyday language. Take for instance the following five examples of the word *desi* 'native Indian, not foreign' (from Hindi देशी *desī*):

Go *desi* on Independence Day with the latest range of *khadi salwar kameezes*, *kurtas* and skirts by Rohit Bal and Malini Ramani[.]
(*Cosmopolitan (New Delhi) 15 August 2001: 86*)

Bollywood, in turn, has more than one reason to pause and ponder this season. With a lull having set in after the storm, all is quiet on the desi tinsel town front.
(*Times of India 10 August 2001*)

Yes, the Indians are coming. And going. And staying in the land of the angrez, and they are making the gora more desi than you can imagine.

(Times of India 22 September 2002)

The Laloo–Rabri duo also has a large number of dogs. Both deshi and videshi, remarked Laloo.

(Times of India 20 December 2002)

Swati probably wasn't used to eating desi khana any more.

(Dé 1995: 92)

These citations are a good example of the maxim that words change with the company they keep. The phrase 'go desi', the immediate context of 'all quiet on the desi tinsel town front' and the proximity of the slang terms *angrez* and *gora*, all serve to make the first three examples of *desi* appear quite slangy. In contrast, the contexts of the final two examples are not nearly so informal. Slang words exist on a continuum of formality, but their positions on that continuum are not fixed. Another word that demonstrates this fluidity is *guru* (from Hindi गुरू *gurū*). This has long been in English slang or informal language, but for the most part in Indian English *guru* is used without any sense of informality, keeping company with such reverent words as *ashram*, *sadhu*, *temple* and the like. Yet consider the following example: 'When I sent a frantic e-mail about how my hair was coming out in bunches to an aunt, who's my naturopathy guru, she replied: drink milk' (*Cosmopolitan* (New Delhi) 15 August 2001: 14). This is exactly the slangy way in which the word is used in other major varieties of English (Dalzell and Victor 2008b: 312).

Other common borrowings from Hindi found in Indian English slang are *bakra* 'a fool, a victim of a ruse, a patsy' (from Hindi बकरा *bakrā*, literally, a goat); *chutia* 'a fool' (from Hindi चूतिय *cūtiya*, from चूत *cūt* cunt); *phirangi* or *firangi* 'foreign' (from Hindi फ़िरंगी *firangī*, from Persian); *ekdum* 'immediately; completely, absolutely' (from Hindi एकदम *ekdam*) and the initialism *KLPD* 'masculine sexual frustration, "blue balls"; hence, any disappointment', in which the letters stand for the Hindi phrase खड़े लंड पर धोखा *khaṛe laṇḍ par dhokhā*, literally, 'a betrayal of the penis'.

Moving away from Hindi we find the verb *thulp* 'to hit, to whack', possibly a blend of *thump* and *pulp*. Of unknown derivation is the term *pondy*. Richter (2006: 57) suggests that it is a clipping of the English word *po(rnograhpy)* to which the suffix *-ndy* (as in 'trendy', 'handy', etc.) has been added: a Partridgean etymology at best. Another etymological mystery is *poondy* 'chasing, or sexually harassing, women'. It has been suggested that this is an extended use of the Tamil word for vagina, *pundai*, or is related to *pondy*. Both are plausible, but lack supporting evidence. The suggestion that *poondy* is connected with American English *poontang* is also unsubstantiated.

The final word perhaps should be left to *dekko* 'a look' (from the Hindi imperative of the verb देखना *dekhnā* 'to look') as it bears witness to the incredibly complex situation that has arisen from the long history of language contact between English and the vernacular tongues of the subcontinent. This ungrammatical nominalization of the Hindi imperative dates from the colonial period, where it was in common use in Anglo-Indian English (Rao 1954: 29). Hindustani imperatives were frequently used as infinitives by the British in India (Yule and Burnell 1886: xix), and from there the verb was converted to a noun. Outside India, the term was kept alive by its continued use in the British armed forces (Mügge 1920: 219; MacDonald 1927: 97) and thence made its way to Australian and New Zealand slang. It occurs in Australia, for instance, from the 1930s and began to be commonly used from the 1950s onwards (Lambert 2004: 61), generally without any knowledge of its Indian origins. Its presence as a part of the slang lexis of other varieties of English is well documented in countless dictionaries. What has eluded lexicographers to date is the presence of *dekko* in modern Indian English slang, where it is not uncommon. It appears in Indian English as early as 1856 (*Allen's Indian Mail* 1856: 39) and may have been in continuous use since the colonial era, but the available evidence is scant. My earliest record of its use in post-Independence Indian English is 1951 (Singh 1992: 511), where it is used by a speaker who had spent time in England. That *dekko* is used as a noun and not an imperative in Indian English slang indicates that this is not a modern loan from Hindi or a case of contemporary code-switching. However, significantly, in Indian English slang *dekko* has a greater collocational valency than in other varieties of English, for not only can one have a *dekko at* something, as in British, Australian and New Zealand English, it is also possible to have a *dekko on* something, which is not found outside Indian English.

Indian English slang is vibrant, ever-changing and expansive, and keeping abreast of it promises to be an engaging occupation for anyone who chooses to take it up. Little has been done and consequently much is left to do. As the words covered here demonstrate abundantly, each slang term has its own history, its own milieu, its own complexities and nuances. Due to India's incredibly multilinguistic environment, semantic, etymological and orthographical challenges abound, and great care needs to be taken in assessing, describing and recording the Indian English slang lexis, of which we have only just begun to scratch the surface.

PART III
English influence on the slang of other languages

Julie Coleman

The chapters in this section take the notion of 'global slang' one step further by considering the influence of English on the slang of other languages. They are particularly concerned with countries in which English is learned as a foreign language (Kachru's expanding circle). However, English influence operates very differently in the languages discussed in these chapters: Norwegian, Italian and Japanese. While these findings cannot be generalized to other linguistic contexts, they may offer predictions against which evidence from these contexts could be tested.

These chapters identify a number of important factors determining how English influences the slang of other languages, including the age at which English is taught in schools, how far speakers of the host language are exposed to Anglo-American culture (and particularly whether films and television are dubbed or subtitled), what economic or social advantages are attached to speaking English or using English terms when speaking the host language, whether a similar writing and spelling system are used, how far the grammatical systems of English and the host language are compatible with one another, and also how closely English and the host language are related to one another. The three languages discussed in this section illustrate how these factors interact with one another in specific linguistic contexts. Again, future research might make it possible to quantify the effect of these factors in relation to one another.

In all three countries discussed, it tends to be younger speakers who have been provided with the most thorough education in English, and this association between English and youth may go some way towards explaining why English loans often have slangy connotations. These young people are also exposed to English through social media and the internet, which means that many loans may be occurring through written rather than spoken contact (though spoken contact also occurs online). For example, Mattiello (Chapter 13) and Stanlaw (Chapter 14) document the use of *LOL* 'laughing out loud' and other internet acronyms in contemporary Italian and Japanese slang. Stanlaw also documents the interplay between English influence and mobile phone technology in Japanese slang.

Sometimes the influence of English on the slang of other languages is a straightforward process by which terms from English slang are adopted into another language with the same meaning and similar social functions. Thus we find some of the same slang reported here as in chapters discussing English slang in English language contexts, such as *nerd* 'a socially inept or studious (male) individual' (in Norwegian) and *joint* 'a marijuana cigarette (in Italian). However, in contexts in which English is a foreign language, loanwords from Standard English can also function as slang in their new linguistic context, such as *parent* 'one's mother or father' (in Italian), *rage* 'to rage or ravage' (in Norwegian) and *turu* 'true' (in Japanese).

Whether from Standard English or slang, these chapters find that English loans are generally assimilated into the grammatical system of the host language. In Norwegian, this involves the acquisition of grammatical gender and conformity with generally used grammatical inflections. For example, the English noun *hacker* 'one who breaks computer code (maliciously)' is grammatically masculine in Norwegian. However, Mattiello notes that English loans in slang and in Standard Italian behave differently in this respect. For example, the slang term *gayo* 'a gay male' acquires both masculine determiners and a masculine inflection in Italian, while loans from Standard English tend to acquire gendered determiners but not inflections.

In Japanese, the grammatical integration of English loans involves the use of an extensive range of markers indicating the relationships between words within sentences, as well as verbal inflections indicating tense, mood and politeness levels. English loans are also assimilated into the phonological rules of Japanese by clipping. For example, *apartment* becomes *apāto* in Japanese, while *department store* becomes *depāto*.

A second level of influence sees loans from English subject to further development in the host language, so that a new term or usage develops that, although clearly derived from English, would not be recognized as English by native speakers. This can involve semantic change. For example, Hasund and Drange (Chapter 12) find that *kjip*, from English *cheap*, is used in Norwegian with the senses 'inexpensive' and 'tight-fisted', which are found in English, as well as with the sense 'stupid', which is not. Stanlaw reports that *rimo-con*, from *remote control*, is used with the sense 'a person (usually a husband) who is remote controlled' in Japanese. Mattiello finds that the English word *carpet* is used with the sense 'a submissive person' (parallel with English *doormat*) in Italian.

Loans from English are also used in affixed and compounded forms in the slang of other languages. Examples from the chapters in this section include *snacksy* 'good, tasty, sexy' (in Norwegian), *bi-jogā* 'a beautiful female jogger' (in Japanese) and *baggy pantaloni* 'low-slung trousers' (in Italian). Loans from English can also be used with different grammatical functions in other languages. Examples from the chapters in this section include *digg* 'candy, sweets' (in Norwegian) and *fashion* 'fashionable' in Italian.

Calques offer a further means by which English can influence the slang of other languages. For example, Mattiello finds that *Maria Giovanna* is used with the sense 'marijuana' in Italian, on analogy with *Mary Jane*. Far more frequent were the examples of English usages influencing the meanings of cognate terms in other languages. For instance, Norwegian *eie* 'to own' has developed the sense 'to defeat, to outperform' under the influence of English *own*, in computer gaming. Similarly, Italian *stonato* 'out of tune; tone-deaf' has acquired the sense 'intoxicated by drugs or alcohol' by association with English *stoned*.

In Italian, the spelling of loanwords is adapted to represent Italian pronunciation, which means that English loans do not influence Italian spelling. However, the chapters by Stanlaw and by Hasund and Drange explore the influence of English spelling on slang usage in the other two languages discussed in this section. In Norway, slanginess is emphasized by Norwegianizing the spelling of loans from English, so that <båring> is more slangy in written Norwegian than <boring>. Conversely, native Norwegian terms with English cognates can be rendered slangy by Anglicizing their spelling, in *perfekt* <perfect> and *idiot* <idjit>. In Japanese, the influence of English on the written form is far more complex, not only because English is written in a different script, but also because written Japanese uses three other orthographic systems in combination with one another.

Although the influence of English on the slang of other languages is largely lexical and orthographic, these chapters do provide evidence of English influencing grammar too. For example, Stanlaw notes that English *now, was* and *will* are used as explicit markers of tense in Japanese texts. Mattiello notes increasingly flexibility in the use of *farsi* 'to do' under the influence of its English equivalent.

None of the authors in this section feels that the language they discuss is threatened by its adoption of loans from English. On the contrary, each of these languages is enriched by the addition of another level of playfulness and informality. Slang derived from English is used alongside native slang, and both remain productive in their own right.

It is clearly beyond the scope of a single volume to survey the influence of English slang on the slang of all of the world's languages. However, work in this field is by no means restricted to the languages represented here. For example, Diniz de Figueiredo (2010) observes many of the phenomena found in the languages considered here in his study of the influence of English on the slang of Brazilian Portuguese, including the use of Standard English terms as slang and post-borrowing morphological and semantic development. For example, Standard English *boy* is used with the slang sense 'spoilt (or rich) boy' in Brazil, where it is also suffixed in the gendered forms *boyzinho* (masculine) and *boyzinha* (feminine). Sears' (2012) study of an English-language multi-lingual school found that a group of 'cool' older students used 'American slang' to rebel against their parents and teachers at the same time as distancing themselves from students with less fluency in English. Ndlangamandla (2010: 71) also finds that English slang is used to create solidarity among young people in a multi-lingual African context, while Swift and Wallace (2011) emphasize the social significance of slang fluency in adult non-native speakers' use of English as an inter-lingual language. Conversely, among a minority linguistic group in an English-speaking country, the rejection of English-speakers' slang can symbolize an individual's refusal to assimilate to the majority culture (Nguyen and Brown 2010).

12

ENGLISH INFLUENCE ON NORWEGIAN TEENAGE SLANG

Ingrid Kristine Hasund and Eli-Marie Drange

Introduction

This chapter deals with English influence on Norwegian teenage slang and reports the findings from research on written and spoken data from 1997 until 2007. The written data comprises a Norwegian slang survey from a Nordic research project on teenage language called *Language Contact and Teenage Language in the Nordic Countries* ('Språkkontakt och Ungdomsspråk i Norden'), henceforth UNO. The Norwegian slang survey was conducted in 1997–8, but to the best of our knowledge it still represents the only research based on a written slang study in modern Norwegian. In order to supplement the data with more recent slang, we have searched for English slang in three recent dictionaries of Norwegian slang, *Slangordboka 2005, 2006* and *2007*. The spoken data comprises two corpora of audio-recorded spoken language: the UNO-Oslo corpus of spoken teenage language (compiled as part of the UNO project in 1997–8) and the NoTa corpus (Norsk Talespråkskorpus – Oslodelen 'Norwegian Speech Corpus, the Oslo part'), collected between 2004 and 2006. We thus have both written and spoken data from the two periods 1997–8 and 2004–7.

Data

English influence on Nordic teenage slang was one of the main research topics in the UNO project. UNO was part of the research programme Norden og Europa ('The Nordic Countries and Europe'), funded by the Nordic Council of Ministers. Two types of data were collected: (1) a comprehensive written slang survey and (2) audio-recorded spoken language corpora. The written slang survey was implemented among students in secondary and upper secondary schools in socially and regionally dispersed cities in Norway, Sweden, Denmark and the Swedish-speaking areas of Finland (Kotsinas 2000: 26–7). In Norway, the written slang survey was conducted in 1997–8 in the cities of Oslo (east Norway), Bergen (west Norway) and Tromsø (north Norway) (Drange and Hasund 2000: 201). Prior to this, a pilot study was conducted in the city of Kristiansand (south Norway). Including the pilot study, a total of 435 students filled out a questionnaire during one school lesson. The questionnaire provided 55 expressions (e.g. *jente* 'girl', *penger* 'money' and *stygg* 'ugly') for which the students were asked to list all the slang expressions they knew. The expressions were selected to represent semantic areas where slang expressions are common in adolescent language, such as expressions describing persons, evaluative expressions, expressions for desires and vices, body parts, money and the use of money, different types of activities, swearing (expletives) and insults/ expressions of abuse. The students were also asked to add as many other slang expressions as they could think of. In addition, the students were asked to provide information about their age, gender, place of residence, language background, etc. The Norwegian material consists of a total of 25,336 slang expressions (single words or phrases), entered in an SPSS database. The vast majority of the slang expressions were quoted by several students, which means that the total number of different expressions is far lower than 25,336. Following Kotsinas (2000: 27), we esti- mate that as little as 10 per cent of the total number of expressions (approximately 2,500) are different expressions.

In order to supplement the UNO research with some more recent data, we have searched three dictionaries of Norwegian slang for English expressions, *Slangordboka 2005, 2006* and *2007*. The material for these dictionaries was compiled through a written survey where adolescents from all over Norway were invited to send their slang expressions to *Kunnskapsforlaget*, one of the main dictionary publishers in Norway. The dictionaries contain 4,500, 5,000 and 7,300 entries respectively.

It is reasonable to assume that slang expressions mentioned by several students in the written slang survey are well known and frequent in teenage language. However, a written slang survey does not reveal how often or in what situations teenagers use slang, or whether they use them actively at all. In order to answer such questions, one needs access to spoken conversational data (Hasund 2006: 50–1).

As part of the UNO project, spoken language corpora were compiled in some of the Nordic countries. In Norway, the spoken corpus was compiled in 1997–8 and consists of approximately 18 hours of self-recorded conversations (in dyads, triads and groups) between teenagers aged 14 to 19 from different parts of Oslo. A total of 45 informants participated, some of whom recorded conversations with friends who were not informants, giving a somewhat higher total number of speakers in the corpus. The corpus compilation was designed to get an even balance as regards gender and social class. This aim was only partly achieved (Drange and Hasund 2000: 198–9), due to the inevitable complications involved in teenage self-recordings: the informants were given the recording equipment and instructions, and after a week the research team returned to collect the equipment. Despite a certain lack of balance as regards the social categories, the UNO corpus has all the advantages of self-recorded teenage speech: it is spontaneous, informal and as 'natural' as recorded speech can get. The corpus has been transcribed and consists of 206,854 words of transcribed text (Hasund et al. 2012: 41). This chapter focuses on the Norwegian part of UNO (both written and spoken), with limited reference to the other Nordic countries.

While the UNO-Oslo spoken corpus consists of teenage language only, the NoTa corpus consists of spoken data from both adolescents and adults, recorded in 2004–6. A total of 144 respondents from Oslo and the surrounding areas participated in semi-structured interviews and in dyadic conversations with (typically) a friend, a classmate or workmate. The researcher organized the recordings and was present as an observer in the dyadic conversations. The corpus consists of approximately 90 hours of recordings and 790,000 words of transcribed text (Hasund et al. 2012: 41). The NoTa corpus is evenly balanced regarding the respondents' age (from 15 to 51+), gender, place of residence and socio-economic background, and thus provides us with the opportunity to compare our teenagers' speech with the speech of adults. Furthermore, since this second corpus was collected some years later than the first, it allows us to adopt a diachronic perspective.

Findings

Before focusing on the Norwegian slang survey, we shall briefly look at the Norwegian, Danish, Finnish and Swedish data sets in comparison. As regards the percentage of English expressions in the different data sets, Kotsinas's (2002: 41) results are presented in Table 12.1.

Table 12.1 shows that the percentage of English expressions is highest in the Danish data and lowest in the Swedish. In all four data sets, English has a special position in relation to the Nordic languages, as slang expressions from other languages account for only a small percentage of the loanwords. In the Norwegian data, for instance, slang expressions from other languages such as Arabic, Berber and Spanish amount to only 3 per cent of the total number of expressions (Drange 2002: 9).

In the Norwegian slang survey, Kotsinas (2002: 49–50) found that the most frequent English expressions are *party* (n = 303), *nerd* (252), *happy* (143), *in* 'popular' (127), *cash* (114), *babe* (112), *bitch* (108), *crazy* (83), *pay* (82), *shop* (72), *cut* (70), *ugly* (69), *spaced* (68), *bored/boring* (61), *dope* (59), *hip* (59), *fag/faggot* (56),[1] *nigger* (56), *fuck* (50), *ok* (46), *rock* (46), *weird/weirdo* (44), *money* (40), *hangover* (32), *super* (30),

TABLE 12.1 Number of informants, total number of expressions and frequency of English expressions (Kotsinas 2002: 41)

Country	Informants	Total expressions	English expressions
Denmark	297	26,755	6,216 (23.2%)
Norway	435	25,336	5,467 (21.6%)
Finland	261	18,782	3,424 (18.2%)
Sweden	2,105	134,490	22,966 (17.1%)

sure (30), *sexy* (29), *fatso* (28), *shut up* (28), *buy/buye*[2] (26). These expressions occur in all four languages, with the exception of *dope* and *sexy*, which occur in three of the data sets. This indicates that the English influence is quite similar in the Nordic countries as regards lexicon. It should be noted that many of the expressions are not slang in English, e.g. *party*, *happy* and *money*. When used in the Nordic languages, however, they are slang: they are typical of informal language and they would not be used in more formal contexts.

It should be mentioned that Hasund (2002: 144) found *kul* 'cool' to be a frequent slang expression in the Norwegian data, although it does not appear in Kotsinas's list. This might be because *kul* is generally regarded as a loanword in Norwegian but as a native word in Swedish.

Spelling raises some interesting questions regarding words' degree of integration into Norwegian in adolescent usage. What is clear is that Norwegian adolescents exploit the Norwegian language system's potential for creative, expressive and humorous purposes in their spelling of English loanwords. The issue of loanword spelling is a sensitive one in Norwegian, and proposed spelling reforms tend to cause heated debates. For example, the famous *beiken-feiden* 'the bacon feud' from 2004 (Språkrådet [the Norwegian Language Council] 2004) was a heated debate in the media and among scholars following Språkrådet's proposal to change the spelling of the English word *bacon* to the Norwegianized form <beiken>. The proposal was rejected in the 2005 spelling reform (though several other loanwords were Norwegianized in the same reform), and to this day *bacon* is still spelled <bacon> in Norwegian.

Hasund (2000, 2002) demonstrates that the students use two main strategies in their spelling of English loanwords in the Norwegian slang survey. The first and most common strategy is to use Standard English spelling, e.g. <boring> 'kjedelig'. The other strategy is Norwegianization based on the English pronunciation, e.g. <båring>. Only a few spelling variants do not fit within these two strategies: <boaring> 'boring', <weardou> 'weirdo' and <goodlucking> 'good-looking' seem to be failed attempts at Standard English spelling or 'hyper-Anglification' rather than attempts at Norwegianization. The same is probably true for the variants <beach> 'bitch' and <cheek> 'chick', but these spellings may indicate a humorous distancing effect. <Beach> may also reflect the pronunciation represented as <bi-atch> in English.

If we include all English expressions in the data, the percentage of expressions spelled in Standard English is around 75 per cent. Considering that Norwegians in general have a high competence in English, this is not surprising. Since the 1997 school reform, English teaching has been obligatory in Norwegian schools from the first grade (age 6), and before the reform it was obligatory from the fifth grade (age 11). Even kindergartens are increasingly exposing children to English songs, nursery rhymes and computer games. Norwegians are constantly exposed to English in the media; dubbing in film is still not widespread in Norway, except in children's television. In the slang survey, this popularity is evident in the fact that even well-established Norwegian words are sometimes transformed to be more

English-looking and thus more exciting, fun, modern, etc., as when the Norwegian word *idiot* is spelled <idjit> to reflect an Anglicized pronunciation. In particular, the letters c, x and z seem to be almost magical when it comes to adding an English (or at least, un-Norwegian) flavour, transforming boring old Norwegian words such as *perfekt, sigarett* and *danse* into something more cool: <perfect>, <cigarett> [sic] and <dance>. We do not know how these words would be pronounced by the students who wrote them in the slang survey, but it is not unlikely that they would go for an English pronunciation. This seems to fit well with Graedler and Johansson's (1997: 9) description of English in Norwegian as carrying both prestige and sales potential.

Most of the expressions not spelled in Standard English are conscious (and some very creative and humorous) attempts to represent their pronunciation in Norwegian. One informant, for instance, explained, 'Some of the words I have written the way I pronounce them'. Others have added the Standard English spelling form in parentheses, as if to show that the Norwegianization is deliberate and *not* due to a lack of competence in English spelling:

<*feis* (egentlig 'face')> 'actually "face"'
<*øgli* (fra ordet 'ugly')> 'from the word "ugly"'
<*oåt eva* ('whatever' skrevet slik jeg uttaler det)> 'written the way I pronounce it'

In sum, the results indicate that the students not only have a high competence in English (including spelling), but also a high metalinguistic awareness and the ability to exploit the use of English for creative, expressive and humorous purposes. On the one hand, therefore, it seems important to be able to know and use correct English. On the other hand, it is unimportant that *snack* does not have the inflectional form *snacksy* in English (in Norwegian, *snacksy* is slang for 'good, tasty, sexy') or that *digg* is not a noun or an adjective in English (the noun *digg* means 'candy, sweets' in Norwegian and the adjective *digg* means 'tasty, good, nice'). The main point seems to be that they at least look or sound English, which is enough to give them the desired 'snob value' of English (Graedler and Johansson 1997: 26).

As a contrast to this admiration of everything English, we also find some critical perspectives in the Norwegian slang survey. One of the students listed *party* as slang, adding the comment 'said ironically'. In the spoken language corpus, one of the informants said: 'we don't really use that many slang words, *pardeh* and stuff like that'. The spelling <pardeh> reflects the Americanized pronunciation of 'those who use slang too much' (Hasund 2002: 151).

Nearly all the most frequent slang expressions from the UNO written survey are also listed in the more recent data (*Slangordboka* 2005, 2006 and 2007). The only exceptions are *cut, boring, nigger, hangover, sure* and *sexy* from UNO, which are not listed in the 2005–7 dictionaries. However, we know from our native-speaker knowledge that these are all still in use in present-day Norwegian. The following well-known slang expressions found in the *Slangordboka* (and still in use today) were not found in the UNO written or spoken data:

anyway
awesome 'very good'
bling-bling 'expensive, often flashy jewelry'
keeg (*geek* 'nerd, unpopular' backwards) 'cool, popular'
gæsse (*sag* backwards + infinitive suffix *-e*) 'to wear one's trousers higher than the
   waist line'
random 'unexpected, strange, unknown'
sweet 'good'

In addition, several slang expressions that originated from the world of computer games/mobile telephones and other technological innovations did not appear in the UNO data:

noob 'amateur, beginner'
eie translation loan, 'own' from gaming
podde 'to put music on an iPod'
mpis 'mp3-player'
sæppern (*zapper*) 'remote control'
lægg (*lag*), 'slow/stupid person'
mob 'mobile phone'

It seems reasonable to conclude that there are more English expressions in present-day Norwegian than in the 1990s: new expressions enter while old expressions remain.

We will now look more closely at the English expressions used as slang in spoken Norwegian, specifically their frequency and their phonetic and morphological integration into Norwegian. Finally, we will discuss slang on phrase and clause levels and give some examples of the pragmatic function of the expressions. We will present previous research on the UNO-Oslo spoken corpus (Drange 2009) as well as some new results. We will also refer to relevant findings from other contemporary studies based on the NoTa-Oslo corpus (Lea 2009).

Both single words and phrases are used as slang in Norwegian, as shown in the following two examples:

EVA: jeg ble helt sånn *impressed* jeg [I got totally like *impressed* I]
'I GOT LIKE IMPRESSED'

(Talking about cigarette smoking)

ANI: *can I have some* trekk? [*can I have some* puff?]
'CAN I HAVE A PUFF?'

In UNO and NoTa, the words that are used most frequently are adjectives, including *kult* 'cool', *teit* 'tight', *kjip* 'cheap' and also *chill* used as an adjective meaning 'great, cool' (Lea 2009: 47).

TABLE 12.2 The ten most frequent English expressions in the UNO-Oslo spoken sub-corpus

English expression	Variants and Norwegian adaptation	Number
cool	kul	123
	dritkul (shit cool), dødskul	
	(dead cool), småkul (small cool)	
	all meaning 'very cool'	
tight	teit	27
	driteit (shit tight) 'very stupid'	
fuck	fuck	18
	fuck off, so fuck, fuck you	
cool it	kuler-n	14
shit	shit, bullshit, oh shit, shit happens	14
	shit på (shit on) 'never mind'	
dig	dig	13
cheap	kjip	13
sorry	sorry	11
yeah, yes	yeah, yes	11
happy	happy	10

Drange's (2009) study of UNO and Lea's (2009) of NoTa investigated the frequency of foreign expressions in the two corpora. Drange (2009: 165) found 10.31 English expressions per 1000 words, including names of trademarks, films, songs and so on. Lea (2009: 11) excluded trademarks and found 1.12 foreign expressions per 1000, of which 92.2 per cent were English. Both studies include English expressions that are not used as slang, which means that the frequency of slang from English is even lower than the results given.

Drange (2009) is based on a sub-corpus of 100,000 words from UNO. Although this provided a representative selection from the main corpus, some of the expressions with a high frequency in the written slang corpus, like *crazy*, do not appear in the spoken corpus. Table 12.2 shows that adjectives and interjections are most frequently used. Lea (2009: 11) also found that the most frequent expressions are mainly adjectives and interjections.

Drange (2009: 143) found that there is a tendency to maintain a pronunciation close to standard (British or American) English pronunciation. Since the English and Norwegian sound systems are close, it seems that informants sometimes vacillate between the two. The same expressions may therefore be pronounced in different ways by the same speaker, as 'fuck':[3]

ASIF: sier vi *fuck* /fʌk/ også han bare *fuck* /føk/ *fuck* /føk/ han bare *fuck* /fuk/
[say we *fuck* he just *fuck* *fuck* he just *fuck*]
'WE SAY FUCK AND HE JUST FUCK FUCK AND HE JUST FUCK' [OSUNGU1B1]

As stated by Graedler (2002: 64), there is no systematic integration of English vowel phonemes in Norwegian. The examples from UNO support this statement, since the English vowels are pronounced in different ways in different contexts.

Regarding English consonants, the most common pattern is maintaining the phonemes that do not exist in Norwegian, as /tʃ/ and /dʒ/:

THOMAS: bare prøv å *touch* /tøtʃ/ meg [Just try to *touch* me]
'DON'T YOU DARE TO TOUCH ME' [OSVGGUJE1B1]

WAQAS: så kom han ut igjen etter fem minutter igjen på *DJ* /didʒey/-*rommet*
[Then came he out again after five minutes again at *DJ*-room-the]
'THEN HE CAME OUT AGAIN AFTER FIVE MINUTES IN THE DJ ROOM' [OSUNGUJE1A1]

We also find some examples where English pronunciation is used in Norwegian expressions or already integrated English expressions. Here the pronunciation is used to attract the attention of the interlocutors, sometimes turning standard Norwegian expressions into 'English slang':

KRISTOFFER: … å *cut* /køt/ opp med lyden … [Oh *cut* up with sound-the]
'OH CUT GET UP THE SOUND' [VEUNGU1B1]

The English word 'cut' has already been integrated to Norwegian as /kut/, but in this example the pronunciation is changed to /køt/, an example of 'hyper-Anglification', turning the word into English slang.

Regarding the morphological integration of English expressions in Norwegian, a sign of morphological integration of common nouns is when English nouns are used with Norwegian determinants of gender. According to Graedler (2002: 69) between 80 and 90 per cent of all English nouns adopt the masculine gender. In Drange (2009), all common nouns are integrated into the Norwegian grammatical noun system and all have masculine determinants of gender, as in:

MARI: *dreadsen* hang etter –n på golvet [Dreads-the hung behind him on floor-the]
'THE DREADS HUNG DOWN BEHIND HIM ON THE FLOOR' [OSVGGUJE1A1]

MARI: en liten bitteliten hangover lissom [a small very-small hangover like]
A SMALL, VERY SMALL HANGOVER, LIKE

In Lea (2009: 93), 77 per cent of nouns were masculine, 2 per cent were feminine and 21 per cent were neuter.

When looking at other word classes, Drange (2009: 157) found that verbs and adjectives are normally integrated into the Norwegian grammatical system. All the verbs from the UNO study are integrated as weak verbs, the normal way of integration as stated by Graedler (2002: 71). In UNO we also find an example of the English noun *party* used as a verb, probably influenced by the Norwegian *fest* (n.) 'party' and *å feste* (vb.) 'to party':

KAROLINE: men hva er det dere skal for noe i helgen da skal dere *party* eller [but
what is it you are-going-to-do for something in weekend-the then shall you *party* or]
'BUT WHAT ARE YOU GOING TO DO IN THE WEEKEND – ARE YOU GOING TO PARTY'
[VEUNGUJE1A1]

As shown above, adjectives are the most frequent category in the UNO-Oslo
spoken corpus (Drange 2009: 152). Table 12.2 shows adjectives used with Norwegian
words as prefixes. They also adapt to the noun in gender and number:

SANJA: se meg da (laughter) den *teite* stilen [look me then (laughter) that silly style]
'LOOK AT ME THEN (LAUGHTER) – WHAT A SILLY STYLE' [OSVGJE1A4]

The examples from UNO show that English expressions are normally integrated
into the Norwegian grammatical system when used in Norwegian sentences.

In this chapter we deal with English expressions used as Norwegian slang. As
stated in the introduction, one of the reasons why English expressions are used in
Norwegian slang is that English has prestige. In the UNO spoken corpus, one of
the informants stated that 'we are quite English-centered' [vevgje1a1]. Another
reason for using an English expression is to mark a distance to what the speaker is
saying. For instance, *nude* can be used to avoid the embarrassment of *naken* 'nude'
in Norwegian. In the example below, Karoline uses English to distance herself
from the meaning of the word:

KAROLINE: vi har sett deg *nude* asså vi [we have seen you *nude* [particle] we]
'WE HAVE SEEN YOU NAKED' [VEUNGUJE1A1]

English expressions may occur as single words, but also as phrases or clauses.
Phrases and clauses are typically used in connection with more or less prefabricated
quotations from song lyrics, advertising, etc. in what is sometimes called the
'quoting game' (Johansson and Graedler 2002: 260). For example, Karoline O. uses
English to create distance from her attraction to a boy:

KAROLINE O.: det er liksom bare det at, *he turns me on* ikke sant [it is like just it that,
he turns me on not true]
'IT'S JUST LIKE, HE TURNS ME ON INNIT' [VEUNJE1B1]

English is also used in a playful way in Norwegian, frequently with reference to
movies and songs with English texts:

ANI: de svarte fiskene, gode [the black fish, good]
'THE BLACK FISH, YUMMY'
ANNE: *the black fish* [the black fish]
'THE BLACK FISH'

ANI: *here comes the fish in black* [here comes the fish in black]
'HERE COMES THE FISH IN BLACK' [OSUNJE1B1]

Here the informants are eating some candy that looks like small black fish. Ani says that she likes the black fish, and Anne repeats the same phrase in English. When listening to Anne, Ani recalls that one of the themes earlier in this conversation was the movie *Men in Black*, and she makes a new expression associated with this (in fact, this conversation is full of constructions based on the formula 'here come the X in black', from the *Men in Black* theme song).

Conclusion

In this chapter we have shown that English is by far the biggest source of imported slang in Norwegian, as well as in the other Nordic languages. The English influence is not new; it took off after the Second World War and is steadily increasing (Johansson and Graedler 2002: 78). Norwegians' exposure to English, in particular from Anglo-American popular culture, is huge. In 2005, the Norwegian Language Council developed a new language policy with the aim of securing the future of the Norwegian written language in face of globalization and the threat from English, and there have been speculations and debates about whether Norwegian will survive as a national language.

In view of the research presented here, we conclude that the Norwegian language is changing, but that it is not under any immediate threat of extinction. One reason is that Norwegians are, after all, not that competent in English (although we like to believe so). In the written slang investigation, there is a lot of slang from English, and English is indeed the main source of imported expressions, accounting for about 20 per cent of all imported expressions in the Norwegian, Danish, Swedish and Finnish datasets. However, when we analyse the spoken data, consisting of everyday conversations between teenagers, we find that the frequency of slang expressions from English is not very high.

Furthermore, we find that the English influence is found first and foremost on the lexical level: teenagers tend to adapt loanwords to the Norwegian grammatical system (e.g. by using Norwegian inflectional endings) and use them in clauses with a Norwegian syntactic structure. We also find English phrases and clauses, but most of these are borrowed as fixed quotations from film, music, etc., and are as such cut off from the 'ordinary' Norwegian sentence structure. The speakers express a high degree of metalinguistic awareness, and often flag the English expressions as special effects of various types.

As regards spelling of English expressions in the written slang investigation, there is vacillation between Standard English and Norwegianized spelling, but the majority of the expressions have Standard English spelling. Here, too, we find expressions of metalinguistic awareness, as when one informant wrote <øgli> as a Norwegianized spelling of 'ugly', adding 'from the word ugly' as information to the research team (so that we would know that she was aware of the Standard English spelling). Our written data confirms that English has prestige in Norway, and this is particularly visible in cases where old Norwegian words are 'pimped up' with English (or at least, un-Norwegian) letters.

It is evident that the speakers' metalinguistic awareness will disappear when the expressions no longer are perceived as English, as in the case of *kul* 'cool' meaning 'great, fun'. In Graedler and Johansson (1997: 104), *kul/cool* is dated back to the 1980s as an Anglicism, but today it has completely lost its English flavour. It is still, however, perceived as a slang word, although it is increasingly losing its slang status too, in particular among younger people.

If we compare our data to the situation in present-day Norway, we find that the biggest change has to do with the speed and amount of borrowing. With so many Norwegian children now having their own smart phones and iPads, the influence from English is now stronger than ever. The type of slang expressions seems to be the same: new slang expressions are still a mixture of expressions that are slang in English (e.g. *awesome*) and expressions that are not slang in English, but are used as such in Norwegian (e.g. *rage*). Furthermore, our impression is that the influence is still mainly on the lexical level.

Finally, it should be noted that our data and methods yield a somewhat different type of data than what is provided in many of the other chapters. First, we have studied slang used by school teenagers. This means that our main focus has been on slang used by 'ordinary' Norwegian teenagers who are in the school system, not dropouts or any particular subculture. For this reason, we do not have much data on, for instance, drug slang or hip-hop slang (it does appear, but not very frequently), which would have been interesting in light of some of the other chapters in this book.

Second, we have used a mainly quantitative approach, focusing primarily on the most frequently used slang expressions in our data. The most frequent expressions are often the most common expressions, and they are usually not the most creative or exciting. Although a study of such unusual expressions would be very interesting, our main purpose has been to give an overview of the general slang use in Norwegian and to show the most widespread English expressions.

Notes

1 *Fag* and *faggot* are not necessarily related etymologically, but Kotsinas does not address this question.
2 *Buye* is a Norwegianized form with the infinitive suffix *-e*.
3 We have used a simplified orthographic transcription in all the examples.

13

THE INFLUENCE OF ENGLISH SLANG ON ITALIAN

Elisa Mattiello

Introduction

This chapter intends to investigate both the influence of English slang on Italian current usage and some innovative aspects introduced by the Italian variety. The assumption from which the paper starts is that the contact between the two lexical varieties is not accidental, in that the semantics, the morphology and even the phonology of English slang have massively affected Italian slang vocabulary and inspired the creation of neologisms by analogy with preexistent patterns.

Italian slang is not an exclusively indigenous phenomenon. A diachronic and synchronic study of dictionaries and glossaries of Italian slang (e.g. Forconi 1988; Giacomelli 1988; Ambrogio and Casalegno 2004; Casalegno and Goffi 2005) shows that English has had a strong influence on the language spoken by Italian teenagers, drug addicts (e.g. *Ho fumato un joint e sono intrippato.* [I smoked a joint and I am PREFIX-trip-PARTICIPLE SUFFIX] 'I smoked a marijuana cigarette and now I'm hallucinating') and similar social sub-groups in society, as well as on the informal speech Italians adopt in unofficial situations, with their intimates and peers (e.g. *A: Ti piace la mia nuova cover del cellulare?* [you like the my new cover of mobile phone] 'Do you like my new mobile cover?' *B: Molto fashion* [very fashion] 'It's very fashionable').

The popularity of Anglo-American rap songs, detective stories, comics, magazines, adverts and films has played a key role in the proliferation of new Italian slang words influenced by English. For instance, when British or American films are dubbed in Italian, English slang words tend to be borrowed or adapted to the target language.

More recent developments such as internet blogs, chat rooms and social networks have also contributed to the propagation of slang words of English origin into Italian: e.g. on Facebook, *Ti ho taggata nella foto di ieri* [you I tag-g-PAST TENSE in the photo of yesterday] 'I tagged you in yesterday's photo'.

In Italy, English is recognized as a lingua franca in many different (specialized) fields and widely studied as a foreign language from secondary school. The young even consider English an elite language, selective of a restricted minority of speakers, and consider its use as a symptom of the freshness and privacy characterizing slang. Thus, young Italians call the members of their *gang* 'social group' *brothers*, they go to *raves* 'clandestine lively parties', dancing *break* or *jungle*. Italian *junkies* 'drug addicts' buy from their *pusher* 'drug dealer' a dose of *crack* or *ecstasy*. Teenagers argue with their *parents* and often use such English expressions as *quiko* (← *quickie*) 'a brief sexual encounter' to exclude adults from their conversations. Italian people also use English slang words to offend others (e.g. *lesbo* 'lesbian', *nigger* 'black person'), or alter unpleasant loanwords adding the jocular augmentative suffix *-one* to them (e.g. *suckerone* ← *sucker*). Therefore, Italian slang can be viewed as a hybrid language, whose speakers exploit the exotic flavour of (non-)Standard English to be trendy, to show off, to insult or to identify with a social group and exclude outsiders.

Yet Italian has also idiosyncratically developed its own slang vocabulary, introducing linguistic and cultural adaptations which characterize it as an autonomous variety. Borrowings, for instance, are often graphically adapted to the Italian phonetic system (e.g. *gayo* ← *gay*), or they may undergo metaphoric extensions, as in *dope* referring to 'sound, rhythm' in Italian music slang (e.g. *il dope che la rima crea* [the dope that the rhyme creates] 'the sound that rhyme creates', Sottotono cited in Ambrogio and Casalegno 2004: 149; compare English slang *dope* 'a narcotic drug').

As a result of the different grammatical systems, English slang words are often adjusted to the native language rules. Loanwords in Standard Italian (e.g. *il mouse, la star*) generally have no marker of gender beyond the use of the appropriately gendered determinative article. However, loanwords in slang more commonly also acquire an explicit marker of gender, such as the *-o* in *gayo* 'a male homosexual'.

Moreover, calques may originate sets of new formations that are not in English slang: e.g. the Italian slang verb *farsi* [to do-REFLEXIVE] 'to take drugs', after English slang *to do*, attracts the neologism *farsi col naso* [to do-REFLEXIVE with the nose] 'to inhale cocaine', whereas the past participle *fatto* [done] 'drug-intoxicated' derives the new formation *fattone* [done-AUGMENTATIVE] 'one who habitually takes drugs', and the creative similes *fatto come una pera, come una pigna, come una zucchina* [done as a pear/as a pine cone/as a courgette] 'completely under the influence of drugs'. Lastly, loanwords, such as the acronym *LOL* (← *laughing out loud*), may be the base of some new derivatives used by Italian teenagers on the internet, namely, *lolloso* [lol-ADJECTIVE SUFFIX] 'amusing' and *lollare* [lol-INFINITIVE VERB SUFFIX] 'to amuse oneself' (*L'Espresso* online).

Italian teenage slang is particularly rich in this type of original form: e.g. by analogy with the English slang intensifiers *dead* and *to death* (as in *to be drop dead gorgeous, to love somebody to death*), Italian teenagers use the expression *da morire* [to die] 'very, extremely' (as in *essere bello da morire* 'to be really handsome', Mattiello 2005). Furthermore, teenage slang is the source for some adverbial uses of English adjectives: e.g. the calque *duro*, from *hard*, is often used with an intensifying function in teenage talk, as in *fatto duro* [done hard] 'completely under the influence of drugs' (Giacomelli 1988; Ambrogio and Casalegno 2004). Italian slanguage also abounds in innovative intensifiers that have no English equivalents (e.g. *a bestia* [to beast], *un casino* [a mess], Mattiello 2005).

In the past, Giacomelli (1988) suggested that, although the contact between English and Italian slang is undeniable in the case of direct borrowings (*flash*, *freak*, *pusher*) and of some intensifiers (*duro*, *peso*, *tosto* [hard]), the relationship between these two varieties is often accidental. For instance, he claims that the connection between the Italian drug slang words *buco*, *erba*, *fumo*, *nero*, *sniffare* and their English counterparts (*hole*, *grass*, *smoke*, *black*, *to sniff*) is weak, vague, unnecessary or even unreal (Giacomelli 1988: 44, 197).

The position I take in this chapter is different. On the one hand, I claim that some similarities between English and Italian slang terms could have arisen by coincidence and/or independent figurative developments. For instance, English *grass* (or *herb*) and Italian *erba* could have been independently associated with the idea of 'marijuana', because of the consistency and colour of the drug. On the other hand, the possibility of influence is strengthened by the existence of definite calques from English in this field. For instance, the Italian term *cavallo* acquired the sense 'opium' when *Trainspotting* was translated in Italian: *Quasi tutti i tossici che conosco in Inghilterra se lo fumano il cavallo, invece di bucarsi.* (Welsh 1993, trans. Zeuli 1996: 250, cited in Ambrogio and Casalegno 2004: 82) 'Maist English junkies ah know smoke horse rather than shoot it up.' Hence, I am not basically disagreeing with Giacomelli (1988), but claiming that Italian has evolved since 1988, and the interlinguistic contact with English is at present favoured by many factors, including the internet, which helps long-distance communication.

Methodology and database collection

Most of the Italian data used in this chapter are drawn from studies and dictionaries on youth slang, especially from Ambrogio and Casalegno (2004). A large part is taken from less recent studies on Italian slang (Forconi 1988; Giacomelli 1988), including the language of homosexuals (compare Rodríguez González 2008), prostitutes, drug addicts, the underworld, rock stars, as well as teenagers' and students' vocabulary. A considerable part, consisting of unpleasant, offensive and vulgar slang words, is taken from the lexicon of Italian insults (Casalegno and Goffi 2005; compare Monti 2012). The above-mentioned works have the strength of gathering items collected from heterogeneous sources, including recent literature, song lyrics, film scripts, magazines, newspapers, internet websites, questionnaires submitted to students, confessions, interviews and ex-drug addicts' diaries. Some of these works, however, have the limitation of not being up to date and, therefore, of not being entirely representative of Italian current usage. To obviate the latter limitation, I have collected my own empirical data from young Italians through questionnaires.

The informants were 29 young people – 13 young men and 16 young women – coming from different areas of Tuscany and central Italy. First, they were given a list of Standard Italian words/expressions and they were asked to provide synonymous slang words that they commonly use with their peers or intimates. Then, they were asked to suggest contexts where these same slang words are used.

Although fabricated contexts cannot guarantee the spontaneity of recorded conversations (compare Hasund and Drange, Chapter 12), they have been used to corroborate the existence and actual usage of the slang expressions offered by previous works, and to discover original recent expressions.

The English data that have been used for a comparison with the Italian examples are drawn from Ayto and Simpson (2005), Dalzell and Victor (2008b) and *The Oxford English Dictionary* (OED), as well as from experiments and tests on native speakers of English (Mattiello 2005, 2008).

Italian slang: what it is not and what it is

A primary terminological distinction is in order to identify and define the phenomenon of Italian slang. Let us start with what it is not.

As Coleman highlights in the introduction to this volume, slang is neither standard nor colloquial language. Although it is difficult to distinguish between Standard or colloquial Italian and Italian slang, some features that characterize the slang variety, such as secrecy or privacy, are not distinctive of standard speech. Consider, for instance, the word *bomba* [bomb]. In Standard Italian, this word refers to 'an explosive device', but, by metaphoric extension, it is also used in colloquial language to designate something dangerous for one's health, as in *bomba calorica* [bomb caloric] 'a high-calorie food'. In drug slang, *bomba* takes on a different meaning ('a drug, especially to be smoked'); and in youth slang it variously designates 'a strong alcoholic drink', 'a fast motor vehicle', 'a forceful blow with the fist', 'an exceptional person', 'great energy' or 'a lie' (Ambrogio and Casalegno 2004). Hence, whereas all Italians understand the standard meaning of *bomba* and almost everyone understands its colloquial use, only restricted groups understand its slangy use.

Furthermore, the concept of slang should not be conflated with that of other nonstandard varieties. In particular, Italian slang does not overlap with cant (Coleman 2004a, 2004b, 2009a; Thorne, Chapter 6). Yet the clandestine and cryptic terminology of the Mafia, Camorra and other organized secret societies (e.g. *bianca* [white-FEMININE] or *neve* [snow] 'cocaine', *lavoro* [job] 'a crime') is now part of criminals' slang vocabulary.

Also, Italian slang is not the jargon of a small privileged minority, such as physicians, lawyers or linguists. However, the private use of many slang words, such as those belonging to hip-hop culture (e.g. *freestyle* 'the art of performing a rap song', *jam* ← *jam session*) (compare Pułaczewska 2008), makes slang comparable to technical vocabulary, because of its specificity and inaccessibility to those who are not affiliates.

Nor is Italian slang the same as dialect or vernacular. Nevertheless, in Italian, the same concept may be expressed through different slang words depending on the speaker's origin: compare Lombard *pistola* [gun] and Sicilian *minchione* [dick-AUGMENTATIVE], both referring to 'a stupid person'.

I also distinguish specific from general slang. Specific slang is language that speakers use to show their belonging to a group and establish solidarity or intimacy with other group members, whereas general slang is language that speakers deliberately use to break with the standard language and to change the level of discourse in the direction of informality (Mattiello 2008: 39–40). Thus, the specific slang word *roba* (← *stuff*) is commonly used by criminals to refer to 'stolen goods' and by drug addicts or drug dealers to designate drugs. On the other hand, the general slang words *meloni* and *palle* (or *balle*), from English slang *melons* (1972; compare *boobies* 1934, in Ayto and Simpson 2005) and *balls*, are used by anyone who wants to refer to 'a woman's large breasts' and 'a man's testicles' in a jocular or colourful tone. However, the same Italian slang word may be either specific or general depending on its distribution, frequency and context of use: e.g. *scimmia* (← *monkey*) refers to one's 'addiction to drugs' among young speakers, but it refers to 'inebriation' in general slang.

The borderline between slang and colloquial Italian is also blurred. For instance, the words *gay* and *tette* ('female breasts', compare English slang *tits*) are 'colloquial' rather than slang, while the derivatives *tettona* [tit-AUGMENTATIVE] and *stettata* [NEGATIVE PREFIX-tit-PARTICIPIAL SUFFIX] 'a woman with large/small breasts' deserve the label 'slang', in that they are limited to teenage use (Ambrogio and Casalegno 2004).

Slang is often an ephemeral, short-lived language. As a result, some Italian slang words are old-fashioned: e.g. nowadays nobody would use the words *piedipiatti* to refer to 'a policeman', *canarino* for 'a police informer' or *verdone* for 'a banknote' (Forconi 1988). These words were widespread in the 1950s, as calques of Anglo-American slang *flat-foot*, *canary* (in the phrase *to sing like a canary*) and *greens*, but they are now dated.

Other words are simply long-lasting, but still in use, although with a semantic extension (Adams 2009: 15). For instance, the word *allupato* [PREFIX–wolf–PARTICIPIAL SUFFIX] has a long history. According to Banfi (1992: 100), it was used before the nineteenth century to mean 'starving', but it is reported in Forconi (1988: 16), Ambrogio and Casalegno (2004: 9–10) and Casalegno and Goffi (2005: 6) with the meaning of 'sexually aroused', which seems to be influenced by the English slang noun *wolf* 'a sexually aggressive man' and the verb *to wolf* 'to act in a sexually aggressive manner'.

Lastly, the concept of Italian slang does not completely overlap with youth or college language (Eble, Chapter 3; Coleman, Chapter 4). Yet the latter represents a large portion of the slang lexicon, especially that imported from abroad. The freshness and creativity of teenagers and adolescents are prolific in terms of slang hybridisms – e.g. *drunkato* (← *drunk*) and *preppina* (← *preppy*) – which are not used by older generations.

The contact between English and Italian slang

A marked contact between English and Italian slang is in direct borrowings or loanwords, i.e. non-adapted, adapted and false Anglicisms (Pulcini 2008, 2010; Pulcini, Furiassi and Rodríguez González 2012). The words *cool* and *OK*, for instance, are currently used among young Italians to define something or someone 'fashionable'. The English–Italian contact is also evident in indirect borrowings or calques. Some of them are semantic calques: e.g. Italian drug slang *stecca* and *linea* (also *riga*) have been coined after English slang *stick* 'a marijuana cigarette' and *line* 'a dose of cocaine', because of the drug's shape before smoking or inhalation. Others are morphological calques – e.g. of English slang derivatives (*rappatore* ← *rapper*), compounds (*ragazza squillo* ← *call girl*), phrases (*fuori di testa* ← *off one's head*) – or even phonological calques (*stonato* ← *stoned*), based only on phonic resemblance.

The impact of English slang on Italian is also seen in equivalent semantic patterns. Like English neo-semanticisms in slang (Mattiello 2008), Italian ones also follow some regular associative patterns. Thus, by analogy with a series of English slang words for 'extremely drunk or drug-intoxicated' (Eble 1996), Italian slang *collassato* 'collapsed' literally, *disintegrato* 'disintegrated', *distrutto* 'destroyed' and *scoppiato* 'burst' allude to the destructive effects of drugs or alcohol.

Loanwords and calques also provide the base for numerous neologisms or creative coinages which are obtained by analogy with existing patterns. Furthermore, English and Italian slang tend to share the most productive semantic areas involved in the creation of slang words.

The two varieties are comparable from a pragmatic perspective, too, especially in terms of equivalent functions, effects, users and contexts of use. But these aspects are not investigated in this paper.

Non-adapted loanwords

Italian slang non-adapted loanwords have different origins, since they are borrowed either from the different regional varieties of English slang or from Standard English. Borrowings from British slang include: *glam* (← *glamorous*), *punk* 'a fan of punk rock music', *rave(r)* and *skin(head)*. The hybrid formation *baggy pantaloni* (Ambrogio and Casalegno 2004: 25) comes from the English noun modifier *baggy* ('a loose fashion briefly popular with ravers') and the Italian noun for 'trousers', with an influence also in word order (see 'hybrid loans' in Pulcini et al. 2012).

Most Italian slang loanwords come from US slang and especially belong to hip-hop culture: e.g. *b-boy* 'a break-dancer', *freestyle* (n. converted from the v. *freestyle* 'to improvise and perform a rap lyric'), *rap* and *rapper*. Other Americanisms belong to the drug culture: e.g. *fix* 'an injection of heroin', *flash* 'a sudden onset of drug-induced effects', *speed* 'an amphetamine' and *weed* 'marijuana (cigarette)'. Still other Americanisms are used to offend others (e.g. *bozo* 'a fool', from the US figure of Bozo the Clown) or to define people with special characteristics (e.g. *freak*, also adapted as *fricchettone*). The initialism *a.k.a.* (← *also known as*) and the acronym *LOL*, both frequent on the web, come from American slang, as well as the above-mentioned expressions *cool* and *OK*.

Italian slang loanwords may alternatively have originated from contact with Standard English. For instance, young Italians use *boy* (in the sense of 'boyfriend', normally preceded by a possessive adjective), *cash*, *fanzine* (← *fan* and *magazine*), *moment*, *news*, *overdose* (not necessarily related to drugs; compare Zucchero Fornaciari's song 'Overdose (d'amore)'), *regular* and *situation*.

False Anglicisms

Some borrowings from Standard English are false (or pseudo-)Anglicisms derived from a 'semantic shift' (Furiassi 2010: 44–6) in that they are made up of English lexical elements, but re-interpreted in Italian slang. For instance, the following expressions acquire a novel (figurative) meaning: *after hour* 'a party which starts at dawn and lasts all day' (a compound ellipsis from *after-hours party*, Furiassi 2010: 41–3, 137–8), *airbag* 'large breasts', *carpet* 'a submissive person', *fight* 'a struggle among rappers', *mister* 'a drug dealer' (compare colloquial Italian 'football coach'), *stress* (in *che stress* 'expressing annoyance') and *tilt* (in *andare in tilt* 'to lose control of the situation').

Adapted Anglicisms

There is a group of Italian slang borrowings that are 'adapted loanwords' (Pulcini, Furiassi and Rodríguez González 2012), i.e. Anglicisms which undergo some orthographic, phonological and/or morphological integration into the structures of Italian. Anglicisms with orthographic and phonological integration are <diler> (*dealer*), <flesc> (*flash*) and <fric/frik> (*freak*). The Anglicism *okappa* is instead obtained via letter pronunciation of *O.K.*, by analogy with English slang *okay/okey* (Mattiello 2008: 152). The Anglicisms *dopa* (← *dope*) and *grungio* (← *grungy* 'filthy, dirty') exhibit a morphological integration of gender through the final vowel *-a* (feminine) or *-o* (masculine).

Semantic calques

Semantic calques in Italian slang are existing words/expressions in Italian, some-times formally similar to the English ones, which acquire the meaning of English slang words/expressions. Of course, when the two languages have the same words (e.g. Italian *acido*–English *acid* 'LSD'), it is difficult to establish the source and the target, or slang meanings may have been autonomously attributed to them.

The main semantic areas involved in Italian neo-semanticisms presumably having an English origin are drugs and drug-intoxication (e.g. *albero di Natale* [Christmas tree] 'an assortment of multi-coloured pills', *mamma* [mother] 'a drug dealer' and *pasticca* [pill] 'a tablet of MDMA'); alcohol and drunkenness (e.g. *andato* [gone] and *pieno* [full], both meaning 'drunk'); criminality and corruption (e.g. *pulito* [clean] 'drug-free or unarmed', *roba* and *sputare* [to spill] 'to confess'); and sexuality and sexual organs (e.g. names for sexual organs: *cosa/-o*, *micia* [pussy] and *palle* [balls]; verbs meaning 'to have sex with': *farsi* [to do] and *fottere* [to fuck]). Other important categories include body parts (e.g. *meloni/cocomeri* [(water)melons] 'breasts' and *ruote* [wheels], in teenage slang 'legs', compare the meaning 'shoes' in criminal slang); craziness (e.g. *essere fuori di melone* [to be off one's melon] 'to be off one's head'); (attractive) young people (e.g. *pollastra/pollastrella* [chicken] 'attractive young woman', now dated, and *schianto* [smasher]); stupid or despicable people (e.g. *animale* [animal] 'a person displaying vulgar manners', *spastico* [spastic] 'incompetent', also converted to n., and *vacca* [cow] 'a degraded woman'); valueless people/things (e.g. *cacata/cagata* [cack] 'shit; rubbish' and *zero* 'a person of no significance'); friends and mates (e.g. forms of address: *fratello* [brother] and *sorella* [sister]); and parents (e.g. *vecchio/-a* [old-MASCULINE/-FEMININE] 'father/mother').

Some calques also exhibit a semantic extension as compared with the meaning they have in English slang. For instance, in youth slang, the word *botta* refers not only to 'sexual intercourse', like its English slang counterpart *knock*, but also to 'falling in love' and to 'high price' (compare *costare un botto* 'to cost an arm and a leg' in Mattiello 2005: 287). Similarly, the Italian slang word *cavallo* is used by drug addicts to indicate either 'the effects of a drug' or 'opium', and in the underworld to indicate 'a drug dealer': all these senses are probably connected with the English slang meaning 'heroin' (compare Giacomelli 1988). Moreover, the noun *storia* is not only used for 'a love story', but also for 'a drug experience', 'a difficult situation' and 'a marijuana cigarette' in *farsi una storia* (Ambrogio and Casalegno 2004).

Morphological calques

Further evidence of the influence of English slang on Italian is in morphological calques, i.e. borrowings which preserve the structure of the source word/expression, but use the morphemes of the target language. They may be derivatives (e.g. *rappatore* [rap-p-AGENT SUFFIX] 'rapper', *sveltina* [quick-DIMINUTIVE SUFFIX] 'quickie'); compounds (e.g. *Maria Giovanna* [Mary Jane] 'marijuana', *quattrocchi* [four-eyes] and *sessantanove* [69]); or phrases (e.g. *avere una scimmia sulla schiena* [to have a monkey on one's back], *gioielli di famiglia* [family jewels], euphemistic, now dated, and *incipriarsi il naso* [to powder one's nose], used in Volfango De Biasi's film *Come tu mi vuoi* 2007 with the meaning 'to sniff cocaine').

Some Italian compounds are adapted to the Italian post-modifying system (e.g. *tacchino freddo* [turkey cold] 'cold turkey') or to the Verb-Object structure (e.g. *fottimadre* [fuck-mother] 'motherfucker', *leccaculo* [lick-arse] 'arse-licker'). The plural suffix *-s* is attached to an Italian base in *genitors* [parents].

Italian slang has also inherited some extra-grammatical formations from English, that is, morphological calques of formations that are not rule-governed but lie outside standard grammatical rules in that (a) their structure does not obey the regular patterns of English grammar (e.g. their morphotactics is obscure), or (b) they do not derive new words, but rather informal variants of existing ones (Mattiello 2008, 2013). Examples include the clippings *coca*(ina) [cocaine] (on *coke*), *comu*(nista) [communist] (on *Commo*) and *frate*(llo) [brother] (on *bro*).

However, since Italian is a post-modifying language, in clipped compounds it is the right-hand element which is normally deleted. So, English *water-closet* is shortened into the false Anglicism *water* ('an ugly or despicable person') rather than the more transparent *closet* (Furiassi 2010: 42) by analogy with Standard Italian *night* (← *night club*).

Phonological calques

Calques are rarely based uniquely on a resemblance with English pronunciation. A relevant case is the Italian adjective *stonato*, which, like its American slang equivalent, is used to mean both 'intoxicated on a drug' and 'very drunk' (Adams 2009: 15). According to Forconi (1988: 216) and Manzoni and Dalmonte (1980 cited in Giacomelli 1988: 173), the origin of *stonato* is by sound similarity with the English *stoned*. Indeed, unlike other cases in which the association may be semantic (see semantic calques above) in that both slang and standard meanings correspond in the two languages, the Standard Italian word *stonato* ('out of tune; tone-deaf') has a different meaning from Standard English *stoned* ('wounded or killed with stones').

Another case which deserves attention is the Italian slang word *parenti*, used by young people to refer to their 'parents'. In the standard language, Italian *parenti* 'relatives' and English *parents* are false friends. Thus, although the two concepts are related by a hyponym-hypernym relationship (i.e. 'parents are a type of relatives'), the similarity between *parenti* and *parents* is only phonological.

New slang words

The empirical data collected from tests on young Italian speakers shows that the above-mentioned loanwords and calques of various types can give rise to many new coinages by analogy. Analogy does not impose constraints on either the input or the output of a morphological process, and admits many new words on the basis of their similarity with pre-existing items and patterns (Mattiello 2013: 50–3).

Among new derivatives, many slang verbs, such as *brekkare* [break] and *lollare* are analogical with standard *ballare* 'to dance', while the reflexive verbs *cannarsi* and *robarsi* are analogical with *drogarsi* 'to take drugs'. Other new words are past participles (e.g. *impasticcato*, on *drogato* 'drug user'), deadjectival nouns (e.g. *gayezza* 'homosexuality', on *debolezza* 'weakness'), infixed nouns (e.g. *rappettaro* 'rapper', on *rockettaro* 'rocker') (Grossmann and Rainer 2004).

Sometimes Anglicisms acquire an Italian alterative suffix having the function of expressing playfulness or non-seriousness (Dressler and Merlini Barbaresi 1994). For instance, the suffix *-one* (or feminine *-ona*) often conveys a jocular or displeasing flavour to Italian slang words, as in *dikone* (← *dick*) and *tettona*, comparable to standard *testone*, from *testa* 'head'.

Similarly, new nominal compounds are produced in Italian slang by analogy with existing slang compounds of English origin. This is the case with the exocentric compound *leccapiedi* [lick-feet], based on *leccaculo*, or with the appositional compound *biancaneve*, obtained from two drug names, but jocularly alluding to the protagonist's name of the story *Snow White and the Seven Dwarfs*.

Phrases whose head or modifier is an Anglicism are also analogical with existing patterns: e.g. *farsi una canna* or *farsi un joint* 'to smoke a marijuana cigarette' are analogical with *farsi una sigaretta* 'to smoke a cigarette'; and *fuori di cervello* is based on slang *fuori di testa*.

Conclusions

Borrowings are not the only evidence of the influence of English slang on Italian. Partially in contrast with Giacomelli's (1988) claims, this study has shown that the relationship between the slang spoken by English people and that currently used by Italian people is not accidental, but clear, strong and necessary, especially to understand the meaning of more obscure slang words and the mechanisms whereby slang neologisms are constructed.

The semantic associations behind the meanings of many Italian slang words are not always transparent. They may be more opaque and require the activation of more complex cognitive processes, unless one knows that the corresponding English slang words are used with the same meanings.

Anglicisms in Italian may be pure loanwords, morpho(no)logical or orthographic adaptations or false Anglicisms, with English words acquiring a new meaning in Italian slang. Calques can similarly be of various types, with semantic ones being the predominant category.

Anglicisms may even give rise to new Italian slang words or phrases which combine the heritage from English slang with the creativity of Italian speakers, and at the same time confirm that slang is '*The People's Poetry*' (Adams 2009: viii).

14

SOME TRENDS IN JAPANESE SLANG[1]

James Stanlaw

Introduction

In this chapter I will discuss some of the recent developments in slang terminology in Japanese. While there are many slang terms associated with various Japanese subcultures – for example, the *yakuza* gangster underworld, workers in the sex trade, *otaku* 'geeks' interested in *manga* comics and *anime* animated films, and teenagers – I will focus mainly on the use of English in Japanese slang in general. English pervades all areas of Japanese language life, but I will focus on three trends as exemplars for observing some of the social and linguistic processes involved in Japanese linguistic creativity: (1) the rising popularity of so-called *KY-go*, a mixing of scripts and spoken forms that also demonstrates connections to social changes and pressures Japanese young people are now facing; (2) the development of *Lu-go*, a style of speech created by a popular celebrity which intentionally mixes the English and Japanese languages together; and (3) the influence of the mass media and events (like the 2011 earthquake and tsunami) on language change. I believe there are several themes readily apparent: the goal of much of Japanese slang is linguistic economy – to make spoken or written forms shortened and more efficient, either morphologically (e.g. through truncation or abbreviation) or socially (e.g. through the use of jokes, puns or other references which do not need to be explicitly stated). Also, in almost all cases, spoken Japanese slang creation and usage has a close connection to script and orthography. Finally, rather than strictly being used as static identity markers, Japanese slang tends to be ephemeral, open-ended and productive.

Some processes of Japanese slang creation.

The Japanese, of course, are quite aware of the changeability and permeability of their language. There are many Japanese–Japanese slang dictionaries (e.g. Yomekawa

2003; Kindaichi 2009; Dutcher 2009; Netto-go Kenkyū Iinkai 2009; Kitahara 2012). A perennial bestseller is the huge 1500-page annual word almanac *Gendai Yōgo no Kiso Chishiki* ('Encyclopedia of Contemporary Terms', published by Jiyū Kokuminsha; Kendai Yōgo no Kiso-Chishiki Editorial Board 2013). All these help the average person keep up with the latest, and fast-changing, linguistic developments. There are also about two dozen English–Japanese slang dictionaries, and numerous websites.

But an important feature of the Japanese language is the presence of English (Stanlaw 2004, 2010). At least 5 per cent of the daily vocabulary used in everyday Japanese is taken from, or inspired by, English (Hashimoto 2010). In special registers these numbers can be substantially higher. And much of this widely available English is used in the production of slang terms or neologisms of all kinds.

Truncation is a common phenomenon seen in borrowing and slang creation in Japanese. This happens to hundreds of English loanwords: e.g. *apāto* (アパート 'apartment'), *depāto* (デパート '*depart*ment store'), *rimo-kon* (リモコン one, usually a husband, who is '*remo*te *con*trolled'). This can happen in terms that are combinations of English and native Japanese terms as well. For instance, in the list of the top 60 new slang terms in 2011 monitored by word almanac publisher Jiyū Kokuminsha was *one-kyara* (おねキャラ). Among fans of daytime talk-show television, it refers to the male *characters* (キャラ *kyara*) acting as women – with the female prefix *one-* coming from *o-nē-san* (お姉さん), a term meaning 'older sister' but often used for ladies in general, like the English *Miss*. What is funny about *one-kyara* is that they often wax extraordinaire on topics thought to be restricted to the speech of women such as clothes, make-up or perfume. Another similar popular neologism last year was *bi-jogā* (ビジョガー), a beautiful woman who jogs. This comes from the native Japanese *bijo* (ビジョ a 'beauty') and the English *jogger*. Truncations can take place initially, medially or word-finally. Among groups of rebellious young women (Miller 2004: 232) the English loanword *konpanion* (コンパニオン one's romantic partner or 'companion') becomes *panion* (パニオン).

These days, Japanese teenagers are even adding certain features to their language that did not exist before. For example, linguists generally say that Japanese technically only has two tenses, past and non-past. But among young smartphone texters or Twitter users, the English auxiliaries 'now' (ナウ *nau*), 'was' (ワズ *wazu*) and 'will' (ウイル *uiru*) can be used to indicate time. So a Tokyo night-lifer might tweet *Roppongi nau, wazu Shinjuku, uiru Shibuya* (六本木ナウ、ワズ新宿、ウイル渋谷) which could be translated as 'I am in Roppongi *now*; I *was* in Shinjuku, but I *will* be in Shibuya later.'

The Japanese writing system and kanji-henkan

The other thing that is noticeable about Japanese slang creation and usage – and that makes it rather unique in the world – is its close connection between speech and writing. Written words are very important to Japanese speakers, even in spoken or aural contexts. Most native speakers would say that the 'real' Japanese is the written form. But there are four orthographies commonly in use, and this allows speakers of Japanese to be almost infinitely creative: (1) Sino-Japanese *kanji* characters (generally used for most nouns and some verbs), which were borrowed from China over the course of several centuries starting in the mid sixth century C.E. – meaning each character today has at least two (native Japanese and borrowed Chinese) readings; (2) the *hiragana* syllabary (used for auxiliary words and bound-morphemes or for things for which *kanji* do not exist); (3) the *katakana* syllabary (used as kind of an italics, or as a way to render foreign names or places into Japanese); and (4) *rōma-ji*, or roman letters (used in a wide variety of contexts, everything from advertising copy to sports jerseys). Thus, theoretically, everything in Japanese could be written in four ways. For example, the name of the country, Japan, is written as 日本 in *kanji*; にほん in *hiragana*; ニホン in *katakana*; and *Nihon* in *rōma-ji*. Any of these four scripts can appear together; in fact, few Japanese sentences have less than two. However, which script is used, and why, has always been a thorny issue in Japanese, and, again, playing with orthographic convention can be a form of wordplay in Japanese (e.g. making a spoken pun or joke whose punch line centers around how some word is written or pronounced).

Another direct contributor to the process of Japanese slang creation is the way Japanese scripts are entered in most computers, smartphones or other digital devices. I'll call this the *kanji-henkan* process for reasons that will become obvious momentarily. The most commonly used technique today for word processing Asian-language scripts is to use a regular Western roman-lettered keypad (or one equipped with keys allowing for phonetic syllabary entry). The user types in a lexeme or morpheme phonemically in Japanese. Then a set of possible Sino-Japanese characters with this reading appears in a side menu, and the user then chooses the correct one by highlighting it and pressing a hot key – the *kanji-henkan* (漢字変換), or 'changing it into Sino-Japanese *kanji* characters' key – to replace the phonetically typed form in the text. This is really not especially cumbersome because programs have become so context-sensitive that the list of available choices offered is already drastically reduced even at the first step, so typing or texting in Japanese is actually not much slower than typing in English. But what is more important here is that certain digital entry shortcuts, tricks and alternative scripts become available for Japanese slang creation and usage – both as written and spoken forms. Some of these are discussed below.

Digital slang and KY-go

Japan is one of the most digitally connected nations in the world. All this has fostered a whole new linguistic world of digitally inspired graphic and quasi-spoken forms. This is especially true for Japanese teenagers and young adults.

The first thing to notice is that – besides truncations – abbreviations abound in Japanese slang. In English the internet has given Brits and Americans a whole litany of abbreviations which have become almost mainstream worldwide. LOL ('laughing out loud'), FWIW ('for what it's worth') and BTW ('by the way') are just a few of the most common (and clichéd). Japanese, too, uses this device, but it operates very differently than in English, with many twists and turns.

For example, the Japanese phrase *yoroshiku onegaishimasu* (よろしくおねがいします) 'Please give my best to …' is often shortened in everyday speech to simply to *yoroshiku* (よろしく). In cell-phone, tablet or computer usage, this gets even more truncated to *yoro* and is written in either *hiragana* (as よろ) or *katakana* (as ヨロ). We might also see the roman alphabet used. *Kon-nichi wa* (こんにちは) – 'good day' – and *kon-ban wa* (こんばんは) – 'good evening' – are common ways of saying hello. Both are simply truncated to *kon*. But instead of being written in full Japanese script, the first syllable is often written as a mixture of *hiragana* and roman scripts: こn.

These forms can be blended in almost limitless ways. For instance, another way of writing *yoro* – the short form of *yoroshiku* – could be *yr*. Another way is *46*. The numbers *4* and *6* are pronounced as *yon* and *roku* respectively in Japanese. Thus, '46' in this context is intended to be pronounced *yon-roku*. It is very common for Japanese people to use the pronunciation of numbers as mnemonic devices in this fashion (e.g. choosing a close-sounding word when trying to remember, say, the numbers to the combination of a bicycle lock). While this may seem like very complicated wordplay to an outsider, this is very transparent to most Japanese and, in the proper contexts, it is blatantly obvious. For example, the pronunciation of the numeral 5 in Japanese is *go*. Thus, in the context of online gaming, *55* means the loanwords '*Go Go!*' or 'let's get started.'

So in even these few simple examples, we see the interesting – though very common – mixing of scripts (native Japanese orthographies and roman letters) and languages (Japanese and English) to create a plethora of new terms and phrases. In fact, some of these devices have become so typical and institutionalized now that they have been given their own special names, like *KY-go* (KY語) – literally, 'KY language'. In 2007 this neologism was first introduced to refer to a person who was always lagging behind the pace of the conversation, referring back, say, to a topic from which all the other speakers had moved on. Such a person was said to *kūki o yomenai* (空気を読めない) – literally, not being able to 'read the air' of the discourse, always being somewhat out of it.

The K and Y came from the initial letters of this phrase. It has since come to mean the technique of using roman-letter initials to refer to native Japanese phrases and words. There are hundreds, if not thousands, of such terms. At two different times, Taishūkan Publishers collected some 44,000 different examples. While some are no doubt nonce forms, many are frequently used.

For instance, *am* (pronounced *ēmu*) stands for a farewell parting, *Ato-de mata, ne* (後でまたね), 'I'll see you later, OK!'; *IW* is *imi wakaranai* (意味わからない) – or the more informal *imi wakan-nai* (意味わかんない) – implying 'I don't get it,' or 'I don't understand the meaning.' Another example, where each syllable within a word is given its own roman-letter abbreviation, is *kwsk* (*kuwashiku*, 詳しく), to explain 'minutely' or 'in detail'.

English loanwords, of course, can also be directly involved in this process. The term *erg* (*erogu* エロゲ) stands for *ero-gēmu* (エロゲム). *Ero* itself is a productive truncation of 'erotic' (*erotikku*, エロテイック) and is found in many coinages, such as the famous word *ero-guro-nansensu* (エログロナンセンス) referring to the liberal early 1930s when parts of Tokyo were alive with much 'erotic grotesque nonsense'. An *erg* is itself short for another English loanword, *adaruto gēmu* (アダルトゲーム) or 'adult game,' usually a video or computer game with sexually explicit content.

But it must be remembered that these are not simply the substitutions of a roman initial letter of Japanese word to create a new expression. For example *wktk* stands for the phrase *waku-waku teka-teka* (ワクワクテカテカ), literally, 'nervous or trembling with excitement' (*waku-waku*) and 'brightly' (*teka teka*). This is from the title of the theme song to the popular television program *Marumo no Okite* ('Marumo's Rules'). It can refer to the excitement one feels doing something challenging, like getting up on stage to sing a song. Here the *wk-* stands for two words (*waku waku*) and not just one, as does the *-tk* for *teka teka*.

The term *JK* can have several interpretations. First, it can stand for *jōshiki-teki ni kangaete* (常識的に考えて), or 'thinking logically or sensibly'. It can also mean *jōdan kitsui* (冗談 きつい), 'you've got to be kidding,' or *jōdan wa kao [dake ni shite]* (冗談は顔 [だけにして]), 'It's just that your face is a joke and there is nothing that can be done about it.' It can also mean *jōshi kōsei* (女子高生), or 'senior high school girl'. Seeing as how KY-go is a popular sport among high school girls, this term is not a surprise. Keeping in this light we see that, besides a cash machine, *ATM* means *Aho-na Tō-chan mō iranai* (アホな父ちゃんもういらない), 'I don't need my stupid dad anymore!' Another example is *PK* (*pantsu kuikomu* パンツ食い込む, *pantsu kuikonderu*) 'underwear [pants] creeping up into one's private parts', referring to a condition so unfashionable that people can see pants stuck in the butt under clothes.

Both sexes, and the young and old, often use the term *MK5* (*maji kiruru 5* [go] *byōmae* マジキレる５秒前). This means 'five seconds before I really lose it', as in describing a situation where someone's increasing temper or impatience is getting the better of them. Note that here the numeral *5* is used for the spoken form *go*. Numerals also appear in other places. For example, *3M* (*maji de mō muri* マジでもう無理) means 'I just can't stand it anymore.' Here, however, the 3 is not meant to be pronounced; it stands for the three repetitions of the initial m- in the *maji*, *mō* and *muri*.

As we can see, English borrowing abounds in KY-go. Sometimes, whole English words are taken in, rather than just abbreviating Japanese terms. Such an example is *TM* (*toraburu mēkā* トラブルメーカー), or 'trouble maker', already a common loanword in Japanese. Other times, the use of English is more creative. *WK* is actually pronounced *shirakeru* (しらける). These letters come from the English word '*w*hite *k*ick.' Why this is used might be a little hard for a native English speaker to fathom, but it is pretty simple for Japanese who are very used to this kind of spoken and graphic linguistic wordplay. The Japanese word *shirakeru* means to cast a chill over something, to make a situation uncomfortable or unpleasant. It is normally written as 白ける. The first character for the first two syllables of this word – *-shira* – is written as 白, and this actually means 'white' when presented just by itself. The second two syllables – *-keru* – are written as 蹴る and when pronounced by themselves mean 'to kick'. In other words, *shirakeru* ('cast a chill') can be imagined as being composed of *shira* ('white') and *keru* ('kick'). Using the first letters of the English glosses '*w*hite' and '*k*ick' yield the term *WK*. Such linguistic verbal and orthographic puns are found not only in KY-go but also in much of the Japanese language.

While such KY-go terms, and other *keitai-go* ('mobile phone terms'), are ubiquitous among young people, Yoneyama (2008) believes that they sometimes have a cost. Because these slang terms are constantly being created and changing, one needs to always be in touch and connected to others to keep up with the transformations and vicissitudes inherent in living in such a globalized high-tech country – with a corresponding language in a constant state of flux. To her, it is not coincidental, then, that the KY phenomenon can be associated with school bullying in Japan. As she points out, bullying is epidemic throughout the nation in spite of the many well-intended attempts to curtail it. Again, the KY label – *kūki o yomenai* – refers to those who are not able to 'read' the social context around them. Thus, the use of nonce-forms of KY-go known only among certain cliques provides a means to exclude others, especially the weak and less popular. Digital IT communication, then, provides new ways of relating to others and pushing notions of friendship to new heights. But these benefits may not always be equally distributed.

Lu-go

The life of Lou Oshiba (ルー大柴 *Rū Ōshiba*) has been quite colorful and controversial. His real name is Ōshiba Tōru (大柴 亨), and he was born on 14 January 1954 in the cosmopolitan Shinjuku ward of Tokyo. He is primarily known as a comedian and film actor, though he has dabbled in many things. But lately he has been gaining special attention for his advocacy of the 'Lou language' – (*Lu-go* ルー語) – a unique blending together of English and Japanese in certain prescribed ways. His blog, Ōshiba, soon became very popular, especially among young teenagers interested in popular culture and learning English. It has been through this forum and the rest of the internet that he has propagated Lu-go, though he also has written several books on it.

In its simplest forms, Lu-go involves the replacement of certain key words in a Japanese sentence with their English correspondents while keeping the Japanese grammar and word order intact. For example (Oshiba 2007a: 9) the sentence 'I love you' can be rendered in Japanese as:

私 は	あなた を	愛 しています
watashi -wa	anata -o	ai -shiteimasu
I [subject marker]	you [direct object marker]	love [verbal auxiliary indicating tense, politeness level, mood, etc.]

Note that Japanese is a verb-final language, so the word order here is subject-object-verb. In Lu-go the sentence might use three English replacements, and come out as:

I は	you を	love しています
I -wa	you -o	love -shiteimasu

But with native pronunciation, and writing the English words in the *katakana* syllabary, the real Lu-go would look more like:

アイ は	ユー を	ラブ しています
ai -wa	yū -o	rabu -shiteimasu

Oshiba (2007b) gives many examples. For instance, here are some well-known phrases, expressions and proverbs loosely based on the well-known *karuta* Japanese children's card game translated into Lu-go. The first is a well-known proverb:

> Japanese: 嘘から出たまこと
> transliteration: uso kara deta makoto
> meaning: from lies come truth (≈ *many a true word is spoken in jest*)
> Lu-go: 嘘からでたトゥルー
> transliteration: uso kara deta turū

Here the English loanword *turū* (from *true*) replaces Japanese *makato*. In the following example, Oshiba changes *kakusu* ('to hide') to the English loanword *hide* and *shiri* ('bottom' or 'hip') to the English loanword *hip*, leaving the original meaning intact but more humorous:

> Japanese: 頭 隠して 尻 隠さず
> transliteration: atama kakushite shiri kakusazu
> meaning: to hide the head but not the bottom (≈ *we can only be partially successful in hiding our faults*)
> Lu-go: 頭ハイドしてヒップ隠さず
> transliteration: atama haido-shite hippu kakusazu

This next example is also a well-known proverb.

> Japanese: 犬も歩けば棒にあたる
> transliteration: inu mo arukeba bō ni ataru
> meaning: 'A dog, too, if he walks, will run across a stick' (≈ *even an unintelligent person can achieve something by chance*)
> Lu-go: 犬もウオークすればポールにヒットする
> transliteration: inu mo uōku-sureba pōru ni hitto-suru
> meaning: 'A dog, too, if he walks, will hit a pole.'

The humor is intentional and is also transparent in Japanese; this is because the English vocabulary is rudimentary and the original phrase well known, providing an easily discerned context.

It is difficult to accurately judge the popularity and ultimate influence of Lu-go. At one time, Oshiba's blog was one of the top 50 in Japan, actually ranked 33rd (Toto 2008). Some 2000 hits were made to his website in 12 February 2013, so his is still a visible presence. Is this due to Oshiba's celebrity as comedian and movie star or is it due to his writing in, and about, Lu-go? He has produced a series of DVDs for English learners (with catchy titles and locales like *English Together Hawaii*), three books and numerous games, records and YouTube clips promoting international communication and English (albeit largely through Lu-go). Nonetheless, what are we to make of Lu-go and its presence? Certainly Oshiba is an idealist who believes that this pop-pidgin approach to viewing English could aid in improved learning of Standard English. However, in the end, this may not be successful. As Moody and Matsumoto (2012: 121) argue, '[The] relexification of Japanese sentences ... is entirely consistent with the ways that iconic language contact has influenced ... English in Japan. It does not attempt to address the basic sociolinguistic reality of English in Japanese society: that English is studied universally, but rarely used communicatively.' That is, in the end Lu-go appears to be simply another variant of Japanese slang.

Japanese slang, neologisms and the media

Everywhere in the world, television and the popular media are rich sources of slang, and if anything, Japan is even more adopting and creative. Current events, of course, dictate much of the new slang in a language. The *Higashi Nihon Daishinsai* (東日本大震災 the Great East Japan Earthquake and tsunami) in Fukushima in 2011 prompted the coining of dozens of new terms. Many of these incorporate English. Among the top twenty, according to the Jiyū Kokuminsha word almanac, are:

afuta 4 (アフター 4 'after 4'): work activities conducted 'after 4:00', in spite of the new standard finishing-time the government and many companies enacted to save electricity and divert power to northeast Japan where it was needed.

zero de wa nai (ゼロではない '[probability of a nuclear fuel meltdown] is not zero'): statement often repeated by the master of understatement Madarame Haruki of the Cabinet Office for Nuclear Safety regarding the situation of the Fukushima reactors.

hotto supotto (ホットスポット 'hot spots'): areas where contaminated radioactive material accumulated.

merutodaun (メルトダウン 'meltdown'): the possibility of fuel rods in the Dainichi Nuclear Power Plant melting down and causing the facilities to explode, casting a tremendous amount of radioactive material into the environment.

Concluding thoughts

As Coleman (2012: 11) says, 'Now you and I know what slang means. Of course we do.' But are things quite as obvious in the 'slang around the world' (Coleman 2012: 206)? How is English incorporated into Japanese slang? Is it English slang terms that are adopted into Japanese slang? Or Standard English terms? Or made-in-Japan English terms? Or something else? Most of the time it is unclear because it is hard to know into which category a term falls. For example, Moody and Matsumoto in their analysis of Lu-go claim that *Katakana Eigo* – that is, English words (*eigo*) nativized by being written in the *katakana* syllabary – constitutes 'a lexicon distinct from either Japanese or English' (2012: 112) and thus might not qualify as slang at all.

How much slang is there in Japanese, and how much of it is English-based? Again, this is a very difficult question, and one hard to quantify. Most statistics gathered on English in Japanese (e.g. Hashimoto 2010) are hard pressed to distinguish slang terms from standard forms, and the orthographic wordplay found on the internet so far has defied corpus analysis (but see Jerry 2008; Kitahara 2008, 2012; Netto-go Kenkyū Iinkai 2009). I would say that all those presented here are recognizable to most Japanese.

So what, then, is the role of English in Japanese slang? In their *Bad Language* classic, Andersson and Trudgill argued that slang is predicated on the following features: Slang is:

> operating below the neutral stylistic level
> typical of informal situations
> typical of spoken situations
> lexical rather than grammatical
> not dialect
> not swearing
> not register
> not jargon
> creative
> ephemeral
> conscious and intentional
> group related
> possibly ancient
>
> *(Andersson and Trudgill 1990: 69–81)*

Such lists – while long-standing, going back to Eric Partridge – are of course arbitrary. Nonetheless, the Japanized English discussed here fulfills most of these criteria.

But the digital age has made such definitions of slang somewhat outdated. The internet, texting, tweeting, social networking – these have all redefined communication, and indeed what is language and orthography. Japan is at the forefront of the charge. As a major technologically innovative force, interacting in the globalized economy in a culturally plural world, Japan might represent the future of how transnational communities will interact: mixing native and borrowed languages, developing new scripts, bending media of all kinds and allowing for almost limitless creativity by individual users. While not having Japan in mind when he said '[t]his is your brain on slang', Adams (2009: 173) draws attention to an important but often overlooked aspect of slang research: its cognitive side. 'If slang is in the brain, isn't it likely there for a reason?' (Adams 2009: 173). No doubt; it is a tool. Slang, then, offers an opportunity for users – creators – to linguistically re-imagine and re-construct their world, in ways not possible with the usual grammatical and sociolinguistic confines. In this sense, the Japanese have been imagining themselves, and re-imagining themselves, using slang and English for well over a century. I doubt they will stop now.

Note

1 Data for this chapter were gathered from numerous dictionaries, almanacs and other printed materials, as mentioned throughout the text. The internet, of course, is now a major font of important linguistic resources, as Coleman (2012: 291–3) and others have shown. I have used it freely. Japanese television is another major storehouse of slang, and in the interest of science, I spend hours watching it. While no formal ethnographic interviews or surveys were conducted, having a readily available pool of family and friends to pick on was invaluable. And speaking of which, I wish to thank several Japanese-speaking colleagues – including Nobuko Adachi, Roger Thomas and Michiko Thomas – who always give me much needed advice and commentary, and often save me from making egregious and embarrassing errors. I also wish to thank the reviewers of this paper, including Julie Coleman and James Lambert, who made numerous detailed, thoughtful and helpful suggestions for clarification and improvement. As usual, Nobuko Adachi's assistance was invaluable, and I could not have written this chapter without her help.

PART IV

Slang and the internet

Julie Coleman

The chapters in this section return to a subject mentioned in many earlier chapters, namely the influence of the internet and particularly of social media on the development of slang. They explore whether online slang is a good representation of spoken slang, and although they generally agree that this cannot be taken as read, they do not argue that slang used online is by any means less to be considered slang because it is found in or even restricted to specific written contexts. For all the written peculiarities of online discourse, it is in some respects closer to spoken language than conventional formal written English. In any case, much online interaction is characterized by its use of inter-related multiple media, so that players of multi-player games may be talking to one player while they are typing to other players about the trolls they are fighting. Many blog writers and posters on Twitter and Facebook upload podcasts as well as written text. In addition, those we engage with using social media are often people with whom we also have, or have had, face-to-face interaction. The people who use obscure gaming slang online probably continue to do so, where appropriate, when they meet fellow gamers socially. Because there is no clear dividing line between the real world and the various virtual worlds we inhabit online, it is unlikely that the slang we use in these contexts is completely unrelated.

Adams (Chapter 15) explores the interplay between traditional media, such as film and television, and online media, such as blogs, social media and websites. The interrogative use of *much* following adjectival and noun phrases (for example, *Patronizing much? Cocaine much?*) provides a case study for the use of evidence from traditional and online media in tracing the spread of a slang form that may have originated in these media. This provides a stark contrast to the type of evidence that has traditionally been available to slang lexicographers. Partridge, for example, was reliant on a few scattered examples of slang forms that made their way into glossaries, memoirs and fictional texts, and on the potentially unreliable information provided by correspondents, a methodology that was criticized even by his contemporaries (Coleman 2011b: 129–46). Partridge's glimpses of a slang form were equivalent to the tips of icebergs, and from these he had to construct an account of something bigger and unseen: actual slang usage. Contemporary slang lexicographers have much more evidence of slang usage available at their fingertips. It is still only a sample of the whole iceberg of slang usage, but sea levels have fallen significantly, providing us with a much clearer sense of what might remain beneath sight. Chapter 18 returns to the question of tracking slang in the era of big data.

These chapters do not merely consider the use of online material as evidence for slang usage. They also consider the new possibilities for the documentation of slang offered by the internet. Peckham and Coleman (Chapter 16) describe the processes involved in publishing definitions for slang terms in *Urban Dictionary* and give an overview of the type of material submitted as well as of the types of entries that users tend to access. What this reveals is that although the contents of *Urban Dictionary* are by no means exclusively slang, slang terms represent a more significant proportion of the terms consulted than submitted. Unlike wiki-edited online dictionaries, *Urban Dictionary* embraces differences of opinion and does not seek to reach consensus. It thus provides contemporary and future students of slang with invaluable evidence about fluid and complex differences in usage. At the same time, like some of the film and television franchises discussed by Adams, *Urban Dictionary* commercializes slang. In the commercial process, slang is a means by which products (consumer goods, but also media productions) are sold and also a product in itself. It is also a means by which slang users can identify themselves with a product and with the set of values associated with it. This is by no means a new phenomenon: the commodification of slang began in the sixteenth century with the earliest glossaries, and slang has been used effectively in marketing since at least the 1950s.

Victor (Chapter 17) introduces a challenge to the definition of slang presented in the introduction of this volume. For Victor, slang not only transcends the lexical, but also the verbal. His chapter explores levels of informality in gestures. For example, nodding is an acceptable gesture indicating approval or agreement in most social contexts. Clapping is the conventional way to express approval in a theatre or at a presentation of research findings among fellow researchers, but it is not normal in a lecture to students (alas!). Clapping can also express rebellious agreement or a warmer feeling of approval in contexts where clapping is not conventional. Synchronized slow clapping generally signals collective disapproval, but it can indicate a determined collective desire for another encore. There are many less formal ways of expressing approval and agreement, including a single or double raised thumb, or a thumb and forefinger made into a circle (a gesture which can have markedly negative connotations in other contexts). These gestures might be considered colloquial, in that they are widely recognized, but they would be inappropriate in formal contexts. *Urban Dictionary* lists other gestures of approval that are used even more informally and only within restricted groups. Social stigma is attached to their use in groups that do not employ them, to incorrect realizations of them or to their use in inappropriate settings. For example, the gesture identified on *Urban Dictionary* as *shaka* expresses approval by pointing the little finger and thumb outwards from a loosely formed fist which is slowly rotated or shaken. Rotating or shaking the fist too quickly risks ridicule or contempt. A snap of the fingers accompanied by a downward gesture of the hand can also express approval, though an individual who uses this gesture in a formal context will probably look foolish. These gestures are much less widely used and are often associated with specific social subgroups in the same way that slang is. As with spoken slang, gestures are socially fluid. In recent years, in part thanks to its use by President Obama, the *shaka* appears to be spreading into wider usage.

Victor argues that gestures like these should be categorized as slang and that the internet provides the ideal medium for documenting gestural slang. This is both because it can capture movement in a way that line drawings cannot, and also because it is necessary to index gestural slang in flexible ways for a variety of possible users. For example, an individual who has seen an unfamiliar gesture in action will need to access its meaning in an online database via its physical expression. An individual who has seen the gesture referred to in print or heard it mentioned in conversation may want to access it by name. Actors, screenwriters and directors might look for a gesture to indicate a particular emotional response, and would thus need to access the database by meaning.

In face-to-face interactions, slang plays a role in defining and confirming group membership and personal identity. We use slang to show that we are young and rebellious, that we like a particular type of music or that we identify with specific social groups of which we may or may not be members in reality. Within a group, the way we use slang will be influenced by the people we like and spend time with. These same functions operate online. When we blog or tweet or post a comment on YouTube or Facebook, we are projecting ourselves to a presumed audience who will judge us on the evidence available to them. For people we know in the real world, these written manifestations of our personalities are just that: our slang use will be evaluated alongside their sense of who we are as individuals and will also feed into the on-going development of our relationship. If I used current youth slang in a status update on Facebook, my Facebook friends would know that I was doing so ironically. For people we interact with only virtually, our slang use occupies a less nuanced relationship with who we are: our decisions about whether we like or dislike an individual online will be made more quickly and informed more strongly by their use of language. A usage that might be perceived as ironic or humorous by those who know us is understood without that contextual knowledge online. If I used current youth slang in a tweet, those who read it might make assumptions about my age, gender and nationality and/or make a judgement (based on their own usage) about whether or not they have any respect for me. As with a chance encounter in a real-life crowd, these judgements are made quickly and soon forgotten unless they represent shared experience or are reinforced by repeated contact.

Perhaps most importantly in the context of this book, the internet is the means by which slang could, in theory, become truly global. As we have seen in Part III,

English is influencing the slang of many languages, some closely related and reasonably local, others much further away both linguistically and geographically. What sets the internet apart from traditional media is its reciprocity: native and non-native speakers of English interact on equal terms online, and none of them are passive consumers of cultural products, Anglophone or otherwise. Broken English phrases used online and in computer games, such as *a winner is you, all your base are belong to us* and *I kiss you*, have fed into the informal usage of some native speakers online (*Know Your Meme* 2007–13), and viral crazes often use English wherever they originate.

Moreover, online discourse is not conducted entirely in English, even in English-language contexts. *Urban Dictionary* includes definitions for many words from Japanese, including *anime, manga, ninja* and *otaku*. While their inclusion on *Urban Dictionary* does not guarantee usage, cross-referencing with Google Blog Search confirms that these terms are all widely used in English-language contexts online, and that they have given rise to undoubtedly slangy compounds, such as *manga-meister* 'a skilled creator of manga comics', *ninja-wannabe* 'one who aspires to be a skilled practitioner of the martial arts', *slowtaku* (*slow* + *otaku* 'a computer nerd') and *uber-anime* 'a dominant or exceptional form of animation'. We might expect, in the future, to see considerably more evidence of the influence of other languages in global English slang.

15

SLANG IN NEW MEDIA

A case study

Michael Adams

Chambers argues that 'the only obvious [linguistic] effect of mass communication … is the diffusion of catch-phrases' (1993: 138). Although Eble notes that 'expressions used on television can be disseminated nationally in a single night' (1996: 94), Chambers argues that '[s]uch phrases are more ephemeral than slang, and more self-conscious than etiquette. They belong for the moment of their currency to the most superficial linguistic level' (1993: 139). Unlike Chambers, I'm not inclined to dismiss ephemera, slang, self-conscious style or, for that matter, etiquette as superficial. They are all concrete aspects of our daily experience – let's not lose sight of them in the aggregation of linguistic data and its relatively abstract representation.

Chambers has in mind traditional media (television, film, radio), which have surprisingly important relationships to modes of online media. Media of both categories introduce, develop and spread slang – sometimes it's spread thick and sometimes it's spread thin, and thick isn't always 'better' than thin. How does slang behave online and how does its behavior online differentiate it from our grandparents' slang? The web is big, and analysis of language on it fraught with difficulties; I am thus merely probing here, suggesting that we look more into the matter than we have, not arriving at any grand conclusions. Nevertheless, when examining slang online, one notices ways in which some new slang forms and online media cooperate in each other's construction and development, how they fit together in rhetorical symbiosis.

In the interest of probing and, as a result of the probing, observing intersections of the rhetoric of slang and that of online media, I engage in a case study of one slang form. The item in question is X + *much*, shorthand by which I'll refer to combinations of ADJECTIVE + *much* (*Awkward much?*) and NOUN + *much* (*Epic fail much?*). Such combinations are presented as sentences (most often interrogative), but they are not conventional or grammatically well-formed sentences – they are more in the way of editorial exclamation. X + *much* here does not include VERB + *much*

(*Drive much?*), which is colloquial but not slang, and well enough formed once one accounts for ellipsis. I've chosen this particular item because it is very much a media phenomenon: apparently – at least, until earlier evidence is discovered – it originated in television and film, and it has prospered there and in online media, in rhetorical contexts where it proves especially handy as a marker of style.

New media

Recent developments warrant a closer look at the relationship among traditional and new media, especially television and various platforms of internet communication, and also between them and language, namely: the networked nature of media; the persistent intrusion of television and other media into our consciousness; media's adept mediation, even manipulation, of what's familiar and what's novel in English worldwide, given the internet and global distribution of old new media in English; the rise of linguistic activity associated with television and modeled on speech actuated, developed or endorsed in mass media; the rise of social groups devoted to television and film, occasioned by the internet, and the layers of commentary, the 'involved' or 'social' language, even talk about talk they produce in blogs, chat rooms, posting boards and fan fiction, etc.; in effect, the convergence of media in a new paradigm of media, and the reconfiguration of interdependencies between language and media. These factors combine into a potent and qualitatively new force in language use. The average person under 50, fully engaged in the spectrum of traditional and online media, encounters the same actors, the same plots, the same attitudes, the same behaviors, the same ideas, and, significantly, the same innovative language spoken by the same actors expressing the same attitudes, from media venue to media venue – television to billboards to tweets – hour after hour, day after day, year after year.

Most important, speakers who are also consumers of media comment on mediated objects – everything from an episode of a television show to slang in the show – and their relations to one another. Speakers, who are also consumers, are also essentially critics, engaged in critical discourse which is at the same time social activity – they produce as well as consume. When they comment on a mediated object, whether in a blog or a drive-by post, a tweet or a photo caption, they enter the very media they observe, so they also observe themselves ironically, and, when they do so, they are conscious of their verbal (and other) style. This description of behavior in the universe of new media is in search of a theory to ground it, and, fortunately, there is theory ready to do so.

Media convergence and slang as style

Experts in media studies are beginning to assess new media, their convergence and mutual implications, and their influence on various aspects of culture:

> A new knowledge culture has arisen as our ties to older forms of social community are breaking down, our rooting in physical geography is

diminished, our bonds to the extended and even nuclear family are disintegrating, and our allegiances to nation-states are being redefined. New forms of community are emerging, however: these new communities are defined through voluntary, temporary, and tactical affiliations, re-affirmed through common intellectual enterprises and emotional investments. Members may shift from one group to another as their interests and needs change, and they may belong to more than one community at the same time.

(Jenkins 2006: 27)

That is to say, they form communities of practice around media and media-related activity, organize themselves (as humans tend to do) in networks that may sometimes be linguistic networks, for the networks of media consumers Jenkins has in mind assume some of the key attributes of linguistic networks. 'The emergent knowledge culture will never fully escape the influence of commodity culture' (Jenkins 2006: 27); commodity culture tends to organize media in mutually referential, mutually reinforcing, and therefore repetitive ways that might affect network behavior including linguistic behavior. Thus, 'according to the logic of affective economics, the ideal consumer is active, emotionally engaged, and socially networked. Watching the advert or consuming the product is no longer enough; the company invites the audience inside the brand community' (Jenkins 2006: 20). Once inside, the audience is supposed to talk about the brand and, as media converge, 'in' the brand; that is, within the brand community, they talk the brand community's language, which is itself an enactment of the brand.

In a sense, we are all branding ourselves with the language we use, and slang is especially helpful in enacting our brands – it is often self-conscious and iconic. Consider some of the criteria Coupland applies to stylization: 'Stylised utterances project personas, identities and genres,' so 'stylization is therefore fundamentally metaphorical. It brings into play stereotyped semiotic and ideological values associated with other groups, situations or times' and 'invites attention to its own modality.' It also 'instigates, in and with listeners, processes of social comparison and re-evaluation (aesthetic and moral)' (Coupland 2007: 154), what I'll call 'verdictive' speech below. Not all stylized utterances are slang, but all slang utterances are to some degree stylized, and, where Coupland's criteria converge with Jenkins' media theory, we can see more clearly how X + *much*, perhaps representing slang generally, operates within new, newer and newest media.

X + *much*

If you trip on the pavement, your sarcastic friend asks, 'Walk much?' Colloquial, interrogative sentences of this form, VERB + *much*, are unexceptionable: they are transparently elliptical (that is, *Walk much?* is an elliptical version of (*Do you*) *walk much?*); and they observe rule-governed relationships among lexical categories, since adverbs like *much* modify verbs like *walk*. From the 1970s forward, however, *much* moved from colloquialism to slang, as speakers combined *much* with adjectives (*Confused much?*) and nouns (*Lapdog much?*) in ways that are not merely elliptical and seem – or indeed are – ungrammatical, and so carry unconventional pragmatic meanings beyond the sum of their components' lexical meanings.

The earliest known instance of ADJECTIVE + *much* is 'Underdeveloped much?' uttered in a sketch on *Saturday Night Live* on 7 October 1978. A decade later, the film *Heathers* (1989) introduced 'Jealous much?' used so often since that it has become a catch phrase. On 10 March 1997, 'Morbid much?' introduced the ADJECTIVE + *much* pattern on the television show *Buffy the Vampire Slayer* (1997–2003; hereafter *Buffy*), and it was soon established as significant in the idiom of the show (see *OED* s.v. *much* (adv.) in sense B.1.h). Such sentences may appear to be elliptical in the VERB + *much* way, but they aren't. It isn't clear, sometimes not even in context, whether a speaker of such a sentence means, for instance, "Are you intensively jealous?" (adverbial *much*) or "Are you often jealous?" (adjective *much*). The pattern doesn't violate any rules (adverbs can modify adjectives), but English speakers find the pattern unusual and slangy.

For some, ADJECTIVE + *much* wasn't transgressive enough: by 1998, NOUN + *much* had developed, for instance, in items like 'Tuna much?' in the film *Jawbreaker* and 'Meanwhile, *My Best Friend's Wedding/Friends* much?' Out of context, such items are incomprehensible, not nearly elliptical. Adverbs don't modify nouns, and it isn't easy to reinterpret *much* in these contexts as adjectival. In fact, these are expansive semantic gestures compressed into tight non-sentences. The most important meanings in these utterances aren't articulated directly, but are understood – a very slang characteristic, since being hip to meaning marks one as belonging to an in-group; if you don't get it, then you obviously belong to the out-group. At the beginning of the *much* timeline, the gestures in question are generally critical, accusatory, dismissive; X + *much* started as invariably interrogative, with lifted intonation on the *much* but, by *Buffy*'s 'Broken record much' (24 October 2000), speakers had twigged to the declarative potential of the form, which is perhaps more intensely whatever it would have been as a question.

The history of *much* illustrates the interaction of media and slang. We have no evidence of ADJECTIVE + *much* before that *Saturday Night Live* episode in 1978; it's therefore possible – though impossible to prove – that ADJECTIVE + *much* originated in traditional visual media and was perpetuated in them, especially by means of reruns, DVDs and now streaming video, all of it commodified, all of it, for some fans, at least, constituting an endless loop of contact with particular slang items or practices. *Buffy* reinforced the ADJ + *much* pattern both directly, by using it frequently and prominently in its own text and thereby endorsing it, and indirectly, by 'encouraging' its use among fans of the show. This 'encouragement' came in many forms, from dissemination of the pattern in related print media (such as novels derived from the show, the official fan magazine, etc.) to development of the pattern in various chat rooms and posting boards devoted to the show.

Following Jenkins, the system of representation and re-representation (including discussion of representations) promotes slang. Slang is a type of branding: characters are branded with it just as media brand and cross-brand with it. Those who use slang they observe in media are branding themselves, too. Thus, it is no accident that Julie Benz, who played the vampire Darla on *Buffy* and *Angel*, played Marcie in the film *Jawbreaker* (1999), while Rose McGowan, who utters "Tuna much!" in *Jawbreaker* is the subject of discussion on the celebrity gossip website *The Superficial* (21 March 2007), with one poster writing of her appearance, "Wow. Cocaine much?" (for more on X + *much*, see Adams 2003: 198–200; 2009: 169–72).

X + *much* works for people who know who Rose McGowan is, those who recognize and affiliate with a certain brand of culture, one that includes all of these shows, films, celebrities and the advertising in which they participate, for, as Danesi points out, 'The term "branding" is used … to refer to the process whereby the messages of brand advertising and those of other cultural sectors are no longer seen as different' (2006: 91), which is consistent with Jenkins's theoretical position. After observing the brand in an array of mediated objects, one can participate in the brand, by using the language embedded in those objects in one's own web discourse, say, commenting on them on a posting board like Television Without Pity and thereby further mediating them. As Mark Peters (2006) shows with reference to that site, X + *much* is not the only form useful in such branding, but online media seem to be X + *much*'s natural habitat.

Three perspectives on X + *much*

There are many ways to examine a slang form on the internet. For instance, on 9 June 2009, Jackson Samuel wrote in *Urban Dictionary* (s.v. *much*) that *much* is 'used on the end of adjectives to make retarded sentences' – like 'Retarded much?' – and that 'if you want to sound like a conformist then go ahead [and use it].' It's not clear from the evidence that X + *much* is an ideal instrument of conformity, but it does help those who use it to fit into some groups and stand out from others, which means it's good slang. Here follow three other short takes on X + *much*, by which I hope to show two things: ways in which the behavior of X + *much* supports the descriptive and theoretical positions I've taken so far, and ways in which X + *much* and online discourse cooperate with each other.

First perspective

First, we observe X + *much* in a very likely but overlooked virtual place, Usenet archives available via Google Groups. I searched there for several variations on the pattern, some first recorded in *Heathers* or *Buffy*, some not. The results suggest the effect of media convergence on both particular items and on the formative pattern, and they also suggest some things about why X + *much* is so useful in some varieties of what the experts call Computer Mediated Communication.

Jealous much?, which occurred in *Heathers* and is the second recorded ADJECTIVE + *much* form, is the only form active between 1989 and 1997. As far as I can determine, there are no instances of X + *much* anywhere between 1989 and 1997, except

TABLE 15.1 Usenet use of some X + *much* forms

	1998	1999	2000	2001	2002	2003	2004	2005	2006
Jealous much?	61	97	108	105	103	64	89	75	93
Pathetic much?	14	8	8	8	3	2	4	1	2
Insane much?		1	1		2	2	2	1	1
Awkward much?		1	1	1					2
Self-righteous much?	2				2				2
Passive aggressive much?			3	2	5	4	2	4	5
Self-absorbed much?				1	2	4	3		
Fucked up much?					1		2		

Jealous much? in Usenet archives. Two Usenet citations for *jealous much* appear in 1994 and there are two more in 1995, fourteen in 1996 and twenty in 1997. During the *Buffy* years, however, use of X + *much* in Usenet explodes, and it persists even after *Buffy* was off the air, as described in Table 15.1. As in 1997, *Buffy* aired during only a few months of 2003; in figures for those years, we arguably see an onset and offset of influence in Usenet use of *Jealous much?*

Interestingly, *jealous much* has persisted on Usenet since *Buffy* became history. One might suspect that the rise in X + *much* in Usenet groups corresponded not to media influence but rather to increases in the number of users or groups, but then one notes the decline in post-*Buffy* use, which may confound that suspicion. While we can't ignore the figures, we can't raise them to the status of a correlation or shake the possibility that it's all just a remarkable coincidence. Thus, I'm not suggesting that *Buffy* itself provably influences Usenet X + *much*; rather, *Buffy* is a marker of media convergence, and we're observing the transmutation of brand into style. The post-*Buffy* figures do suggest, however, that *Jealous much?* is a durable form, just the sort of item Eble had in mind – introduced on television, further actuated in film and television, and established by online media like internet posting boards and chat rooms.

The tally in Table 15.1 also records a remarkable coincidence of X + *much* and media context: 52 per cent of the 38 tokens occurring in Google groups between 1981 and September 1997 occurred in groups devoted to television, film, gaming or popular music. Between October 1997 and the December 2002, 46 per cent of 494 tokens occurred in such groups (now including those devoted to celebrity gossip, radio, etc.); 13 per cent of the tokens occurred in groups devoted explicitly to television or particular television shows. Post-*Buffy*, 38 per cent of 321 tokens occurred in media-focused groups, 15 per cent in television-related sites. In both of the last cases, while *Buffy*-related sites generate tokens, they do so at an insignificant level, so *Buffy* itself is not the most salient media context for X + *much*. Of course, in spite of media's self-involvement, there are plenty of things to discuss in new media besides media, which doesn't change at all the media-centeredness of the activity or the implication of language in media convergence.

TABLE 15.2 Randomly accessed instances of X + *much* (as of 25 January 2013)

ADJECTIVE + *much*	NOUN + *much*	NAME + *much*
Absent much?	Abs much?	Rachel Berry much?
Absentminded much?	Asshat much?	Ally McBeal much?
Affectionate much?	Bikini much?	Meredith Grey much?
Anal much?	Cocaine much?	
Asinine much?	Coke much?	
Baked much?	Douche much?	
Bitter much?	Douchebag much?	
Black much?	Epic fail much?	
Blazed much?	Fake tan much?	
Brownish black much?	Geek much?	
Coked out much?	Glassy eyes much?	
Coked up much?	Hottie much?	
Cute much?	Jigaboo much?	
Dramatic much?	Lapdog much?	
FUBAR much?	Munchies much?	
Fucked up much?	Natural high much?	
Gacked much?	Nerd much?	
Goth much?	[N-word] much?	
Happy much?	Patriotism much?	
Jewish much?	Slang much?	
Lame much?	Slut much?	
Neurotic much?	Stoner much?	
Overprotective much?	TMI much?	
Precocious much?	Uncle Tom much?	
Pretentious much?	Upskirt much?	
Psychotic much?	Weed much?	
Reckless much?		
Shitfaced much?		
Stoned much?		
Two-faced much?		
Viral much?		
Wasted much?		

Clearly, outside of *Jealous much?*, instances of any one collocation appear infrequently, and even the pattern X + *much* (covering all the instances in Table 15.1, as well as those in Table 15.2, and more) is quite rare, exactly what we would expect of a form that does the work X + *much* does. It is a stylistic coruscation introduced into commonplace web discourse in order to announce a brand identity or at least a brand affiliation. As such, X + *much* cannot be an ubiquitous form, but that's all right, because '[a]cts of speaking and the meaningful variation they articulate are *not* inherently linear. It can be argued that the basic unit of analysis for language variation is the individual occurrence of the individual linguistic variant' (Coupland 2007: 41). Numbers and frequencies have their place, but each instance of X + *much* or any other such arresting slang should be gauged in its own discursive act.

Second perspective

Though X + *much* is not used frequently on the web, at least, not relative to better established slang, X + *much* forms are nonetheless easily found. Google helps us to recover such ephemeral items, which are designed to further a speaker's communicative goals in specific contexts, and are then left as lexical detritus in cyberspace. I once set myself the challenge of finding as many of what I thought were unlikely -*y* suffixed forms (*Jesusy, saviory, cathedraly, mixed signally, four lettery*, etc.) as possible, day after day, in one hour on the web (Adams 2009: 166–9); when I started each session, I thought, surely, this time, I won't find many such forms, but I always did – there can't really be an infinite number of them, but they seem inexhaustible. Less rigorously, I've tested the web randomly for X + *much* forms, some of them similarly unlikely above and beyond the unlikelihood of the pattern in the first place. Table 15.2 provides a list of some forms I've found.

The items listed in Table 15.2 suggest another way of looking at X + *much*: we can think of the combination as a function, with *much* as the constant and X as a variable coefficient. The 'value' of the coefficients is partly thematic. We could argue for decades about how the themes should be characterized – how fine-grained they should be, and what terms label them most accurately – but for now, just as a means of illustrating the matter, let me propose categories like Affect (*Jealous much?* or *Precocious much?* or *Over-protective much?*), Vice (*Cocaine much?* or *Gacked much?*), Insult (*Asshat much?* or *Lapdog much?* or *Uncle Tom much?*), Racism/Ethnic Animosity (*Jewish much?* or *Jigaboo much?* or *[N-word] much?*). Racism/Ethnic Animosity might be a subcategory of Insult, and the relationship between those categories a problem we confront when, for instance, we realize that *Uncle Tom much?* belongs in both of those categories.

Again, all X + *much* forms are, in speech act terms, verdictive – they judge or evaluate, so while we can distinguish different themes among the items listed in Table 15.2, their functions in discourse are strongly similar. In the case of NAME + *much*, the topics and quality of verdicts are obscure, because grasping them requires primarily pop-cultural rather than lexical knowledge, which may explain why examples of that combination are probably much less frequent than the others. To determine the relative frequency of the grammatical categories in various new online media, one would have to construct a corpus of web text that included blogs, tweets and posting media (YouTube, Pinterest), logically the next step beyond the probing recorded here.

Third perspective

The verdictiveness of X + *much* is significant because arguably the form is especially well suited to certain online contexts – it conveys attitude and a wide array of rhetorical stances, from affiliation to scorn, very efficiently. Most people use the web to comment, to judge content others have placed on the web, and they like to do so with whatever flair they can muster. X + *much* is a sharp, quick cut, often meant to be devastating, and because it breaks the rules of English it asserts an above-the-law superiority on its users' parts. As already noted, X + *much* is too obtrusive to be used frequently. It is a nice addition to the blogger's verdictive repertoire, and many of the forms reported in Table 15.2 appear in blogs, for instance, *Asinine much?*, *Dramatic much?* and *Asshat much?* They aren't always critical or self-deprecatory: *Affectionate much?* refers approvingly to a child's behavior.

The blogger shares stylistic opportunities and pressures with those who post or chat. Rettberg insists that 'blogs are conversational and social, they are constantly changing and their tone tends to be less formal and closer to everyday speech than is the general tone of print writing' (2008: 33), but while she's right about tone, she's not quite right, IMHO, about blogs as conversation. It's because they aren't, because they start as statements, as actions, but not as components of interactions, that X + *much* and similarly sparkling slang can work in them. As opposed to novels and essays, blog posts are short, so certain types of slang can shine there as they can't in print media. And, of course, blogs can anchor interactions: 'Most blogs allow and encourage readers to leave comments, and almost all use links to link to sources and to other bloggers discussing similar topics' (Rettberg 2008: 21).

This is yet another iteration of the networked nature of media, a precondition for convergence found even before blogs: '"the market" had already become interconnected, with television viewers discussing plot turns with hundreds or thousands of other viewers online, readers writing reviews of books they'd bought at Amazon.com and people discussing good or bad customer service in online discussion groups and mailing lists' (Rettberg 2008: 129). Of course, commentary recapitulates language that carries cultural capital in 'the market'. It is a short step from 'Markets are conversations' to 'Conversations are markets', as they surely are on the web.

In two emerging media, X + *much* is particularly apt. One must not overstate the case: it's not uniquely suited to them, nor is it especially useful relative to, or to the exclusion of, other rhetorical strategies or other linguistic forms. But X + *much* fits well with them, and the fit may explain X + *much*'s unlikely resilience. The first is Twitter, the second photo and video captioning.

While *Jealous much?* is used on Twitter by leaps and bounds more often than other X + *much* forms (indeed, perhaps more than all others together), the top three are originally from old new media, perhaps also *Self-involved much?*, used on *The Sopranos* on 28 March 1998. Forms like these demonstrate the power of media

TABLE 15.3 Approximate Twitter hits for select X + *much* forms (as of 20 August 2012)

Jealous much	145,000
Pathetic much	16,500
Broken Record much	10,900
Self-involved much	2,730
TMI much	2,300
Munchies much	1,100

convergence in the recycling, recapitulation or re-contextualization of slang items and formative patterns. Verdiction is the dominant strategy, and Affect the dominant theme – Twitter is used often to criticize behavior, it's a medium of gossip. Thus, *Munchies much?* is lowest ranked because when it's gossipy, it implicitly approves drug-related behavior, but otherwise, it's not – accusing someone of jealousy is always verdictive, but asserting that someone has the munchies is not reliably so. Use of *TMI* 'too much information' *much?*, while negatively verdictive, is probably inhibited because it uses two radical shortening strategies at once. This last should be an advantage, as it consumes fewer of a tweet's 140 characters, so it's no surprise that the longer items, though thematically appropriate to the medium, are less though not least favored.

X + *much* is also handy for captioning photos (on personal blogs, social net-working sites, Flickr, Tumblr and Pinterest, for instance) and videos (primarily YouTube), because it packs a lot of attitude into the fewest possible words, in the cases of NOUN and NAME + *much* short-circuiting conventional grammar in the process. Sometimes the photos and captions are a means of representing oneself, sometimes others; when others it's possible to pass judgment, but when oneself the tendency is to self-congratulate or brag about whatever the pictures represent. So, Melissa Araujo, a fashion designer, captions a picture of her modeling one of her designs, 'Black much?' to convey the color purity of her black ensemble. Or, for reasons never entirely clear to me, when photos of someone named Rebecca Black rose to the status of memes, the site funnyjunk.com captioned one of them 'Rebecca Black much?' with the further comment, 'Viral much?', thus amplifying the verdictive effect of the slang pattern in perhaps the only new medium in which the piling on of X + *much* is possible. And, on various posting or social networking sites, revelers have tagged photos – whether during the reveling or just after isn't always clear – 'Weed much?', 'Wasted much?', 'Baked much?', 'Wrecked much' or 'Shitfaced much?' This all suggests a semantic development away from verdiction and towards the bragging I mentioned above. In other words, the slang and the media are developing rhetorically, not in parallel, but cooperatively.

Conclusions

Looked at one way, the three perspectives just taken on X + *much* and by impli-cation slang on the web, amount to a truism: in whatever media it operates, slang accommodates the media, or it won't be successful, won't accomplish what slang is supposed to do. Nevertheless, the web affords fresh opportunities for mediated and even commodified communication, so the motives underlying use of X + *much* are rather different from those underlying slang in traditional media. The nominalist in me resists the truism as an abstraction – the devil is in the details – and here I've tried to suggest the value of examining the details of language use in new media, both old and new, more often and more intensively than we tend to do.

The techniques of variationist sociolinguistics have their place, but they should not lose sight of what Johnstone has called linguistic self-expression, the conscious choice of forms for any number of reasons, including working both within and around the constraints posed by the new circumstances of web discourse and media convergence. 'How', she asks, 'can linguistic work be done in such a way as not to lose sight of people speaking?' We should see the study of language generally, and slang particularly, as partly 'the study of verbal art,' an intersection of 'language, identity, and individuality' (Johnstone 1996: 179–80). Perhaps Chambers is right, then, to frame the production of lexical ephemera in media as of 'the most superficial linguistic level', since what isn't structural is, after all, superficial – not that there's anything wrong with that. The superficial level is where one finds people speaking.

16

URBAN DICTIONARY AND THE DOCUMENTATION OF CONTEMPORARY SLANG

Aaron Peckham and Julie Coleman

Urban Dictionary was first launched in 1999 as a parody of *Dictionary.com*, which originally also provided the model for its appearance. In contrast to *Dictionary.com*, all of *Urban Dictionary*'s content was written by amateurs, originally by the friends of its founder. It was thus set up in opposition to established authority and is, by its nature, irreverent. It was also designed to provide an alternative source of authority for settling arguments about the meanings of words that were not included in more formal online lexicons. From the beginning anyone could submit a word and definition, so the authority lay in *Urban Dictionary*'s contributors: in the speakers of the informal language it seeks to document.

Urban Dictionary is frequently cited by journalists commenting on a current linguistic or cultural trend. For example:

> [U]rban dictionary defines geeks as 'people you pick on in high school and wind up working for as an adult.'
>
> *(Reshmi 2012: online)*

> Creative Industries at the Nelson Marlborough Institute of Technology is ending 2012 with a whole lot of Hooplah.
>   Urban Dictionary defines 'Hooplah' as 'commotion, disturbance, hype, excited talk or gossip'
>
> *(Pearson 2012: 2)*

> Aargh: A word that proclaims sorrow, annoyance, anger, depression, hopelessness – The Urban Dictionary
>
> *(Sherman 2012: 21)*

A *Nexis* search for 'urban dictionary' in the category of 'major world newspapers (English)' found almost four hundred citations, excluding similar articles, peaking in

2010 at over ten a month worldwide. Most are of the type quoted above, in which *Urban Dictionary* is cited as if it speaks with a single authoritative voice: as if it were a conventional dictionary. However, some journalists do evaluate *Urban Dictionary* and its contents. For instance:

> Almost perversely, *Urban Dictionary* avoids most of the standard dictionary apparatus. You won't find information about parts of speech, etymologies or even standard spellings in it. Its sensibility, in fact, borders on the illiterate, which must be a first for a dictionary. It's also packed with redundancies and made-up entries.
>
> *(Heffernan 2009: MM16)*

Urban Dictionary plays another function for traditional journalists and online commentators, by which it allows them to provide access to obscene definitions without taking responsibility for publishing them. For example:

> We'd suggest that anyone who doesn't know what 'tossing salad' means as a slang term visit Google or Urban Dictionary at their own risk, and then enjoy this unexpectedly naughty 'Today' bit.
>   Check out the video below!
>
> *(GossipCop 2012: online)*

Urban Dictionary data is also useful to other professionals, including the officials who check that Nova Scotia number plates do not contain obscure contemporary slang (*CBC News* 2012: online) and the publicity agents who wish to promulgate fake slang to promote their product (*Jezebel* 2012: online). So frequently do journalists and other commentators turn to *Urban Dictionary* that it is occasionally used as a generic term. For example, an account of the reliable batting record of cricketer Faf du Plessis commented that:

> So sure is he, the phrase 'to Faf about' may well have to be redefined in urban dictionaries.
>
> *(Lalor 2012: 39)*

At the time of writing, 1.4 million unique words are defined on *Urban Dictionary*. About 1,400 new definitions are submitted each day, approximately 40 per cent of which are definitions for headwords that were not previously defined on the site. Although many of these are slang and a significant proportion appears to be made up, they also include a great many of the highest frequency words in English, including *a*, *the*, *and* and *or*, as well as lexical items including *table*, *book*, *to run*, *to sing*, *happy* and *quickly*, all of which are defined in their standard uses. In recognition of its lexical inclusivity, *Urban Dictionary*'s tagline changed from 'the slang dictionary you wrote' to 'the dictionary you wrote' in 2009; to emphasize the fluid nature of *Urban Dictionary*'s contents, it became 'the dictionary you write' in April 2013.

People can engage with *Urban Dictionary* on four different levels: as users, voters, authors or editors. Approximately 37 million individuals access *Urban Dictionary* each month, and popular audience measurement tools such as Google Analytics, Quantcast and Crowd Science reveal some sociological information about these individuals: 58 per cent are male; and 61 per cent live with their parents; 70 per cent live in the United States, with the United Kingdom accounting for 8 per cent, Canada 5 per cent and Australia 4 per cent. Hong Kong, Singapore, Germany, Malaysia and Ireland account for less than 1 per cent each. In short, those who consult *Urban Dictionary* are characteristically native English-speakers, who are young and male. The terms they consult most frequently are shown in Table 16.1.

Table 16.1 demonstrates that over this time period, the words most frequently consulted fell into four main groups. First are the widely used current slang terms such as *swag* 'cool; coolness', *twerk* 'to gyrate the buttocks' and *ratchet* 'unattractive; an unattractive woman'. Acronyms and initialisms make up a significant proportion of these, including *yolo* 'you only live once', *smh* 'shake my head' and *milf* 'mother/ mom (etc.) I'd like to fuck'. The second group consists of words that are not slang, but are of lasting or passing interest to *Urban Dictionary* users, such as *sex* and *no shave November*. The third group are phrases such as *funny sex positions* and *name meanings*, which indicate that users also approach *Urban Dictionary* as an encyclopaedic reference work. Predictive searching probably explains the high frequency

TABLE 16.1 Most frequent look-ups in *Urban Dictionary* in the second half of 2012

July	August	September	October	November	December
swag	swag	swag	swag	swag	swag
yolo	yolo	yolo	ratchet	ratchet	ratchet
hipster	ratchet	ratchet	yolo	poo butter	yolo
ratchet	hipster	hipster	hipster	yolo	hipster
sex	sex	sex	sex	hipster	sex
douchebag	douchebag	pleb	gangnam style	no shave November	kiki
bootylicious	bootylicious	felching	douchebag	sex	molly
smh	smh	gangnam style	felching	douchebag	gangnam style
brony	trolling	stahp	bootylicious	bootylicious	bootylicious
molly	molly	douchebag	photobomb	gangnam style	douchebag
milf	fap	bootylicious	smh	molly	swerve
H.A.M	milf	molly	twerk	swerve	lion style
trolling	brony	smh	swerve	smh	twerk
Rule 34	ftw	mfw	donkey punch	twerk	smh
derp	cunt	milf	molly	donkey punch	donkey punch
cunt	Rule 34	swerve	trolling	funny sex positions	rule 34
otp	derp	trolling	milf	kiki	cunt
ftw	canoodling	unt	cunt	blumpkin	sosa
slang	MFW	spooning	derp	cunt	trolling
noob	otp	derp	butt chugging	trolling	derp

of particular phrases in these searches, in that a user who began to type *funny* in the search box might opt to explore *funny sex positions* when that phrase was suggested to them even if it were not the intended look-up. Finally, current news and media events are reflected in the high frequency of look-ups for items such as *gangnam style* and *pleb*.

Where there is more than one definition for the same word or phrase in *Urban Dictionary*, their order is determined by the number of 'thumbs up' or 'thumbs down' votes provided by users. Approximately 3 per cent of *Urban Dictionary* users vote for or against a definition on any given day. Because many of the words submitted are rarely, if ever, consulted (compare Tables 16.1 and 16.2), the proportion of definitions receiving a vote is lower still, at 2.7 per cent (*Urban Dictionary Blog* 18 April 2013).

Only 0.1 per cent of those who consult *Urban Dictionary* ever submit a definition. However, the numbers are still substantial: of a total of 4.2 million authors who have submitted definitions, approximately 30,000 are active each month. Between them, they have submitted over 7 million definitions since 1999 (as of 24 April 2013).

The top 20 most frequently defined (and approved) words for *Urban Dictionary* in the second half of 2012 are shown in Table 16.2.

TABLE 16.2 Top 20 terms submitted and approved in the second half of 2012 (number of approved entries in brackets)

July	August	September	October	November	December
yolo (14)	one direction (10)	swag (7)	romnesia (9)	jailhouse c-section (16)	haylor (7)
muddy lizard (11)	tinky (8)	yolo (7)	swag (8)	learned the clarinet at school (12)	scrub (5)
swag (10)	swag (7)	peasant (5)	teacup pigging (7)	asmdss (10)	one direction (5)
urban dictionary (5)	yolo (7)	splooge mcduck (5)	trailer turd (6)	swag (6)	yolo (5)
emo (5)	heavy nova (6)	daniel (4)	binder (6)	chris (6)	jordan (4)
love (4)	dubstep (6)	obama (3)	binders full of women (6)	ophie (5)	brandon (4)
cunt (4)	defranco-fy (4)	troll (3)	sarah (4)	hannah (5)	belieber (4)
sarah (4)	connor (4)	touchception (3)	romney (4)	anna (5)	onision (4)
ethan (4)	rageboner (4)	swaggot (3)	love (4)	austin (4)	ratchet (4)
dutch hat (4)	snoop lion (4)	brandon (3)	dylan (4)	sarah (4)	haley (4)
one direction (4)	legitimate rape (4)	republican (3)	emily (4)	amanda (4)	cornball brother (4)
mason (3)	katie (3)	directioner (3)	sydney (3)	jock (3)	michael jackson (4)
loki'd (3)	kyle (3)	love (3)	ratchet (3)	kyle (3)	justin bieber (3)
morgan (3)	jennifer (3)	claudia (3)	jason (3)	jordan (3)	jake (3)
jake (3)	i see how it is (3)	shamboiling (3)	michael jacksoning (3)	hipster (3)	julia (3)
nerd (3)	jordan (3)	ching (2)	fucktard (3)	harry (3)	lauren (3)
hipster (3)	ashley (3)	cod (2)	blowjob (3)	ethan (3)	jacob (3)
fish (3)	friendzone (3)	camellia (2)	hkangela (3)	daniel (3)	hannah (3)
alice (3)	gangnam style (3)	bussy (2)	unicorn (3)	emily (3)	december 21, 2012 (3)
derp (3)	alexandra (3)	chinese fire drill (2)	michael jackson syndrome (3)	andrew (3)	cute (3)

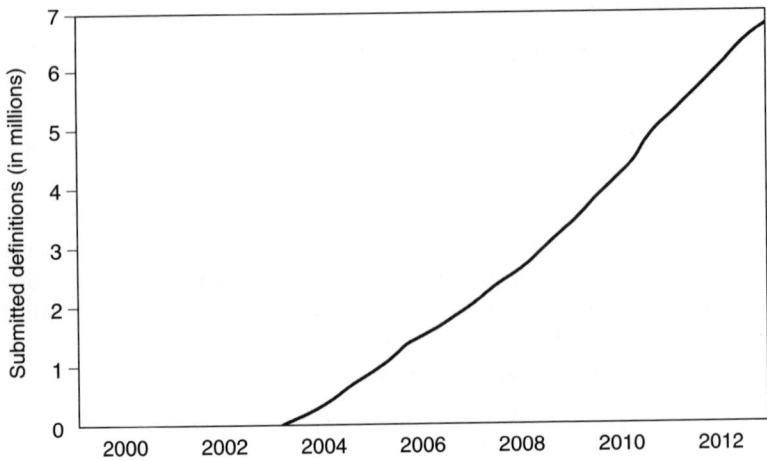

FIGURE 16.1 Number of separate definitions submitted to *Urban Dictionary* since 2000

The most striking difference between Tables 16.1 and 16.2 is that the names of people, known and unknown, and also of bands and tracks are contributed with great frequency but not consulted at a comparable rate. While contributors might want to record their feelings about people and groups, it is less likely that other users will feel the need to look them up on *Urban Dictionary*, though they might consult other sites for celebrity information, gossip and opinion. For example:

> **katie** the name katie is usualy given to one who happens to be exceptionaly well at pleasing their partner. Katie's happen to be very good at making the opposite sex rather 'turned on'. one would not regret having been with a katie.
> i want a girl like katie, one who can turn me on and tease me but do a good fuckin job at it; mmmbaby!
> *(Urban Dictionary: logan! 26 November 2007)*

> **Michael Jacksoning** Using your god-given talent to make the world a better place.
> I'm going to ask others use their Michael Jacksoning powers to Heal the World.
> *(Urban Dictionary: Barbarella123 24 October 2012)*

Temporary hot topics are also represented on this list. For example:

> **Binders full of women** Where Mitt Romney gets his women from
> Joe: Bit of a sausagefest we've got going on here, we need to find some ladies!
> Mitt: Not to worry, I've got binders full of women we can choose from!
> *(Urban Dictionary: laleph 16 October 2012)*

Legitimate rape Legitimate Rape, as defined by the Republican Party, is rape in which upon penis having entry into the vagina, a mutated tiger shark with a laser beam attached to its head jumps out of the vulva and viciously attacks the male genitalia.

'If it's a legitimate rape, the female body has ways to shut the whole thing down.' – Todd Akin

(Urban Dictionary: I3laze 1 25 August 2012)

These terms do not figure in Table 16.1 as being frequently consulted, but their inclusion is potentially invaluable to future researchers in many fields once these transitory references have become incomprehensible.

Slang terms make up a relatively small proportion of the frequently contributed items during this period. Phrases such as *teacup pigging* and *learned the clarinet at school* appear to represent concerted campaigns, because in each case several definitions were submitted within a single day or across a few days, sometimes by the same user. While *Urban Dictionary* is a great resource for information about slang words already encountered in real life, it would be unwise to learn otherwise unevidenced slang from it.

Contributors to *Urban Dictionary* submit their definitions by filling in a form. They are reminded to provide background information in the definitions and to 'write for a large audience'. They are also warned that inside jokes and definitions 'naming non-celebrities' will be rejected, though this warning is not always followed through. An example of use is required and authors can insert links to definitions by placing other slang terms within square brackets. A final box, labelled 'Tags', is designed for synonyms, antonyms, related words and alternative spellings. Before definitions are submitted for review, the author is required to provide a valid email address.[1]

Once definitions have been confirmed by email, they are reviewed by the fourth category of *Urban Dictionary* user: the editors. Like authors, editors are merely site visitors who have chosen to visit a particular page. Editors are not employees of *Urban Dictionary*, and there is no sign-up process. The volunteer editor system was introduced in 2005 and by 2012 9,000 editors were actively reviewing definitions. On average, each editor reviews 20 new definitions, on a taxi-rank principle. Definitions are published with four 'publish' votes or rejected with two 'don't publish' votes, which means that each definition will generally be reviewed by between two and five editors before it is rejected or published. Editors also have the option of voting 'I don't know', so some definitions will be seen by more editors until they have received a sufficient number of decisive votes. Figure 16.2 shows what proportion of the definitions submitted fall at each stage of this process.

An in-house analysis of the editing process asked editors to explain why they accepted or rejected definitions (*Urban Dictionary Blog* 2 May 2013). This study found that editors are more likely to approve definitions that they describe as funny, clear, accurate or for 'something you would use'. Personal and 'nasty' definitions were more likely to be rejected. This suggests that the volunteer editor system is, on the whole, fulfilling its function.

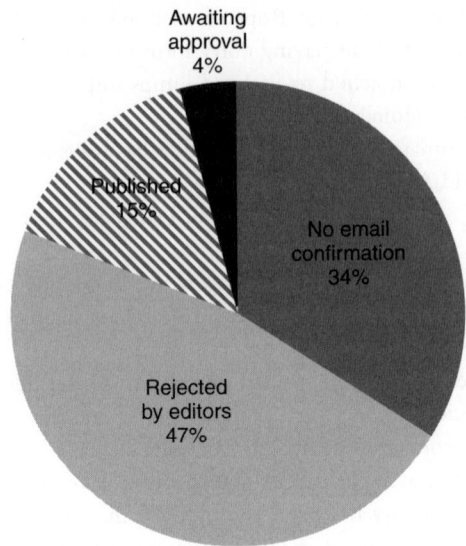

FIGURE 16.2 The fates of the 40,771 definitions submitted during May 2012

Urban Dictionary is not a slang dictionary or even a dictionary at all in any conventional sense of the word. It is still a parody of a standard dictionary in many respects, whether or not this is intended by its authors. Its purpose, unlike *Wikipedia* (for example), is not to reach a consensus of opinion through collaborative writing, but to express and explore differences of opinion. *Urban Dictionary* does not provide a definitive solution to problems of meaning, spelling or usage: it is the reader's responsibility to reach conclusions based on the evidence available. The evidence is constantly changing, and this provides a useful reminder that a living language is always in flux. In a wiki slang dictionary, editors could choose to delete evidence of earlier usage or of variant usage in different parts of the world; in *Urban Dictionary* all submitted evidence remains available indefinitely.

The contents of *Urban Dictionary* are of mixed quality and credibility, despite the volunteer editors' input. Users' strong feelings about what it should and should not be can be assessed by the 440 different definitions provided for the phrase 'urban dictionary'. For example:

> **urban dictionary** A place formerly used to find out about slang, and now a place that teens with no life use as a burn book to whine about celebrities, their friends, etc., let out their sexual frustrations, show off their racist/sexist/ homophobic/anti-(insert religion here) opinions, troll, and babble about things they know nothing about.
>
> *(Urban Dictionary: Lucy 18 March 2005)*

Of the top-rated 50 definitions for *urban dictionary*, 31 make derogatory remarks about the site and/or its users. They make particular reference to obscenity, offensiveness and political bias (of all shades). For the users, these aspects of *Urban Dictionary* may seem negative, but for researchers in these fields they represent an opportunity to move away from toilet-wall graffiti (Green 2003). A further 11 entries remark that *Urban Dictionary* is in decline itself or that it is just one symptom of a more general moral and social decline. Only two entries celebrate *Urban Dictionary* without qualification, while the remaining six focus largely on the site's coverage of sexual terms. It is unclear whether these authors consider that to be a positive or negative feature of the site.

Despite its limitations, *Urban Dictionary* offers slang users the opportunity to document their own usage. Naturally they disagree with one another, and inevitably these disagreements are represented on the site. However, amid the made-up words, the names and the abuse, *Urban Dictionary* also contains a great many useful definitions for contemporary slang terms (Coleman 2011a: 109–28). Even where the definitions are not very good, their combined effect is informative and they offer dated evidence of use.

Urban Dictionary serves many purposes for its varied users. It can help teenagers and pre-teens in the process of growing up: as a safe place to find out about sex, but also to help them understand their peers or the language used in music or online. It can also be useful to adults: parents and teachers can consult it as a guide to understanding their children or students. As has already been noted, it provides lexicographers with dated evidence of slang usage. Learners of English can also use it to supplement their knowledge of contemporary English usage. It is important to take *Urban Dictionary* on its own terms, however, and that means not too seriously. *Urban Dictionary* books (Peckham 2005, 2007, 2012) are rightly placed in bookshops' humour section.

Note

1 Unfortunately, *Urban Dictionary* does not currently collect demographic information separately about its authors or about another category of users mentioned in the next paragraph: its editors.

17

GESTURAL SLANG

Terry Victor

There is a natural tendency to consider slang (and other unconventional forms of expression) as a spoken form that is validated, at least for practical lexicographic purposes, only when used in print and filed in a wordlist. However, we live in a visually literate society; given that non-lexical language, encompassing any inter-personal communication comprised of unformed sounds, both vocal and physical, and primitive gestural expression, must, almost by definition, predate words, we have always done so. Non-lexical slang is a loose categorization of gestures and articulations that cannot unequivocally be counted or collected as conventional expression. The primary constituent of this non-lexical form is gestural slang: a vital and dynamic element of everyday life.

The difference between conventional expression and the informal or slang register is often blurred; the same holds true for gestural expression. Side-stepping the need to develop a precise definition for slang, it is true to say that slang serves a number of purposes in society: essentially as an informal mode of expression that, in addition to meaning, and in varying contexts and degrees, designates inclusion or a lowering of formality. Gestures that conform, however loosely, to that general understanding of slang are a form of cultural shorthand. Together they comprise a significant, yet mainly overlooked, element in unconventional discourse.

As gestural slang is not subject to the same grammatical structures and syntax that form the business of everyday slang lexicography, non-lexical items must, of necessity, be collected and organized by a different set of rules: a process not fully possible until the advent of the internet and associated digital advances. Now, for the first time, it is technically feasible to consider moving-images as lexicographic units and create detailed yet flexible cross-references and taxonomies; hence, my current and on-going development of an interactive online glossary of non-lexical slang that forms the basis of this chapter. In addition to the literal choreography of gestural expression, the online glossary encompasses other types of unconventional, non-verbal expression, meta-linguistic sounds and utterances that serve the same general purposes within the structures of English and American English. The purpose of the online glossary is to provide an accessible academic resource for linguistic study and, also, to offer an interactive element that might encourage the more general user to contribute visual and aural suggestions. There are other, commercial elements that fall outside the parameters of this chapter. Here I will concentrate specifically on gestural slang, and the challenges to be met by its documenter, in the categorization and presentation of this unconventional element of everyday discourse.

Past and present challenges

Lexicography, as with most book-bound endeavours, has always struggled to represent gestures in any but the most stylized ways. In published considerations and glossaries of gestures, a gesture, when illustrated, is invariably captured at its height or at key moments of its expression. This process, while it might be as good as it got, is inevitably less than satisfactory. More often than not, in usage, any gesture's intention is nuanced, signalled by the user's face, body language and, often but not necessarily, accompanying words or sounds. On the printed page, arrows or other diagrammatic embellishments may serve to flesh it out a little but the gestural item has been frozen and catalogued in an un-nuanced form. The best that has been achieved is detailed descriptive text that may suggest variant senses. Until now publishers' limitations of space and technology have required that any gestural icon or illustrative model, whether photographic or line-drawing, is neutral. Contemporary books available in this field have tended, therefore, to put the laws of commerce ahead of the strictures of academic requirement and many of the published titles consulted for this work have had to be resourced from the humour shelves.

In practice, there is little in the way of valuable scholarship that can be drawn on when entering the realm of gestural slang. 'Students of linguistics are everywhere … but the gesture specialist is a rare bird indeed – not so much a vanishing species, as one that has hardly begun to evolve' (Morris et al. 1979: ix). Significantly, much research for the online glossary has had to be done online. Things are changing. The cyber-informality of digital technology has had a profound effect on language (Dalzell and Victor 2012: xiii). It is a reasonable contention that more slang and unconventional English may well now be coined or reinvented on our screens than on the street. Without question, in the fertile grounds of social media, the growth cycle of slang has speeded up. It is a major shift but, despite a reactionary temptation to claim otherwise, the internet has not changed the basis of how we communicate, simply some of the means. Ultimately, it is sound and vision, words and their expression, language and signals. The internet is a powerful tool that enhances our visual literacy and the conventional publishing parameters of serious slang lexico-graphy are moving. However, a third of a century on, while there is evidence that Morris's gesture specialist has evolved, the student of gestural slang is still a *rara avis*.

The challenges presented to any lexicographer, glossarist or textbook writer, past or present, involved in the explication of non-lexical expression are manifold. There are challenges that must come before any consideration of definition: how to display the headword/non-lexical item clearly; how to structure a searchable context.

Although non-lexical expressions may well incorporate lexical items, natural utterances and other physical sounds, and many slang gestures may only exist as illustration of, or accompaniment to, speech, the basic component of a gestural slang item is, self-evidently, visual. The logical (digital) way forward is to replace or accompany a typeset headword with a moving image. This book-bound chapter on gestural slang, however, is without the benefit of any form of pictorial illustration. The limitations are obvious and the reader could be forgiven for shaping a gesture and offering more than one visual comment in this direction.

Some examples of gestural slang

The example gestures that follow (mainly well known but a few less so) show the virtual redundancy of conventional parts of speech as a measure and suggest some taxonomic categories within which such non-lexical items might be collected and classified. The intention is to demonstrate the inherent taxonomic challenges presented by these gestures while focusing on means by which these essential parts of everyday social interaction might now be satisfactorily documented, in a way that is as academically rigorous as a formal dictionary of slang.

Air quotes – *and other mimes and imitations*

'Air quotes eliminate responsibility for one's actions' (Rudnick and Andersen 1989: 98). Were that quotation to be read aloud it could well be encompassed by the hooked fingers that are identified as *air quotes* – but to what purpose? As a simple, practical indicator that the words spoken are, in fact, a quotation, or to signify an ironic editorializing or implied distance between the user and the content? *Air quotes*, a gesture so familiar that it has become, in some degree, contemptible, almost conventional, is structurally imitative. *Air quotes* also stands as a conventional headword in its own right.

In this same general area of categorization are the simple, imitative yet unnamed gestures used for miming a phone ('call me'), indicating a wristwatch (for time or appointment) and, in a restaurant, requesting the bill by mimicking the signing of a cheque/check ('bill, please'). While these gestures are so well established that they might easily be considered all but conventional, the informality of their use in conventional contexts argues for inclusion in the gestural slang register; also, unlike *air quotes*, there is piquancy in the fact that their physical representations of activity have, to varying degrees, been rendered inaccurate by the advance of technology. Obviously, with regard to categorization, these examples cannot be filed by headword.

The wider category of mime and imitative gestures also encompasses a variety of masturbatory and genital allusions. While writing this paragraph a 17-year-old female correspondent has emailed this message: 'I saw an Italian woman in a restaurant do the c**t sign from her belly to one of the staff – reminded me of you.' The offensive *cunt* gesture is formed by bringing the forefinger and thumb of both hands together to form a vulvic symbol which is then roughly pushed toward the subject of the insult (Colville 1985: 113). The asterisks here are the correspondent's own, suggesting a greater comfort with gestural imitation than plain spelling. On the other hand, the specificity and aggression of this gesture make no pretence at euphemism. It may be possible to order this item with the headword *cunt* but, clearly, that is not entirely useful.

Digitus impudicus, digitus infamis – *a superabundance of headwords*

Gestural slang, as distinct from conventional gesture, has certainly been employed for at least 2,500 years: Roman poet Martial and the historian Suetonius both note the *impudent* or *infamous digit* (Martial *Epigrams* VI.LXXX; Morris et al. 1979: 81–2, 152). Expressed with varying degrees of aggression, the single middle finger standing proud is apparently phallic in origin. It is also known as the *highway salute*, the *finger wave*, the *Italian salute*; used in the verb-forms *give the finger*, *flip the bird*, *shoot the bird* (Kener and Zeide 2010: 42), *flip the bone*, *flip (him) off*. The basic gesture may also be accompanied by a spoken statement of direction: *Spin on it! Sit on it! Swivel!* and the punning variation *Oliver Twist!* which may be reduced to *Oliver!* (if gestural slang could encompass the form of rhyming slang that last example is it in that it is the meaningful element, *twist*, that is omitted). In addition to various headwords leading to the same gestural slang, the basic gesture appears in a number of variant, often humorously disguised, forms (Blank and Blank 2004).

Seagulls – *sporting brands, logos and catchphrases*

Brighton & Hove Albion Football Club is popularly known as *the Seagulls*. To demonstrate on-pitch pride and celebration, a player will cross his arms loosely, inner wrist on outer wrist, raised in front of his chest, holding the palms face inward, the hands flapping in a manner intended to represent a seagull in flight. In sport, the field of contest, surrounded – at a distance – by crowds and observed by cameras, is no place for mere words; here a gesture speaks to thousands at a time. Somali-born British Olympic champion Mo Farah employs *the Mobot*, an approximation of the letter M, as a gestural utterance of his signature. Jamaican sprinter, Usain Bolt, has famously developed a physical variant of his punning nickname *Lightning Bolt* as an iconic personal logo or catchphrase. Can a gestural catchphrase be slang? Where else can a lexicographer record the term?

The shocker – *an in-joke*

Best known and defined as *two in the pink and one in the stink* (Brody 2011: 16), this gesture represents the index and middle fingers inserted into the vagina and the little finger in the rectum with the ring finger held into the palm by the thumb. Chad Brody lists 365 alternative rhymes that might accompany this gesture (*two in the slit, one in the shit; two in the tart, one in the fart; two in the cunt, one in the runt;* and so forth), which suggests that imaginative use of this particular gesture requires the crutch of conventional language. The *shocker* can be *given, thrown* (*up*), *rocked, slipped* and *plunged* (Brody 2011: 18). This is a gesture that has inspired T-shirts and bumper stickers, and given title to songs (Warner Drive 2005; Steel Panther 2009), yet its purpose in discourse, for the facets of taxonomy, is restricted to sexual reference, offence and in-joke amusement.

V-sign – *initialism and symbolism*

The gesturer's palm faces inward, the index and middle fingers are raised, spread and, often, jerked upwards. This is the signature gesture of confrontational British slang (Morris et al. 1979: 236): the *two-fingered salute, the fingers, the two up, cunt hooks, the Harvey Smith*. A multiplicity of folk etymologies have been recorded, the most popular of which derives from an alleged historical insult by Welsh archers to their French counterparts. A more likely explanation suggests an anatomical representation of spread legs (compare this with the phallic symbolism of *digitus impudicus*).

As *V for Victory* or *Victory-V*, also familiarly known as *the vick* or *the Vicky*, the same basic sign, given palm in or out, usually palm out, served as Winston Churchill's Second World War visual catchphrase, and, both ways about, was a triumphal gesture in Margaret Thatcher's hands. Palm out, with a different intention, it becomes a *peace sign*. With mischievous intent it can turn into one variation of the *rabbit ears* that adorn unsuspecting photographic subjects. Laterally, it animates as scissors and, in hip-hop and urban culture, becomes *the deuce*, a multi-purpose physical embellishment and gesture of farewell.

As an initialism the *V* is an informal indicator of vodka or Viagra, and may represent the cultural and political symbolism wrapped up in *V for Vendetta*, the influential comic book series (Alan Moore 1982–5, 1988–9) and subsequent movie adaptation (James McTeigue 2005); in informal American Sign Language [ASL] it may indicate a vibrator; conventionally it signals the numeral two (unless you are speaking Latin).

Other gestural initialisms, formed in the manner of ASL or British Sign Language [BSL] alphabet characters: *W* 'whatever', *L* 'loser' and *ML* 'major loser'. However, the textual and spoken *OMG* 'oh my god' is represented in gestural slang as a blend of initialism *and* mime. A good visual citation for *OMG* can be seen in the movie *St. Trinian's 2: The Legend of Fritton's Gold* (Parker and Thomson 2009).

#justsaying – *phrasal gestural slang*

Fuck you, fuck the lot o' yous! – in Australian Sign Language (Auslan) one hand points at the subject then both hands point in a belligerent outward sweep. Australian comedian Adam Hills has a routine about a flight attendant who mischievously incorporates the compound into the gestural vocabulary of her safety demonstration – one hand points to the rear of the aeroplane then both hands indicate the wings. Just saying.

A popular Twitter hashtag 'a keyword or phrase marked with #', the minor-key catchphrase *#justsaying* (or *#justsayin'*) is used as an arch-excuse for expressing whatever text the phrase is attached to. A compound gesture illustrating the spoken phrase *hashtag just saying* was used in the TV sitcom *Hebburn* (Cook 2012). The # is formed by two palm-out *V-signs*, one positioned laterally across the other; the two *V*s are then reversed and pointed down across the speaker's body in a parodic *air quotes,* redolent of hip-hop gestural posturing, and delivered with the attitude of conventionally offensive *V-signs*.

The horns – *sex and goats and rock 'n' roll.*

The index and little fingers are held out while the remaining fingers and thumb are folded into the palm which is faced away from the gesturer. Historically, etymologically, this gesture is an ancient symbol for a man who is betrayed by his wife. Superstitiously, this gesture is seen as a talismanic sign for the devil or devil-goat (Armstrong and Wagner 2003: 161). The occult use, while it may (or not) be considered beyond the unconventional boundaries of non-lexical slang, is the direct source for the most widespread contemporary use of *the horns*: the celebratory gesture of heavy metal fandom, popularized by Black Sabbath frontman Ronnie James Dio, who adopted the gesture he knew as the *maloik* from his Italian grandmother's traditional gestural vocabulary (see Dunn 2005, interview with Ronnie James Dio). The University of Texas has the very similar *Hook 'em Horns* gesture, intended to represent the horns of their longhorn (cattle) mascot. It originated in 1955 and is the reason why pictures exist of George W. Bush apparently making the sign of the devil.

B.l.o.o.d. – *salutes and secrets*

Bloods, a gang originally formed in California but now with US-wide membership, shape the fingers of both hands to spell the word *blood* as a sign of gestural allegiance (Savelli 2009: 87). This type of gestural self-identification can be seen in the *gangsta* posturing of hip-hop culture.

Handshakes cross or signal the boundaries of convention. Barack Obama, for example, employs *fist bumping*, in appropriate circumstances, to lower the level of formality. This category might also include the artificial, elaborate and ritualistic etiquette of some in-group hand-greetings. Freemasons, it is said (and YouTube delights in presenting clips), employ secret handshakes as a discreet means of recognition; a gestural language that connotes inclusion or exclusion, where the difference between slang and jargon is the respectability of its surroundings and the company it keeps. Also worth noting in this general context is a conventional, ritualistic gesture made slangy by the addition of a spoken phrase: the mnemonic *spectacles, testicles, wallet and watch* attached to the Christian *signum cruces*, the sign of the cross.

Salutes: conventional salutes carry official weight, which may then be subverted when adopted into unconventional, slangy and ironic use; unofficial salutes may carry popular, political and iconic appeal – the image of the Black Power salute at the 1968 Olympics has lost none of its punch. Literature, TV and the movies, too, have considerable influence. *Star Trek*'s Mr Spock (Leonard Nimoy) first made the *live long and prosper* Vulcan salute in an episode called 'Amok Time' (Roddenberry 1967). Nimoy derived the gesture, a raised palm with the ring and middle fingers held apart and thumb extended, from Jewish tradition, and it is still in play. A more recent example from a fictional world, especially prevalent as a real-world gesture after the movie *The Hunger Games* (Ross 2012) was released, and which may, or may not, have the cultural impact and longevity of *live long and prosper*:

> At first one, then another, then almost every member of the crowd touches the three middle fingers of their left hand to their lips and holds it out to me. It is an old and rarely used gesture of our district, occasionally seen at funerals. It means thanks, it means admiration, it means good-bye to someone you love.
>
> *(Collins 2008: 24)*

Politically corrected signs – racist, homophobic, disablist, bullshit

A UK-wide survey into BSL found that:

> It is no longer acceptable to sign a slanted eye when talking about the Chinese or to mime a hook nose when referring to Jewish people. The flick of the wrist is now an offensive signal for homosexuals. A finger pointing to an imaginary spot in the middle of a forehead is no longer appropriate as a sign for India.
>
> *(Hill 2012: 15)*

Later in the article Hill writes that some gay deaf people and gay disabled people have reclaimed these traditional signs as a badge of their identity. Many of these gestures, as will be recognized, are not exclusive to the signing community. Other items from the ASL, Auslan and BSL vocabularies have migrated to wider society; the signing for *bullshit*, for instance – arms folded with one hand representing a horned head and the other gesturing an expulsion of effluence – is now a staple of corporate jargon.

Gestural slang obviously represents a far greater body of terms than can be discussed here. In addition to the forms considered above, we can include humorous social-commentaries, physical threats, *talk to the hand*, visual codes, violins, *nudge nudge wink wink*, gestures that illustrate or replace spoken words, racecourse tic-tac, advertising slogans, gestures that encompass the non-lexical, *yadda yadda yadda* (Armstrong and Wagner 2003: 182–4), etc. We might also include:

Ralph Camden's Racoon greeting and handshake, the elaborate mimes that signal 'jerk-off' or 'dickhead', Johnny Carson's golf swing, Vic Reeves' lascivious thigh rubbing and Arsenio Hall's finger-tip-touch greeting.

(Dalzell and Victor 2006: x)

The alphabet and beyond

Gestural slang, a largely unspoken – yet, also, often more than merely spoken – idiom has great power and imagination. Spoken words get replaced, intensified or rendered simply unnecessary by visual puns, allusions and imitations, elaborate in-jokes, parodies, signifiers, codes and secret signs; relatively conventional language and gestures are rendered slangy by delivery and context. What this set of slang, slangy and unconventional terms lacks is the alphabetical consistency of words.

As we have seen, in earlier published considerations and glossaries of non-lexical slang the gesture is, of necessity, invariably shown as an icon (a drawing or photograph) that stands for the complete movement of an articulation. The published catalogue of terms is then compiled thematically or in a pseudo-alphabetic order; thematic collections are variously presented in random or pseudo-alphabetic order within themed sections. In order to achieve an alphabetic ordering descriptive names are given to unnamed gestures and, in some cases, named gestures have been renamed to conform to the specific requirements of a particular work. For example, Morris et al. (1979: 225–40) treat the familiar *V-sign* as the 'Palm-back V-Sign'. The headword is further amended to 'HAND V-SIGN' in Morris (1994: 130). In Armstrong and Wagner (2003: 107–36) 'MASTURBATION' is the headword for *wanker*, a gesture in which the gesturer's fingers are singlehandedly curved around, and up and down, an imaginary penis; while an imitative gesture with a little finger cocked is called 'LITTLE PENIS'; and an offensive or jocular display of bare buttocks is listed under 'THE MOON'. The first two are named according to their physical origins but the third breaks that pattern and relies on a freshly coined noun formed from a slang verb. Croft and Windsor (2010) have a different approach, in that this collection of 54 headwords has a randomly ordered *Contents* as guide. The headwords/chapter headings are, effectively, colloquial or slangy definitions: here 'LITTLE PENIS' becomes 'Tiny willy', the *peace sign* is rendered as 'Peace, maaan!' and *air quotes* are dealt with under the heading '" … … … .!" (air quoting)'. This collection is as easy to navigate as the more academic titles.

In the context of an online-glossary this lack of conventional order is no heresy, simply a starting point. The hierarchical organization of a digital database is not reliant on alphabetic order, nor does it stand comparison with the structural necessities of conventional libraries and wordlists. It is a different process entirely, yet the requirements of any given user may be no more than serendipitous clicking and scrolling: the virtual equivalent of thumbing pages.

The construction of most dictionary entries is determined by a number of factors: any randomly exampled headword may be served by several, differently defined senses and a number of illustrative citations to prove a history and, perhaps, to expand the layers of meaning. The alphabetic model is used whether the dictionary is A–Z, encyclopaedic or thematic, wherein alphabetic order is generally used to organize headwords within themed sections. How else is it possible to marshal the lexicon? How can it be possible to organize the non-lexical in such a detailed fashion, especially when the term to be defined is presented as a moving image? The *Signing Savvy* website (2013) presents short moving-image files to illustrate an alphabetic index; however, here, the image is the definition and it is only possible to find a gesture by browsing the headword list. This is a fine one-way translation tool but the requirements of an online-glossary of gestural slang are less precise.

Although the alphabet retains an important role in the structure of the gestural slang glossary, the practical approach must be to disregard the alphabet and traditional notions of page-turning. To all intents and purposes, a moving-image illustration becomes the headword (for precision: image-word) within a hierarchical categoriza-tion. A user's search criteria will decide the order of presentation. An image-word may be found by a variety of routes, determined by the combination of facets within a taxonomic structure, cross-referencing from a conventional headword or within the text of another entry or, as noted above, random browsing and clicking of thumbnails. The image-word is presented on the screen alongside the conventional textual elements: headword/s (if available), definition, gloss and the other business of building a dictionary entry; quotations, both textual and visual, may be added. This presupposes a suitably codified collection of non-lexical items that can be presented in a form suited to an online-dictionary/glossary-user's needs: a manage-able classification system that accounts for all elements within an entry, including elements within a glossed commentary and its supporting citations.

What follows is a partially developed list of obvious and familiar topic filters, or facets, slanted toward the non-lexical but applicable across the slang lexicon: *alcohol; animal; body and senses; catchphrase; code; commerce; conventional; crime/gang; daily life; drugs; employment; entertainment; food and drink; gambling; hip-hop; location; metaphor; playground/childish; politics; pun; punctuation; race; sex; tic-tac.* Intention: *aggression; comment; derision; euphemism; exclusion; farewell; greeting; inclusion; instruction; insult; invitation; irony.* Within the specific requirements of non-lexical slang, especially with regard to physical articulation, other facets include: *artificial/contrived; descrip-tive; imitative (generic); imitative (mimed action); initialism; musical; signal; sign language/ ASL/Auslan/BSL.* Gestural slang may be further categorized by construction: *sound; speech; compound; finger/s; hand/s; face; whole body/posture;* etc.

The first of the gestural examples given in this chapter is *air quotes*, which might be accessed through the following facets of the taxonomy: *speech; finger/s; hand/s; descriptive; conventional,* as well as by its meaning and purpose: *irony; punctuation.* Seven, possibly eight, search terms would thus combine to classify a familiar and simple gesture to enable users to search for an image-word, without reference to elements of the entry's content that are not contained in the physical description, definition or gloss: if a supporting citation, in whatever form it may be quoted, refers to, for instance, *politics* and/or *employment,* then the search criteria may be refined by eight or nine, possibly ten facets.

Consider this fresh example: a compound of three familiar gestures, two of which we have met above, combined and hidden in the somewhat childish *Shhhhhh! Don't cry. Have a milkshake.* The *Shhhhhh!* element is signed by bringing the middle finger (the *digitus impudicus*) to the lips in a variation of the conventional *shhh!* gesture. *Don't cry* is a disguised, offensive *V-sign* in which the two fingers track imaginary tears down the cheeks. Finally, *have a milkshake* is represented by the *wanker* sign. The searchable facets here, in no particular order: *derisory*; *catch-phrase*; *offence/insult*; *face*; *spoken*; *compound*; *imitative (mimed action)*; *fingers*; *hands*; *food and drink*; *sex*; *playground/childish*. The gesture could also be located by cross-reference from *wanker* and *V-sign*.

Visual citations

Conventional dictionaries routinely use illustrative quotations from printed sources. The following examples are intended to highlight the need to take visual citations from movies, TV, You Tube, etc. The gestural game *cock-muff-bumhole* is a slang variation of the familiar *rock-paper-scissors*. It combines, in play, the *digitus impudicus,* the *V-sign* and a gesture that may mean OK or anus depending on use – a circular shape formed by bringing the tips of the forefinger and thumb together: *muff* smothers *cock*, *cock* fucks *bumhole*, etc. These gestures were created for, and popularized by, UK TV sitcom *Nathan Barley* (Cineastin 2005: 1/1). A similar variation is *rock-scissors-paper-lizard-Spock*. *Lizard* is formed by bringing the tips of four fingers and thumb together in an approximation of a reptile's head, *Spock* is the *live long and prosper* salute: *rock* crushes *lizard*, *paper* disproves *Spock*, *Spock* vaporizes *rock*, etc. (Lorre and Prady 2008: 2/8).

The effect of our online world on non-lexical slang is easily discerned. We all now have the means to collect and casually share moving-images. Gestural slang that might not previously have caught the imagination is successfully propagated in the digital environment; the ephemeral is now recorded. Smaller in-group crazes have inspired the creation of new forms. For example, the arch-mimicry used to convey recognition of a socially awkward situation that has spread across virtual and actual culture – there are 5,260,000 Google results for *awkward balloon*, 2,560,000 for *awkward turtle* and a mere 1,580,000 for *awkward giraffe* (accessed 20 January 2013). Extreme gestures such as *planking*, a whole-body gesture in which the *planker* poses rigidly and face down, often in an unlikely location, have evolved for no purpose other than the recording and sharing of the gesture (Google: 7,810,000).

Conclusion

Gestural slang has, to date and in the main, been pragmatically overlooked by lex-icographers as a practical field of serious study. Now, however, the achievements of our digital age make it possible to encompass the shrugs, clicks and silences of the unvoiced within the greater slang corpus. Wordlists can be supplanted with moving-image and sound files. We have at hand the means to record and publish non-lexical, visual language in ways that have previously been denied to lexicography by the constraints of the printed page. For dictionary user and lexicographer alike, the internet represents a wonderful resource. For this slang lexicographer, in particular, it offers the *thumbs up* to the development and presentation of an academically rigorous glossary of non-lexical slang.

18

GLOBAL ENGLISH SLANG IN THE ERA OF BIG DATA

Julie Coleman

The chapters in this collection have illustrated some of the ways in which English slang is developing in different parts of the world, in the usage of native speakers and learners, sometimes under the influence of other languages, and also through the influence of English on the slang of other languages. Although there are certainly tides in slang usage, largely emanating from the United States at present, these chapters have demonstrated that national and local varieties remain distinct from one another. Young people in Britain may use some American slang terms, but they mix them with slang from a variety of other sources to produce a distinctively local youth language. Norwegian and Italian teenagers may use some English words as slang, but they use them in utterances otherwise made up of their native language. This is unlikely to change: slang tends to operate at the level of specific social contexts, and the slang that is appropriate in one setting will not be appropriate in another.

Less than a century ago, the main challenge facing slang lexicographers was finding sufficient evidence of slang usage. A dictionary-maker like Partridge, undertaking the ambitious task of providing a historical overview of English slang across a broad geographical area, had to rely on dictionaries and glossaries that had already been published and on other forms of written evidence, such as novels, memoirs and newspaper articles. He supplemented his written evidence with the assertions of his correspondents from around the world and by his own observation and first-hand knowledge. His daily routine was structured by the need to find evidence of slang terms to include in his dictionaries:

> Mr. Partridge, an erect, 73-year-old New Zealander … [leaves] his Southgate home before 9 each morning … to spend five hours a day going through periodicals, books and best of all, the day's newspapers … Even on the train

en route to the [British] Museum, he listens to conversations around him …
Hundreds of fans and correspondents write … offering suggestions.

(Nichols 1967: 367)

As we have seen (Scott, Chapter 9), many terms in Partridge's dictionary are included on the strength of their inclusion in just one earlier glossary: on the assumption, that is, that the compiler of that glossary was reliable and trustworthy. Partridge also assumed that slang terms had been in circulation in speech for some time before his earliest written evidence for them, and dated the entries in his dictionaries accordingly (Coleman 2010: 12–14). A contemporary slang lexicographer could not make the same assumptions and faces completely the opposite problem: too much data.

The internet offers contemporary students of slang access to numerous printed sources like those used by Partridge, including many more digitized books and newspapers than any one individual could read in a lifetime. It also offers the high-tech equivalent of eavesdropping on multiple conversations at once. Clearly when an individual writes a blog or a tweet, they are not doing so entirely unselfconsciously, but social media are characterized by more informal language than we would expect to find in a daily newspaper. We have to treat internet evidence with some caution, but we should certainly doubt that a word or phrase is used in a particular way if there is little convincing online evidence for it.

The advantage of having so much data, of course, is that we can fairly easily check the information we find in glossaries. For example, a recent *Urban Dictionary* entry cites *cadabbered* with the sense 'stoned'. That assertion alone, if it had made it into print, would have been sufficient for Partridge to include the word in his dictionary, but it is not supported by any independent evidence accessible through Google, Yahoo or Ask Jeeves. ChaCha returns the answer 'Cadabber is not an English word', and this assertion is supported by negative returns to a Google Blogs search and searches on Twitter and the newspaper databases discussed below.

This lack of online evidence does not mean that the individual who posted *cadabbered* on *Urban Dictionary* was not using it as slang with friends in February 2013, but it does mean that it is unlikely to be much more widespread than that. Across the next few months or years, *cadabbered* may spread to wider usage, and we will then feel fortunate to have this evidence of its early use (*Urban Dictionary* contributors cannot see the future after all). Alternatively, if a small group of friends were using the term, they may already have drifted apart or started using another term instead, in which case no further evidence would be forthcoming. It is also possible that *cadabbered* is one of many fabricated words on *Urban Dictionary* and that it has never been used in spontaneous speech. If that is the case, it is of little interest other than as a demonstration of the pleasure that *Urban Dictionary* contributors take in linguistic creativity. We cannot say with certainty that *cadabbered* is not used, but the absence of independent evidence at present does indicate that the term is not widely spread or frequently used.

For slang terms that are in wider use, there is an abundance of evidence online. When I first began this exploration, I believed that *peng* 'attractive; good quality (with reference to drugs)' was a relatively new term in limited slang usage in the British Midlands. Online evidence demonstrates that it has been more widely used in Britain for at least a decade and that it may be in the process of spreading to the United States (though this process of spreading could halt or reverse at any moment). The following section explains the searches I undertook to discover this information and highlights some of the problems involved in interpreting online evidence.

A ChaCha search quickly revealed that *peng* is both a proper and common noun in Chinese. It is this type of coincidence that can make searching for evidence online particularly time-consuming and frustrating. For example, a Google Blogs search produces more than three million hits for *peng*, most of which are proper names that appear to be irrelevant to this usage. If we want to avoid having to eliminate each hit separately, we will need to find a way to filter out the results we are not interested in.

Restricting the search to pages posted in English does not reduce the hits to manageable numbers because individuals called Peng are frequently mentioned by English-language bloggers. Restricting these searches by region is not particularly useful either, because users of any variety of English can post on sites based in other parts of the world. It is therefore necessary to predict phrases in which *peng* might occur in the sense we are interested in. For example, *bare peng* and *well peng* each produce hits demonstrating that the 'attractive' sense has been in reasonably frequent use since at least 2006. In response to a posting by GoSpelz on Netlog, a social media site, xxlil_cutie_Bootyxx commented 'heyy bbz u r well peng plz add me' (30 September 2006). It is highly unlikely that this represents the first ever use of the term (in fact the search engine presented me with an apparent hit from October 2005 which was no longer accessible), but it does confirm that *peng* has been used with this sense since at least that date. It is worth noting here that even 'well peng' produced false hits because the search engine is not sensitive to capitalization or punctuation. For example:

> Your mentors taught you well Peng … You're a natural!
>
> *(comment by Yelena 6 March 2013 on PengJoon.com)*

> Both these players faced each other at the second round of London Olympics as well. Peng put up a better show that time, forcing the Czech to win the match in three-sets.
>
> *(tennis commentary: Goerges 2012)*

These false hits demonstrate that although online searches offer the possibility of access to huge quantities of data, they also present the serious scholar of slang with a monumental task of sifting and evaluation.

Google searches also revealed that players of the Dead Space computer game (first released in 2008) can collect *peng treasure* as they progress through different levels. *Peng treasure* consists largely of posters or other representations of attractive women, and has a monetary value within the game ('Dead Space 3 Peng Location Guide'). Although the posters appear to be advertising a sleazy product or service within the world of the game, it is unclear exactly what *peng* is. It may be that these posters represent the use of sexualized advertising for some other type of product entirely. Although the game was released by an American company (EA Visceral), two of the three writers credited on *Dead Space* are British. This use of *peng* may have arisen from the British slang usage, but it is impossible to be sure. For some speakers, this gaming use may have re-enforced or shaped their use of *peng* in other contexts.

Google searches *Urban Dictionary* as well as many other sites, and it is necessary to approach *Urban Dictionary* entries with particular caution. There are 44 definitions for *peng*, not all for its adjectival use and not all for this meaning. The earliest, from October 2003, defines *peng* as 'good quality/strong flavour (in drug terms)'. By February 2004, *peng* was also being defined as 'high grade girl', though the supporting citation actually suggests the adjectival use that is supported by several later definitions. The first two definers of this sense either imply or state that it is used in Nottingham, a British Midland city.

The contents of other online slang dictionaries are not generally accessible to Google searches, but they are sometimes worth consulting. In this case, Walter Radar's *Online Slang Dictionary* confirms but does not add anything to the information available through *Urban Dictionary*. *Peng* is defined as 'a very attractive person' (again the citations shows it being used adjectivally), 'sexy, hot, pretty, beautiful' and 'very good', with reference to food. The earliest citation is from December 2005. The absence of *peng* from Chris Lewis's *Online Dictionary of Playground Slang*, which is no longer actively edited, suggests that the term was in relatively limited use before 2010. Although *peng* is listed in Duckworth's *A Dictionary of Slang*, with reference to drugs and women, it is impossible to determine when it was added.

A Google Blogs search turns up further evidence of an association between *peng* and Nottingham, in an article about the establishment of a driving test centre at one of the city's universities: 'A first year psychology student from Nottingham Trent told Impact "that's bare peng"' (Harb 2013). However, this may have appeared at the top of my hit list because Nottingham is not far from where I live and work. Google's analysis of my online behaviour may have predicted that I would be interested in a local story about a university, which means that the prominence of this story has more to do with me than with the significance of the usage. My sense of the geographical distribution of the term is further undermined by an article in *The Times* newspaper, which asserts that *peng* originated among Afro-Caribbean youths in the south-east of England in around 2005 (Rumbelow 2011). This implies that *peng* originated in MLE and spread to other parts of Britain from there. The fact that several other MLE terms have followed the same route adds plausibility to this hypothesis.

Although we might not expect to find slang terms well represented in conventional books and newspapers, it can be worth looking, because the appearance of a slang term in print indicates a relatively high level of visibility. Newspaper archives and Google Books can provide historical depth and geographical specificity that is not accessible in the indistinguishable and near-contemporary data otherwise available online. For example, *peng* is defined as 'good looking' (Tobin 2007), 'sexy' (Dent 2010) and 'attractive' (Brown 2011) in *The Guardian*, and is left undefined in the following arch reference to a political candidate:

> A local paper has also described her as 'peng', believed to be a form of political endorsement.
>
> *(Wintour 2010)*

Ploughing through 51 pages of results for *peng* in *The Guardian* to find these four examples was not a particularly rewarding pastime, but they represent a far greater wealth of evidence than Partridge had for a great many of the terms in his dictionary. They suggest that *peng* was widely enough used by 2007 for middle-class white London-based journalists to have encountered it. The *Nexis* database brings together newspapers from around the world and a search for *peng* alone produced over 3000 results, which is more than the database will display. In this case a combination of *peng* and *slang* produced 94 results, most of which still included the personal name. Nevertheless, they provide further evidence for the use of *peng* from Britain (Walmsley 2007; Mirror Reporter 2011) and the US (Langmead et al. 2011). The US reference specifies that the term is British slang.

Google Trends allows us to analyse the history and geographical origins of *peng* in more detail. The background noise for *peng* is such that there is little evidence of an increase in use between 2004 and 2013. However, if we restrict our search to the United Kingdom, there is a marked upward trend in the use of *peng* during this period, peaking in 2011. If we assume that the background noise remains more or less stable, this increase must be due to the slang usage. The mapping function demonstrates that Google's hits are all located in London until 2009, confirming that this probably is where *peng* originated.

So much for the history of *peng*. What about its contemporary use? Twitter provides extensive evidence of *peng* being used during 2013 to describe not just attractive people (including appealing babies), but also inanimate objects such as clothes, watches and mobile devices, as well as good feelings, good weather, tasty food and a good night's sleep. For example:

> Would you rather lose your left hand or your tastebuds?
>   Standardly I'd chop off my left arm, replace with a hook and eat peng food forever
>
> *(example [sic] 10 April 2013)*

> When you go to a peng girls house for the first time and she has 28 cats #ItsTimeToLeave
>
> *(Murkle Man 25 April 2013)*

Raving all the time, peng weather and BOOMTOWN

(JDuffin 26 April 2013)

Neveah was actually peng when she was born, you know when babies come out looking abit alienish, na mate she was choong

(RUGRAT 26 April 2013)

A surprising number of tweets attest to their posters' extreme dislike of the word and of anyone who uses it, and these comments sometimes associate it with other terms used by speakers of MLE. For example:

your so effin peng i wanna be wiv u u fit girl jheeeezz babe xx ... – I'm sorry I don't understand chav ...

(queen $ame 18 September 2012)

the word 'peng' makes me want to stab myself in the face with a blunt pencil until i die

(real talk 15 April 2013)

Can't stand words like 'peng' 'poe' 'dank' 'bumting'

(Cal 19 April 2013)

Calling a girl 'hot' or 'peng' doesn't get you laid, it makes you look like a prepubesent chav.

(Kira Brennan 22 April 2013)

What Twitter and blogs offer us, then, is an insight into variations in usage and social attitudes. It is clear that some people use *peng* and other people despise them for it. The same was probably true of earlier slang terms such as *groovy*, *fab* and *cool*, but if Partridge had one example of these terms in writing, he would have labelled them, on the strength of that single use, 'British youth slang' or 'American slang', as if one individual could represent the usage of a whole nation or sub-group within it.

For some terms associated with some social sub-groups, it is possible to search for further corroborating evidence. For example, amateur (and some professional) musicians can self-publish their music on a website called bandcamp.com. Almost a thousand hits for 'peng' can be reduced to 277 by excluding *penguin* and *penga* 'money' (in Swedish). Many false hits remain, including a band called Spenghead and an album called Alpenglow, but the few hits that illustrate the slang usage confirm its association with British rap and dubstep: a London rapper called Fresh Pengg and an album from Essex-based drab.one called *Christmas Is Peng*. The Boston-based M|O|D crew released an MP3 EP called *Peng001* (the first of a trilogy differentiated only by the last digit) in 2012, suggesting that the term does have some usage in the United States.

Of course online evidence is not always reliable and it is not useful at all unless it is date-stamped. It is necessary to click through from internet search results to look at the page of origin. Apparent hits do not always materialize, either because the word or phrase has been removed or because it is only included in hidden text concealed in the page's code in an attempt to draw online traffic. Searches may generate large numbers of duplicate hits because the same webpage has been archived more than once, so the estimated number of hits cannot be considered meaningful except in very broad comparative terms. Although the main content of a page may be date-stamped, and although it is this original date-stamp that will appear in the brief summary provided in Google results, users' comments may have been added later, which means that all examples have to be checked separately to determine whether the page date is relevant. Online searches will also produce hits in which posters are commenting on a word or phrase rather than using it themselves (as above for *peng*), and these can provide evidence of attitudes towards a word but not of its continued use.

The modern slang lexicographer does not have to spend all day trawling through websites, however. He (or even she) can ask the websites to send information directly. RSS feeds and email alerts can be used to ensure that new contemporary evidence of usage is brought to their attention. However, this can generate a lot of unhelpful information and would only be useful for terms that are already familiar: it is not possible to set up an RSS feed for 'slang terms I don't know yet'. Nevertheless, email alerts for 'youth slang' or 'new slang' can provide leads for further targeted searching.

Notwithstanding the inherent unreliability of internet evidence, the contrasting levels of evidence available for *cadabbered* and *peng* illustrate that it is possible, given enough time and patience, to use online evidence to explore the usage and distribution of slang words. There is insufficient evidence to convince us, at this stage, that *cadabbered* is genuine slang; but there is considerable online evidence for the use of *peng* going back to 2003. It may have been in spoken use earlier, but we can only base our conclusions on the evidence available to us. It appears to have originated in London and spread to other major British cities from there, with very limited visibility in the United States or elsewhere. Its continued association with chavs supports the idea that the term originated in MLE. Although there is no way to predict the future of *peng*, it has become associated with negative stereotypes and seems unlikely to pass into much wider usage in Britain for this reason. However, its current users and their successors may well continue to defy social convention by using this stigmatized term. In other national contexts, *peng* is likely to have different associations and the lack of stigma may enable it to spread into wider youth slang.

By way of confirmation, *peng* is included in Thorne (forthcoming), while *cadabbered* is not. Thorne defines *peng* as follows:

> **peng** *adj British* attractive. One of the most popular vogue terms of approval in youth slang since the early 2000s and still in use in 2013. Some claim that

it is originally Jamaican, a shortening of 'kushempeng' meaning a high-grade strain of marihuana, referenced in a 1985 song, others think that it is an abbreviation of penguin, the bird being thought quintessentially cute, but this is likely to be a folk etymology. *Compare* **deng**

Jessie's proper peng. There's loadsa peng about.

This provides a final reminder of the limitations of internet evidence: that it is less useful for historical than for contemporary evidence. There will be less evidence for all slang words from before about 2005 because the social media were not yet fully developed.

Conclusions

This volume has brought together chapters dealing with the use of English slang around the world, in contexts where English is used as a native language, where it is learnt as a foreign language and where there is a continuum between Standard English and a local vernacular form. Many terms are cited in more than one chapter, and it has been a deliberate policy not to remove these overlaps. Writers and lexicographers of slang often work within national boundaries. It is right that they should do so because it is necessary to have a detailed understanding of the social and linguistic context in order to understand slang usage fully. However, this can sometimes mean that they are not well informed about the origins and wider use of some of the slang they document. Writers dealing with American slang often assume that all slang used in the United States is American (and in some sense, clearly, this is true); writers dealing with Australian slang often focus on terms that are restricted to national usage and may not acknowledge their co-existence with terms that are more widely distributed (see Coleman 2012: 304–6). These tendencies are rarely stated explicitly and can give a misleading picture both of national usage and of international tendencies.

What this volume has shown is that it is beginning to be possible to talk meaningfully about global English slang. We can understand 'global English slang' to incorporate four different strands. The first of these consists of informal terms shared by speakers of English all around the world, the oldest of which were originally British, the newest largely American in origin. These are the terms that are shared between national forms of English as well as with learners of English. The second strand consists of terms that are restricted to identifiable social sub-groups across national boundaries, such as young people or people interested in particular cultural trends. These terms are often shared online in contexts in which it can be impossible to distinguish between different national forms or between native and non-native speakers. The third strand is made up of English terms employed as slang by speakers of other languages, whether or not they are slang in Standard English. Finally, the fourth strand, the thinnest of all, is the extra-lexical influence of English on informal usage in other languages, whether in speech, writing or gesture. The question that remains is whether any of these phenomena is truly global. A book of this size cannot cover the whole world in adequate detail and there have been some significant omissions. Africa, the Middle East, South America and East Asia are among the regions that offer fertile ground for future research into the use of English slang and the influence of English on the slang of other languages. Moreover, the inevitable delays imposed by the processes of data analysis and publication mean that some of the slang discussed here will already be out of date among some social groups. That is, after all, the essence of slang.

BIBLIOGRAPHY

Abley, M. (2008) *The Prodigal Tongue*, Boston, MA: Houghton Mifflin Harcourt.

Adams, M. (2003) *Slayer Slang: A Buffy the Vampire Slayer Lexicon*, New York: Oxford University Press.

——(2009) *Slang: The People's Poetry*, New York: Oxford University Press.

Ali, R. and Persad, V. (2011) 'A Lexical Semantic Study of Enterprise English Creole', unpublished undergraduate thesis, University of the West Indies, St. Augustine.

Alim, H.S. (2006) *Roc the Mic Right: The Language of Hip Hop Culture*, New York: Routledge.

Allen's Indian Mail and Register of Intelligence for British and Foreign India, China, and All Parts of the East (1856), London: W.H. Allen.

Allsopp, R. (1996) *Dictionary of Caribbean English Usage*, New York: Oxford University Press.

——(2010) *New Register of Caribbean English Usage*, Kingston: University of the West Indies Press.

Ambrogio, R. and Casalegno, G. (eds) (2004) *Scrostati Gaggio! Dizionario Storico dei Linguaggi Giovanili*, Torino: UTET.

'Amy Takes Lessons in Teen Slang', *The Mirror*, 20 April 2011. Available online, by subscription at www.lexisnexis.com (accessed 22 March 2013).

Andersson, L. and Trudgill, P. (1990) *Bad Language*, Oxford: Basil Blackwell.

Armstrong, N. and Wagner, M. (2003) *Field Guide to Gestures*, Philadelphia: Quirk Books.

Ashton, E. (2006) 'Learn Jafaikan in Two Minutes', *The Guardian*, 12 April. Available online at www.guardian.co.uk/education/2006/apr/12/research.highereducation (accessed 12 February 2013).

Ayto, J. and Simpson, J.M.Y. (eds) (2005) *The Oxford Dictionary of Modern Slang*, Oxford: Oxford University Press.

Baillie, J. (1898) *Walter Crighton, or, Reminiscences of George Heriot's Hospital*, Edinburgh: E. and S. Livingstone.

Baker, S.J. (1941) *A Popular Dictionary of Australian Slang*, 1st edn, Melbourne: Robertson & Mullens.

——(1941) *New Zealand Slang: A Dictionary of Colloquialisms*, Christchurch: Whitcombe & Tombs.

——(1943) *A Popular Dictionary of Australian Slang*, 2nd edn, Melbourne: Robertson & Mullens.

——(1943) *A Popular Dictionary of Australian Slang*, 3rd edn, Melbourne: Robertson & Mullens.

——(1945) *The Australian Language*, Sydney: Angus & Robertson.

Banfi, E. (1992) 'Conoscenza e Uso di Lessico Giovanile a Milano e a Trento', in E. Banfi and A.A. Sobrero (eds) *Il Linguaggio Giovanile degli Anni Novanta. Regole, Invenzioni, Gioco*, Bari: Laterza, 99–148.

Bardsley, D. (2009) *In the Paddock and on the Run: The Language of Rural New Zealand*, Dunedin: University of Otago Press.

——(2012) 'On the Turps', broadcast on *Sunday Morning*, 4 March. Available online at www.radionz.co.nz/national/programmes/sunday/audio/2511698/new-zealand-english-it's-creative-edge (accessed 26 March 2013).

Barrère, A.M.V. and Leland, C.G. (1889–90) *A Dictionary of Slang, Jargon and Cant*, Edinburgh: Ballantyne Press.

Barrett, G. (ed.) (2004–) *Double-Tongued Dictionary*. Available online at www.doubletongued.org/tag/india/ (accessed 28 September 2011).

B.E. (*c*.1698) *A New Dictionary of the Terms Ancient and Modern of the Canting Crew*, London: W. Hawes.

Beal, J. (2010) *An Introduction to Regional Englishes*, Edinburgh: Edinburgh University Press.

Beattie, J.H. (1918) *Pioneer Recollections III*, Gore, New Zealand: Gore Publishing Co.

Bedford, F.W. (1859) *History of George Heriot's Hospital, with a Memoir of the Founder, together with an Account of the Heriot Foundation Schools, by William Steven*, Edinburgh: Bell and Bradfute.

Bembe, M.P. and Beukes, A.M. (2007) 'The Use of Slang by Black Youth in Gauteng', *Southern African Linguistics and Applied Language Studies* 25: 463–72.

Bennett, J. (2012) '"And What Comes out May Be a Kind of Screeching": The Stylisation of *Chavspeak* in Contemporary Britain', *Journal of Sociolinguistics* 16: 5–27.

Bergs, A. (2005) *Modern Scots*, 2nd edn, Munich: Lincom GmbH.

B.G. (1999) 'Bling Bling', *Chopper City Ghetto*, New Orleans: Cash Money Records.

Big L (2000) 'Ebonics', *The Big Picture*, New York: Rawkus Records.

Blank, A. and Blank, L. (2004) *Field Guide to the North American Bird*, Berkeley, CA: 10 Speed Press.

Blench, R. (2013) *A Dictionary of Belizean English*. Available online at www.rogerblench.info/Language/English/Belizean%20English%20dictionary.pdf (accessed 20 March 2013).

Brandon, H. (1839) 'Dictionary of the Flash or Cant Language' in W.A. Miles *Poverty, Mendicity and Crime*, London: Shaw and Sons.

Brard, G.S.S. (2007) *East of Indus: My Memories of Old Punjab*, New Delhi: Hemkunt Publishers.

Brody, C. (2011) *The Shocker*, Thousand Oaks, CA: BN Publishing.

Brown, M. (2011) 'English as She Is Spoke? Voice Map Finds American Stresses Not So Loud', *The Guardian*, 10 March. Available online at www.guardian.co.uk/books/2011/mar/10/english-spoke-voice-map-american (accessed 22 March 2013).

Bucholtz, M. (1999) '"Why Be Normal?": Language and Identity Practices in a Community of Nerd Girls', *Language in Society* 28: 203–22.

Calloway, C. (*c*.1938) *Cab Calloway's Cat-alogue. A "Hepster's" Dictionary*, n.p.

Cameron, D. (2007) *The Myth of Mars and Venus. Do Men and Women Really Speak Different Languages?* Oxford: Oxford University Press.

Cary, H.N. (1916) *The Slang of Venery and its Analogues*, Chicago: privately printed.

Casalegno, G. and Goffi, G. (eds) (2005) *Brutti, Fessi e Cattivi. Lessico Della Maldicenza Italiana*, Torino: UTET.

Cassidy, D. (2007) *How the Irish Invented Slang: The Secret Language of the Crossroads*, Oakland, CA: CounterPunch.

Cassidy, F.G. and Le Page, R.B. (1967) *Dictionary of Jamaican English*, Cambridge: Cambridge University Press.

——(1980) *Dictionary of Jamaican English*, 2nd edn, Cambridge: Cambridge University Press.

CBC News (2012) 'Sex, Swear Words Banned on N.S. Licence Plates'. Available online at www.cbc.ca/news/canada/nova-scotia/story/2012/12/07/ns-banned-licence-plates.html (accessed 9 January 2013).

Chambers, J. (1993) 'Sociolinguistic Dialectology', in D.R. Preston (ed.) *American Dialect Research*, Amsterdam: John Benjamins.

Chen, R. (2002) *The Jamaican Dictionary*, 2nd edn, Ontario: Periwinkle.

Chowdhry, P. (2007) *Contentious Marriages, Eloping Couples: Gender, Caste, and Patriarchy in Northern India*, Oxford: Oxford University Press.

Chu, D. (1980) 'Kids that Schools Fail Learn They Can Succeed with Trailblazer John Simon', *People Magazine* 13: 3 (4 February). Available online at www.people.com/people/archive/article/0,20075745,00.html (accessed 14 December 2012).

Cineastin (2005) *Nathan Barley* 1/1, first broadcast 11 February, London: Talkback Productions.

Clark, L. (2006) '"Jafaican" Is Wiping out Inner-city English Accents', *The Daily Mail*, 12 April. Available online at www.dailymail.co.uk/news/article-382734/Jafaican-wiping-inner-city-English-accents.html (accessed 12 February 2003).

Coleman, J. (2004a) *A History of Cant and Slang Dictionaries. Volume I: 1567–1784*, Oxford: Oxford University Press.

——(2004b) *A History of Cant and Slang Dictionaries. Volume II: 1785–1858*, Oxford: Oxford University Press.

——(2009a) *A History of Cant and Slang Dictionaries. Volume III: 1859–1936*, Oxford: Oxford University Press.

——(2009b) 'Slang and Cant Dictionaries', in A.P. Cowie (ed.) *The Oxford History of English Lexicography*, vol. II, Oxford: Oxford University Press.

——(2010) *A History of Cant and Slang Dictionaries, Vol. IV: 1937–1984*, Oxford: Oxford University Press.

——(2011a) 'Online Slang Dictionaries', in Olga Timofeeva and Tanja Säily (eds) *Words in Dictionaries and History: Essays in Honour of R. W. McConchie* [Terminology and Lexicography Research and Practice 14], Amsterdam: Benjamins.

——(2011b) 'Historical and Sociological Methods in Slang Lexicography: Partridge, Maurer, and Cant', in Michael Adams (ed.) *"Cunning Passages, Contrived Corridors": Unexpected Essays in the History of Lexicography*, Milan: Polimetrica.

——(2012) *The Life of Slang*, Oxford: Oxford University Press.

Coles, E. (1676) *An English Dictionary*, London: Samuel Crouch.

Collins, S. (2008) *The Hunger Games*, New York: Scholastic Press.

Colville, M.D. (1985) *Signs of a Sexual Nature*, Northwich: Cheshire Society for the Deaf.

Cook, J. (2012) *Hebburn* 1/3, first broadcast BBC2, 1 November.

Corbett, J. (1997) *Language and Scottish Literature*, Edinburgh: Edinburgh University Press.

——, McClure, J.D. and Stuart-Smith, J. (2003) *The Edinburgh Companion to Scots*, Edinburgh: Edinburgh University Press.

——and Stuart-Smith, J. (2012) 'Standard English in Scotland', in R. Hickey (ed.) *Standards of English: Codified Varieties around the World*, Cambridge: Cambridge University Press.

Cosmopolitan, New Delhi: Hearst Magazines.

Coupland, N. (2007) *Style: Language Variation and Identity*, Cambridge: Cambridge University Press.

Craigie, W.A. et al. (eds) (1931–2002) *A Dictionary of the Older Scottish Tongue*, Oxford: Oxford University Press. Online: *Dictionary of the Scots Language* (2004). Available online at www.dsl.ac.uk (accessed 5 June 2012).

Crawford, E. (1995) *The Hum: Call and Response in African American Preaching*, Nashville, TN: Abingdon Press.

Croft, M. and Windsor, M. (2010) *The Secret Body Language of Girls*, London: Portico Books.

Crowd Science. Available online at www.crowdscience.com (accessed 9 January 2013).

Crowe, C. (1895) *The Australian Slang Dictionary*, Melbourne: Robert Barr.

Crowley, T. (1989) *The Politics of Discourse: The Standard Language Question in British Cultural Debates*, London: Macmillan.

Crystal, David (2007) *The Fight for English: How Language Pundits Ate, Shot and Left*, Oxford: Oxford University Press.

Cuddy Brae: Language At Letham, The Scots Language In A Scottish Primary School (2007). Available online at www.scotseducation.co.uk/reports.html (accessed 5 June 2012).

Dalzell, T. and Victor, T. (2006) *New Partridge Dictionary of Slang and Unconventional English*, London: Routledge.

——(2008a) *Vice Slang*, New York: Routledge.

——(2008b) *The Concise New Partridge Dictionary of Slang and Unconventional English*, New York: Routledge.

——(2012) *New Partridge Dictionary of Slang and Unconventional English*, 2nd edn, London: Routledge. Available by subscription at www.partridgeslangonline.com (accessed 11 January 2013).

Danesi, M. (2006) *Brands*, London: Routledge.

Dawson, S. (1999) *Aussie Slang*, Ringwood, Vic.: Penguin.

Dé, S. (1995) *Snapshots*, New Delhi: Penguin Books.

'Dead Space 3 Peng Location Guide', *Video Games Blogger*. Available online at www.video-gamesblogger.com/2013/02/11/dead-space-3-peng-location-guide.htm (accessed 1 March 2013).

De Biasi, V. (2007) *Come tu mi Vuoi*, Italy: Ideacinema, Medusa Film.

DeCamp, D. (1971) 'Toward a Generative Analysis of a Post-creole Speech Continuum', in D. Hymes (ed.) *Pidginization and Creolization of Language*, Cambridge: Cambridge University Press.

De Klerk, V. (1992) 'How Taboo Are Taboo Words for Girls?', *Language in Society* 21: 277–89.

Dent, G. (2010) 'What I've Learned about Teenagers', *The Guardian*, 29 August. Available online at www.guardian.co.uk/lifeandstyle/2010/aug/29/teenagers-language-music-world (accessed 22 March 2013).

Deverson, T. (ed.) (2012) *New Zealand Pocket Oxford Dictionary*, Melbourne: Oxford University Press.

——and Kennedy, G. (eds) (2004) *New Zealand Oxford Dictionary*, Melbourne: Oxford Univesity Press.

Devonish, H. (2003) 'Language Advocacy and "Conquest" Diglossia in the "Anglophone" Caribbean', in Christian Mair (ed.) *The Politics of English as a World Language*, Amsterdam: Rodopi.

Dictionary.com. Available online at http://dictionary.reference.com (accessed 9 January 2013).

Diniz de Figueiredo, E.H. (2010) 'To Borrow or Not to Borrow: The Use of English Loanwords as Slang on Websites in Brazilian Portuguese', *English Today* 26: 5–12. Available online at http://journals.cambridge.org/abstract_S0266078410000301 (accessed 23 April 2013).

Dollinger, S. (2006–) *Dictionary of Canadianisms on Historical Principles*, 2nd edn. Available online at http://faculty.arts.ubc.ca/sdollinger/dchp2.htm (accessed 25 April 2013).

Dominion Post, Wellington, NZ: Fairfax Media.

Douglas, F. (2009) *Scottish Newspapers, Language and Identity*, Edinburgh: Edinburgh University Press.

Drange, E.-M. (2002) 'Fremmedspråklige Slangord i Norsk Ungdomsspråk', in E.-M. Drange, U.-B. Kotsinas and A.-B. Stenström (eds) *Jallaspråk. Slanguage og Annet Ungdomsspråk i Norden*, Kristiansand: Høyskoleforlaget.

——(2009) 'Anglicismos en el Lenguaje Juvenil Chileno y Noruego', unpublished PhD thesis, University of Bergen.

——and Hasund, I. K. (2000) 'Ungdomsspråk i Norden – en Rapport om den Norske UNO-forskningen', in A.-B. Stenström, U.-B. Kotsinas and E.-M. Drange (eds) *Ungdommers Språkmøter* [Nord 26], Copenhagen: Nordisk Ministerråd.

Dressler, W.U. and Merlini Barbaresi, L. (1994) *Morphopragmatics: Diminutives and Intensifiers in Italian, German, and Other Languages*, Berlin: Mouton de Gruyter.

Duckworth, T. (1996–2012) *A Dictionary of Slang*. Available online at www.peevish.co.uk/slang/ (accessed 22 March 2013).

Dumas, B.K. and Lighter, J.E. (1978) 'Is Slang a Word for Linguists?', *American Speech* 53: 5–17.

Dunn, S. (2005) *Metal: A Headbanger's Journey*, Canada: Seville Pictures.

Dutcher, D. (2009) *Ima-doki no Nihon-go Waei-Jiten: Zokugo, Ryūkōgo, Gyōkai Yōgo Nanige ni tskatte-iru Kotoba o Eigo ni Shitemiru* [A Japanese–English Dictionary of Today: Slang, Popular Words, Business Jargon, and Casual Words Rendered into English], Tokyo: Kenkyū-sha.

Dyson, M.E. (2007) *Know What I Mean? Reflections on Hip Hop*, New York: Basic Books.

Eble, C. (1989) *College Slang 101*, Georgetown, CT: Spectacle Lane.

——(1996) *Slang and Sociability: In-Group Language among College Students*, Chapel Hill: University of North Carolina Press.

Eckert, P. (1988) 'Adolescent Social Structure and the Spread of Linguistic Change', *Language in Society* 17: 183–207.

Edwardes, A. (1966) *The Rape of India: A Biography of Robert Clive and a Sexual History of the Conquest of Hindustan*, New York: Julian Press.

Facebook. Available online at www.facebook.com (accessed 1 May 2013).

Farmer, J.S. and Henley, W.E. (1890–1904) *Slang and Its Analogues Past and Present*, 7 vols, London and Edinburgh: printed for subscribers only.

Farquharson, J.T. (2005) 'Faiya-bon: The Socio-pragmatics of Homophobia in Jamaican (Dance-hall) Culture', in S. Mühleisen and B. Migge (eds) *Politeness and Face in Caribbean Creoles* [Varieties of English Around the World 34], Amsterdam: John Benjamins.

——(forthcoming) *The Jamaican National Dictionary*. Available online at www.jamlex.net/ (accessed 1 May 2013).

Figueiredo, R.B. (1997–2013) *Freelang Romani Dictionary*. Available online at www.freelang. net/online/romani.php (accessed 27 March 2013).

Fitt, M. and Robertson, J. (2003) *The Smoky Smirr o Rain: A Scots Anthology*, Edinburgh: Itchy Coo.

Forconi, A. (1988) *La Mala Lingua: Dizionario dello 'Slang' Italiano. I Termini e le Espressioni Gergali, Popolari, Colloquiali*, Milan: SugarCo.

Fornaciari, Z. (1989) 'Overdose (d'amore)', in *Oro, Incenso e Birra*, Italy: Polydor.

Francis-Jackson, C. (2002) *The Official Dancehall Dictionary: A Guide to Jamaican Dialect and Dance-hall Slang*, Kingston: LMH Publishing.

Furiassi, C. (2010) *False Anglicisms in Italian*, Monza: Polimetrica International Scientific Publisher.

Giacomelli, R. (1988) *Lingua Rock. L'italiano Dopo il Recente Costume Giovanile*, Napoli: Morano Editore.

Gilchrist, J. (1796) *A Grammar of the Hindoostanee Language*, Calcutta: Chronicle Press.

Goerges, S. (2012) 'Petra Kvitova Gusts Away Shuai Peng to Reach the Last Eight: Western and Southern Open 2012'. Available online at http://blogs.bettor.com/Petra-Kvitova-gusts-away-Shuai-Peng-to-reach-the-last-eight-Western-and-Southern-Open-2012-a181331 (accessed 26 April 2013).

Google. Available online at www.google.co.uk (accessed 27 March 2013).

Google Analytics. Available online at www.google.co.uk/analytics (accessed 9 January 2013).

Google Trends. Available online at www.google.com/trends (accessed 17 May 2013).

Görlach, M. (2002) *A Textual History of Scots*, Heidelberg: Universitätsverlag C. Winter.

GossipCop (2012) 'Matt Damon Jokes about "Tossing Salad" on "Today Show"', *GossipCop* (4 December 2012). Available online at www.gossipcop.com/matt-damon-tossing-salad-video-today-show-tossed (accessed 9 January 2013).

Graddol, D. (2010) *English Next India: The Future of English in India*, London: British Council.

Graedler, A.L. (2002) 'Norwegian', in M. Görlach (ed.) *English in Europe*, New York: Oxford University Press.

——and Johansson, S. (1997) *Anglisismeordboka. Engelske Lånord i Norsk*, Oslo: Universitetsforlaget.

Grandison, G. (2012) 'Asafa's Tees & Shorts', *Jamaica Gleaner*, 21 December. Available online at http://jamaica-gleaner.com/gleaner/20121221/social/social11.html (accessed 15 April 2013).

Grant, W. et al. (eds) (1931–76) *The Scottish National Dictionary* and first *Supplement*, Edinburgh: Scottish National Dictionary Association. Available online at www.dsl.ac.uk (accessed 5 June 2012).

Gray, F.G. (1995) *Friday*, Los Angeles: New Line Cinema.

Green, James (2003) 'The Writing on the Stall: Gender and Graffiti', *Journal of Language and Social Psychology* 22: 282–96.

Green, Jonathon (1998) *Cassell's Dictionary of Slang*, London: Cassell.

——(2006) 'Diction Addiction', *Critical Quarterly* 48/3 (Autumn): 99–104.

——(2010) *Green's Dictionary of Slang*, London: Hodder Education/Chambers.

Greene, R. (1591) *A Notable Discoverie of Coosnage*, London: John Wolfe for T.N.

Grose, F. (1785) *A Classical Dictionary of the Vulgar Tongue*, London: Hooper.

Grossmann, M. and Rainer, F. (eds) (2004) *La Formazione delle Parole in Italiano*, Tübingen: Niemeyer.

Gutzmore, C. (2004) 'Casting the First Stone! Policing of Homo/Sexuality in Jamaican Popular Culture', *Interventions* 6(1): 118–34.

Halliday, M.A.K. (1976) 'Anti-Languages', *American Anthropologist*, NS 78: 570–84.

Hankin, N. (2003) *Hanklyn-Janklyn: A Stranger's Rumble-Tumble Guide to Some Words, Customs and Quiddities Indian and Indo-British*, New Delhi: Tara Press.

Harb, H. (2013) '"That's Bare Peng": Driving Lessons At Trent', *Impact*, 22 February. Available online at www.impactnottingham.com/2013/02/thats-bare-peng-driving-lessons-at-trent (accessed 1 March 2013).

Harman, T. (1567) *A Caveat or Warening for Common Cursetors*, London: Wylliam Gryffith.

Hashimoto, W. (2010) *Gendai Nihongo ni Okeru Gairai-go no Ryōteki – Suii ni Kan'suru Kenkyū* [The Amount of Loanwords in Modern Japanese: A Quantitative Study of Changes], Tokyo: Hitsuji-shobō.

Hasund, I.K. (2000) 'Engelsk i Norsk Ungdomsspråk', *Språknytt* 1/2: 8–10.

——(2002) 'Gjør Ungdommen Hærverk på det Norske Språket?', in S. Bjørkås (ed.) *Kulturelle kontekster* [Kulturpolitikk og Forskningsformidling, bind 1. Kulturstudier 24], Kristiansand: Høyskoleforlaget.

——(2006) *Ungdomsspråk*, Bergen: Fagbokforlaget.

——, Opsahl, T. and Svennevig, J. (2012) 'By Three Means: The Pragmatic Functions of Three Norwegian Quotatives', in I. Buchstaller and I. van Alphen (eds) *Quotatives: Cross-linguistic and Cross-disciplinary Perspectives* [Converging Evidence in Language and Communication Research 15], Amsterdam: John Benjamins.

Hawkins, R.E. (1984) *Common Indian Words in English*, Delhi: Oxford University Press.

Hebdige, D. (1990) *Cut 'n' Mix*, London: Routledge.

Heffernan, V. (2009) 'Street Smart', *New York Times* (5 July 2009): MM16.

Herald on Sunday, Auckland, NZ: APN News & Media.

Hi5. Available online at www.hi5.com (accessed 1 May 2013).

Hill, A. (2012) 'Signs of the Times: Deaf Community Minds Its Language', *The Guardian*, 7 October. Available online at www.guardian.co.uk/society/2012/oct/07/british-sign-language-changing (accessed 27 March 2013).

Hilltop Hoods (2006) 'What a Great Night', *The Hard Road*, Melbourne: Obese Records.

Ho, I. (2011) 'Trinidad Youthtalk: A Lexicographic Study of Contemporary Trinidad English Slang', unpublished undergraduate thesis, University of the West Indies, St. Augustine.

Hobart, G.V. (1904) *Jim Hickey*, New York: G.W. Dillingham.

Honey, J. (1997) *Language Is Power: The Story of Standard English and its Enemies*, London: Faber and Faber.

Hotten, John Camden (1860) *A Dictionary of Modern Slang*, 2nd edn, London: J.C. Hotten.

Hughes, G. (1998) *Swearing: A Social History of Foul Language, Oaths and Profanity in English*, London: Blackwell.

Hulme, K. (1986) *The Bone People*, Auckland: Spiral Collective.

Humphrys, J. (2004) *Lost for Words: The Mangling and Manipulating of the English Language*, London: Hodder.

Hunter, J. (2004) *The True Blue Guide to Australian Slang*, Frenchs Forest, NSW: New Holland Publishers.

Hurston, Z.N. (1942) 'Story in Harlem Slang', *The American Mercury* (July): 84–96; reprinted in *Zora Neale Hurston: Novels & Stories* (1995), New York: The Library of America, 1001–10.

Inder, D. (2008) *The Invisible Path: From Violence and Sex to Superconsciousness*, Bloomington, IN: AuthorHouse.

Ings, W. (2008) 'From the Beat to the Soob: The Language of the Male Sex Worker in New Zealand', *NZWords* 12: 1–3.

Irish Slang. Available online at www.slang.ie (accessed 1 August 2012).

Iyer, V. (2007) *Whiskey's Secret*, London: Polyglot Publications.

James, E. (2000) *NTC's Super-Mini British Slang Dictionary*, Chicago: NTC.

Jay-Z (1999) 'Jigga My Nigga', *Ryde or Die, Vol. 1*, New York: Roc-A-Fella Records.

Jenkins, H. (2006) *Convergence Culture: Where Old and New Media Collide*, New York: New York University Press.

Jerry, D.J. (ed.) (2008) *KY-shiki Eigo: Eigo Ryaku-go kara Kendai Amerika ga Mieru* [KY-Style English: Looking at Today's America through English Abbreviations], Tokyo: Taishūkan shoten.

Jespersen, O. (1922) *Language: Its Nature, Development and Origin*, London: Allen & Unwin.

Jezebel (2012) 'Meet the Shallow Looksists Who Fall in Love with Internet Liars' (6 December 2012). Available online at http://jezebel.com/5964747 (accessed 9 January 2013).

Johansson, S. and Graedler, A.-L. (2002) *Rocka, Hipt og Snacksy: om Engelsk i Norsk Språk og Samfunn*, Kristiansand: Høyskoleforlaget.

John Jay College of Criminal Justice (2008) 'Alumni Spotlight: Elizabeth O'Connor', *Alumni Association Newsletter* (August). Available online at http://Johnjay.jjay.cuny.edu/alumninews/alumninewsaugust2008 (accessed 14 December 2012).

Johnson, L.K. (1978) *Dread Beat an' Blood*, London: Frontline.

——(1979) *Forces of Victory*, London: Island Records.

——(1980) *Bass Culture*, London: Island Records.

Johnston, G. (1976) *The Australian Pocket Oxford Dictionary*, Melbourne: Oxford University Press.

Johnstone, B. (1996) *The Linguistic Individual: Self-Expression in Language and Linguistics*, New York: Oxford University Press.

Jones, B. (Forthcoming) *Beyond di Riddim: The Evolution of Language Use in Jamaican Popular Music, 1962–2012*. PhD thesis. University of the West Indies, St. Augustine.

Jones, C. (1995) *A Language Suppressed*, Edinburgh: John Donald.

——(ed.) (1997) *The Edinburgh History of the Scots Language*, Edinburgh: Edinburgh University Press.

Jones, J. (2004) *Certified Gangstas*, New York: Koch.

Jones, J., Game, Lil' Flip and Bezel (2005) 'Certified Gangstas', *Diplomats, Volume 5*, New York: The Diplomats.

Jones, W. (1801) 'A Dissertation on the Orthography of Asiatick Words in Roman Letters', *Asiatick Researches; or, Transactions of the Society Instituted in Bengal for Inquiring into the History and Antiquities, the Arts, Sciences, and Literature of Asia*, 1: 1–56.

Kachru, B.B. (1985) 'Standards, Codification and Sociolinguistic Realism: The English Language in the Outer Circle' in Randolph Quirk and Henry Widdowson (eds) *English in the World: Teaching and Learning the Language and Literatures*, Cambridge: Cambridge University Press.

——(1986) 'The Indianization of English', *English Today*, 6: 31–3.

——, Kachru, Y. and Nelson, C. (eds) (2009) *Handbook of World Englishes*, Oxford: Blackwell.

Kapiti Observer, Wellington, NZ: Fairfax Media.

Kearse, R. (2006) *Street Talk*, Fort Lee, NJ: Barricade Books.

Kendai Yōgo no Kiso-Chishiki Editorial Board (2013) *Kendai Yōgo no Kiso-Chishiki 2013* [Encyclopedia of Contemporary Words 2013], Tokyo: Jiyū Kokumin-sha.

Kener, H.J. and Zeide, M. (2010) *Fingerology: The Complete Guide to the Fingers*, Bloomington, IN: iUniverse.

Kerswill, P. (2005) 'This Is London Speaking', *New Scientist*, 3 December, 50–1.

——(2011) 'Who's an EastEnder Now', *TEDx Lecture*, September. Available online at www.youtube.com/watch?v=hAnFbJ65KYM (accessed 12 February 2013).

Kilgarriff, A. and Grefenstette, G. (2003) 'Introduction to the Special Issue on the Web as Corpus', *Computational Linguistics* 29: 333–47.

Kindaichi, Y. (2009) *Otaku-go Jiten: Manga, Anime, Netto, Gēmu no Saishin & Teibann Wādo ga Maruwakari* [Otaku-Language Dictionary: Understanding Totally the Words in the Latest Standard Comics, Animation, Internet, and Games], Tokyo: Bijutu Shuppan-sha.

Kitahara, Y. (ed.) (2008) *KY Shiki Nihongo: Rōmaji Ryakugo ga Naze Hayaru no ka?* [The KY-Style Japanese: Why Are Romanized Abbreviated Words So Popular?], Tokyo: Taishukan-shoin.

——(2012) *Minna de Kokugo Jiten 3: Jisho ni Noranai Nihon-go* [The Japanese Dictionary for Everybody 3: The Japanese Which Is Not Found in a Dictionary], Tokyo: Taishūkan Shoten.

K Koke (2011) *Are You Alone Fam*, London: Roc Nation.

Know Your Meme (2007–13) Available online at http://knowyourmeme.com (accessed 26 April 2013).

Kotsinas, U.-B. (2000) 'Språkkontakt och Slangspråk i Stockholm' in A.-B. Stenström, U.-B. Kotsinas and E.-M. Drange (eds) *Ungdommers Språkmøter* [Nord 26], Copenhagen: Nordisk Ministerråd.

——(2002) 'Engelska Ord i Nordisk Slang', in E.-M. Drange, U.-B. Kotsinas and A.-B. Stenström (eds) *Jallaspråk. Slanguage og Annet Ungdomsspråk i Norden*, Kristiansand: Høyskoleforlaget.

Kouega, J.-P. (2003) 'Camfranglais: A Novel Slang in Cameroon Schools', *English Today* 19: 23–9.

Kumar, G. (1997) *The Book on Trial: Fundamentalism and Censorship in India*, New Delhi: Har-Anand Publications.

Labov, W. (1972) 'Some Principles of Linguistic Methodology', *Language in Society* 1: 97–120.

Lalor, P. (2012) 'Pace Hostilities Resume among the Best of Friends', *Weekend Australian* (1 December): 39.

Lambert, J. (2004) *Macquarie Australian Slang Dictionary*, Sydney: Macquarie Library.

——(2008) *Macquarie Best Aussie Slang*, Sydney: Macquarie Library.

Langmead, O. et al. (2011) 'The New Teenage Slang', *New York Magazine*, 25 April. Available online, by subscription, at www.lexisnexis.com (accessed 22 March 2013).

Lea, A.H. (2009) 'Lånord i Norsk Talespråk', unpublished MA dissertation, University of Oslo. Available online at www.duo.uio.no/bitstream/handle/123456789/26827/annhlea. pdf (accessed 5 April 2013).

L'Espresso Slangopedia (1999–2012). Available online at http://temi.repubblica.it/espresso-slangopedia (accessed 30 May 2012).

Lewis, C. (2007–10) *Online Dictionary of Playground Slang*. Available online at http://www. odps.org (accessed 22 March 2013).

Lewis, M.P. (ed.) (2013) *Ethnologue: Languages of the World*, 17th edn, Dallas, TX: SIL International. Available online at www.ethnologue.com (accessed 22 April 2013).

Lightnin' Rod (1973) *Hustler's Convention*, New York: Harmony Books.

Lillo, A. (2010) 'Did Dublin's Ben Lang Ever Die? On the Revival of Rhyming Slang in Modern Dublinese', *Lebende Sprachen* 55: 123–38.

——(2012) 'Nae Barr's Irn-Bru Whit Ye're oan Aboot: Musings on Modern Scottish Rhyming Slang', *English World Wide* 33/1: 69–94.

Lonely Planet (2008) *Indian English: Language and Culture*, Melbourne: Lonely Planet.

Looser, D. (2001) 'Boobslang: A Lexicographical Study of the Argot of New Zealand Prison Inmates 1996–2000', unpublished thesis, University of Canterbury, Christchurch, NZ.

Lorre, C. and Prady, B. (2008) 'The Lizard-Spock Expansion', *The Big Bang Theory* 2/8, Burbank, CA: Chuck Lorre Productions.

Lynch, M. (2008) 'Bust It Down', *New York Press* (30 July to 5 August), 10. Available online at http://nypress.com/bust-it-down (accessed 14 December 2012).

Macalister, J. (ed.) (2005) *A Dictionary of Maori Words in New Zealand English*, Melbourne: Oxford University Press.

Macalister, R.A.S. (1937) *The Secret Languages of Ireland*, Cambridge: Cambridge University Press.

McCreary, D. et al. (2001) *Dawg Speak. The Slanguage Dictionary of the University of Georgia*, Athens, GA: The University of Georgia.

——(ed.) (2012) *Dawgspeak: The Slanguage Dictionary of the University of Georgia*, 6th edn. Available online at www.english.uga.edu/dawgspeak/index.html (accessed 24 January 2013).

MacDonald, P. (1927) *Patrol*, London: Fontana Books.

McEneany, L. (2006) 'These Kids Today, with Their Crazy Slanguage', *The Liam McEneany Experience* (7 December). Available online at http://kidliam.blogspot.com/2006/12/these-kids-today-with-their-crazy.html (accessed 14 December 2012).

McGregor, R.S. (1993) *The Oxford Hindi–English Dictionary*, Oxford: Oxford University Press.

MacGreine, P. (1932) 'Irish Tinkers or "Travellers". Some Notes on their Manners and Customs, and their Secret Language or "Cant"', *Béaloideas: The Journal of the Folklore of Ireland Society*, III.ii: 170–86.

MacInnes, C. (1957) 'Young England, Half English', reprinted in C. MacInnes (1961) *England Half English*, London: MacGibbon & Kee.

Macleod, I. (2012a) 'Scottish National Dictionary', in I. Macleod and J. D. McClure (eds) *Scotland in Definition: A History of Scottish Dictionaries*, Edinburgh: John Donald.

——(2012b) 'Twentieth and Twenty-first Century Dictionaries', in I. Macleod and J. Derrick McClure (eds) *Scotland in Definition: A History of Scottish Dictionaries*, Edinburgh: John Donald.

—— et al. (eds) (2005) *New Supplement to the Scottish National Dictionary*, Edinburgh: Scottish Language Dictionaries. Available online at www.dsl.ac.uk (accessed 5 June 2012).

McLeod, W. and Smith, J.J. (2007) 'Resistance to Monolinguality: The Languages of Scotland since 1918', in I. Brown (ed.) *The Edinburgh History of Scottish Literature, Vol. III. Modern Transformations: New Identities (from 1918)*, Edinburgh: Edinburgh University Press.

Macquarie Dictionary (1981) Sydney: Macquarie Library.

McTeigue, J. (2005) *V for Vendetta*, Burbank, CA: Warner Bros.

Mahal, B.K. (2006) *The Queen's Hinglish: How to Speak Pukka*, Glasgow: HarperCollins.

Mahboob, A. and Ahmar, N.H. (2004) 'Pakistani English: Phonology', in E.W. Schneider (ed.) *A Handbook of Varieties of English: Phonology*, Berlin: Walter de Gruyter.

Malkani, G. (2007) *Londonstani*, London: Harper Perennial.

Mann, P. (1975) *Dog Day Afternoon*, London: Mayflower Books.

Marley, B. (1974) *Catch a Fire*, London: Island.

Marston, J. (2004) *Maria Full of Grace*, Los Angeles: Fine Line Features.

Mattiello, E. (2005) '*A Bomb* and *un Casino*: Intensifiers in English and Italian Slanguage', in M. Bertuccelli Papi (ed.) *Studies in the Semantics of Lexical Combinatory Patterns*, Pisa: Edizioni Plus Pisa University Press, 279–326.

——(2008) *An Introduction to English Slang. A Description of its Morphology, Semantics and Sociology*, Monza: Polimetrica International Scientific Publisher.

——(2013) *Extra-grammatical Morphology in English. Abbreviations, Blends, Reduplicatives, and Related Phenomena*, Berlin: Mouton de Gruyter.

Mayhew, H. (1851) *London Labour and the London Poor*, London: George Woodfall and Son.

Mehrota, R.R. (1998) *Indian English: Texts and Interpretations*, Amsterdam: John Benjamins.

Mencken, H.L. (1937) *The American Language*, 4th edn, New York: Knopf.

Mesthrie, R. (2013) 'Where Does a New English Dictionary Stop? On the Making of the Dictionary of South African Indian English', *English Today* 29: 36–43.

Miller, L. (2004) 'Those Naughty Teenage Girls: Japanese Kogals, Slang, and Media Assessments', *Journal of Linguistic Anthropology,* 14(2): 225–47.

Milroy, J. and Milroy, L. (1993) *Real English: The Grammar of English Dialects in the British Isles*, London: Longman.

Miss Kitty (2010) 'English: Yardie Style', *Jamaica Star*, 15 March. Available online at http://jamaica-star.com/thestar/20100315/cleisure/cleisure1.html (accessed 15 April 2013).

Mitchell, H. (1970) *Black Preaching*, San Francisco: Harper & Row.

M|O|D (2012) *Peng001*, self-published. Available online at www.amazon.co.uk/Peng-001/dp/B00AGK0XKQ (accessed 1 March 2013).

Monti, S. (2012) *Dizionario Inglese: Slang & Idioms*, Milan: Vallardi.

Moody, A. and Matsumoto, Y. (2012) 'Lu-go and the Role of English Loanwords in Japanese: The Making of a "Pop" Pidgin', in J.S. Lee and A. Moody (eds) *English in Asian Popular Culture*, Hong Kong: Hong Kong University Press.

Moore, A. (1982–5) *V for Vendetta*, London: Warrior, Quality Communications/Quality Comics.

——(1988–9) *V for Vendetta*, New York: DC Comics.

Moore, B. (1997) *The Australian Concise Oxford Dictionary*, 3rd edn, Melbourne: Oxford University Press.

——(2004) *The Australian Oxford Dictionary*, 2nd edn, Melbourne: Oxford University Press.

——(2008) *Speaking Our Language: The Story of Australian English*, Melbourne: Oxford University Press.

——(2010) *What's Their Story: A History of Australian Words*, Melbourne: Oxford University Press.

Morris, D. (1994) *Bodytalk: A World Guide to Gestures*, London: Random House.

——, Collett, P., Marsh, P. and O'Shaughnessy, M. (1979) *Gestures*, London: Book Club Associates.

Morton, J. (1989) *Lowspeak*, London: Angus & Robertson.

Mügge, M.A. (1920) *The War Diary of a Square Peg: With a Dictionary of War Words*, London: Routledge and Sons.

Mulvey, C. (2010) *Prison Lingo: The Language of the Prison Community*. Available online at www.englishproject.org/resources/prison-lingo-language-prison-community (accessed 1 August 2012).

Munro, M. (1985) *The Original Patter*, Glasgow: Glasgow City Libraries.

——(1988) *The Patter, Another Blast*, Edinburgh: Canongate.

——(1996) *The Complete Patter*, Edinburgh: Canongate.

Munro, P. et al. (1991) *Slang U: The Official Dictionary of College Slang*, New York: Harmony.

Murdoch, S. (1996) *Language Politics in Scotland*, Aberdeen: Aiberdeen Universitie Scots Leid Quorum. Available online at www.scotsyett.com/download/lip.pdf (accessed 5 June 2012).

Murphy, C. and O'Dea, D. (2004) *The Book of Feckin' Irish Slang that's Great Craic for Cute Hoors and Bowsies*, Dublin: O'Brien Press.

Muthiah, S. (1991) *Words in Indian English: A Reader's Guide*, Delhi: HarperCollins.

Myspace. Available online at http://uk.myspace.com (accessed 1 May 2013).

Ndlangamandla, S.C. (2010) '(Unofficial) Multilingualism in Desegregated Schools: Learners' Use of and Views towards African Languages', *Southern African Linguistics and Applied Language Studies* 28: 61–73.

Nelly (2003) 'Tip Drill Remix (E.I.)', in *Da Derrty Versions: The Reinvention*, New York: Universal.

Nelson Mail, Nelson, NZ: Fairfax Media.

Netlog (2004–13). Available online at http://en.netlog.com (accessed 26 April 2013).

Netto-go Kenkyū Iinkai (ed.) (2009) *Hinshutsu Netto-go Techō* [Memos for Frequently Used Internet Words], Tokyo: Shin'yūsha.

New Musical Express, London: IPC Media.

New Zealand Free Lance, Auckland: Geddis & Blomfield.

New Zealand Listener, Wellington: APN News and Media.

Nexis. Available online at www.nexis.co.uk (accessed 9 January 2013).

Nguyen, J. and Brown, B.B. (2010) 'Making Meanings, Meaning Identity: Hmong Adolescent Perceptions and Use of Language and Style as Identity Symbols', *Journal of Research on Adolescence* 20: 849–68.

Nichols, L. (1967) 'In and Out of Books', *New York Times* (12 March), 367.

Norsk Talespråkskorpus – Oslodelen (NoTa-Oslo) [Norwegian Speech Corpus – The Oslo-part], Tekstlaboratoriet, ILN, Universitetet i Oslo. Available online at www.tekstlab.uio.no/nota/oslo/english.html (accessed 5 April 2013).

NWA (1991) 'Niggaz4Life', in *Niggaz4Life*, Los Angeles: Ruthless/Priority Records.

NYC PD (1985) 'Rasta Crime: A Confidential Report', *Caribbean Review* 14.1 (Winter): 12–15, 39–40.

Nyikos, J. (1994) 'An Amendment to Saussure's Principle I Based on Empirical Research Including Regular Iconicity in Irregular Verbs', in Valerie Becker Makkai (ed.) *The Twentieth LACUS Forum 1993*, Chapel Hill, NC: Linguistic Association of Canada and the United States.

O'Connor, E. (2005) *Dictionary of Street Communications* (DOSC1), New York: The DOME Project.

——(2006) *Dictionary of Street Communications* (DOSC2), New York: The DOME Project.

——(2008) *Dictionary of Street Communications* (DOSC3), New York: The DOME Project.

Oliver, P. (1970) *Savannah Syncopators: African Retentions in the Blues*, New York: Stein and Day.

Onwuchekwa, J. (2003) *Yo' Mama! New Raps, Toasts, Dozens, Jokes & Children's Rhymes from Urban Black America*, Philadelphia, PA: Temple University Press.

Orsman, H.O. (ed.) (1997) *Dictionary of New Zealand English*, Melbourne: Oxford University Press.

Oshiba, L. (2006–) *TOGETHER Lou*. Available online at http://ameblo.jp/lou-oshiba (accessed 12 February 2013).

——(2007a) *Lu-go Dai Henkan* [Change into Lu-go], Tokyo: Fuso-sha.

——(2007b) Untitled YouTube clip. Available online at www.youtube.com/watch?v=FF4SUdqjlys (accessed 12 February 2013).

Parker, O. and Thomson, B. (2009) *St Trinian's 2: The Legend of Fritton's Gold*. London: Entertainment Film Distributors.

Partridge, E. (1933) *Slang: Today and Yesterday*, London: Routledge and Kegan Paul.

——(1937) *A Dictionary of Slang and Unconventional English*, London: Routledge.

——(1950) *A Dictionary of the Underworld*, London: Routledge & Kegan Paul/Macmillan.

——(2002) *A Dictionary of Slang and Unconventional English*, 8th edn, Paul Beale (ed.), London: Routledge.

Patrick, P.L. (1995) 'Recent Jamaican Words in Sociolinguistic Context', *American Speech* 70: 227–64.

Pawka, M. (1992–2008) *Rasta/Patois Dictionary and Phrases/Proverbs*. Available online at http://niceup.com/patois.html (accessed 15 April 2013).

Pearson, A. (2012) 'NMIT to Close off with Whole Lot of Hooplah', *The Nelson Mail* (14 November 2012), 2. Available online at www.stuff.co.nz/nelson-mail/news/7948456/NMIT-to-close-off-with-whole-lot-of-Hooplah (accessed 9 January 2013).

Peckham, A. (2005) *Urban Dictionary: Fularious Street Slang Defined*, Riverside, NJ: Andrews McMeel.

——(2007) *Mo' Urban Dictionary: Ridonkulous Street Slang Defined*, Riverside, NJ: Andrews McMeel.

——(2012) *Urban Dictionary: Freshest Street Slang Defined*, Riverside, NJ: Andrews McMeel.

PengJoon.com. Available online at www.pengjoon.com/teach-200000-weekend-part-1/ (accessed 26 April 2013).

Peters, M. (2006) 'Getting a Wiggins and Being a Bitca: How Two Items of Slayer Slang Survive on the Television Without Pity Message Boards', *Slayage: The Online International Journal of Buffy Studies*, 5/4. Available online at http://slayageonline.com/PDF/Peters.pdf (accessed 27 March 2013).

Pettigrew, J. (1995) *The Sikhs of the Punjab: Unheard Voices of State and Guerilla Violence*, London: Zed Books.

Powis, D. (1977) *The Signs of Crime: A Field Manual for Police*, London: McGraw-Hill.

Press, Christchurch, New Zealand: Fairfax Media.

Preston, D.W. (1973) 'A Survey of Canadian English Slang', unpublished MA thesis, University of Victoria.

Pułaczewska, H. (2008) 'Anglicisms in German and Polish Hip-hop Magazines', in R. Fischer and H. Pułaczewska (eds) *Anglicisms in Europe: Linguistic Diversity in a Global Context*, Newcastle: Cambridge Scholars Publishing, 222–46.

Pulcini, V. (2008) 'Corpora and Lexicography: The Case of a Dictionary of Anglicisms', in A. Martelli and V. Pulcini (eds) *Investigating English with Corpora: Studies in Honour of Maria Teresa Prat*, Monza: Polimetrica International Scientific Publisher, 189–203.

——(2010) 'A Dictionary of Italian Anglicisms: Criteria of Inclusion and Exclusion', in L. Pinnavaia and N. Brownlees (eds) *Insights into English and Germanic Lexicology and Lexicography: Past and Present Perspectives*, Monza: Polimetrica International Scientific Publisher, 319–34.

——, Furiassi, C. and Rodríguez González, F. (2012) 'Introduction: The Lexical Influence of English on European Languages: From Words to Phraseology', in C. Furiassi, V. Pulcini and F. Rodríguez González (eds) *The Anglicization of European Lexis*, Amsterdam: John Benjamins, 1–24.

Quantcast. Available online at www.quantcast.com (accessed 9 January 2013).

Queen Latifah (1993) 'U.N.I.T.Y.', in *Black Reign*, Detroit: Motown Records.

Quinion, M. (2006) 'Jafaikan', in *World Wide Words*, 29 April. Available online at www.worldwidewords.org/topicalwords/tw-jaf1.htm (accessed 12 February 2013).

Ramaiah, L.S. (1988) *Indian English: A Bibliographical Guide to Resources*, Delhi: Gian Publishing House.

Ramson, W.S. (1988) *The Australian National Dictionary: A Dictionary of Australianisms on Historical Principles*, Melbourne: Oxford University Press.

——, Hughes, J.M. and Michell, P.A. (1992) *The Australian Concise Oxford Dictionary*, 2nd edn, Melbourne: Oxford University Press.

Rao, G.S. (1954) *Indian Words in English: A Study in Indo-British Cultural and Linguistic Relations*, Oxford: Oxford University Press.

Reshmi, A.R. (2012) 'Why Fall in Love with a Geek', *Times of India* (16 November). Available online at http://timesofindia.indiatimes.com/life-style/relationships/man-woman/Why-fall-in-love-with-a-geek/articleshow/13518928.cms (accessed 9 January 2013).

Rettberg, J.W. (2008) *Blogging*, Cambridge: Polity Press.

Reynolds, R.D.J. (2006) *Jabari Authentic Dictionary of the Jamic Language*. Waterbury, CT: Around the Way Books.

Richter, E. (2006) 'Student Slang at IIT Madras: A Linguistic Field Study', unpublished MA dissertation, Technische Universität Chemnitz.

Roberts, G.D. (2003) *Shantaram*, London: Abacus.

Roddenberry, G. (1967) 'Amok Time', *Star Trek* 2/1, first broadcast 15 September, Los Angeles: Desilu Productions.

Rodríguez González, F. (2008) 'Anglicisms in Spanish Male Homosexual Terminology', in R. Fischer and H. Pułaczewska (eds) *Anglicisms in Europe: Linguistic Diversity in a Global Context*, Newcastle: Cambridge Scholars Publishing, 247–71.

Rose, R. (1995) *The Joy of Words*, Kenthurst: Kangaroo Press.

Rudnick, P. and Andersen, K. (1989) 'The Irony Epidemic [...] An Introduction to the Tiny Conversational Art of Air Quotes', *Spy Magazine* (March), 98.

Rumbelow, H. (2011) 'Peng! As Young Britons Shape the Future of Our Language in Ever More Radical Ways, the UK Is No Longer the True Custodian of the Queen's English', *The Times*, 6 April 2011. Available online, by subscription, at www.lexisnexis.com (accessed 22 March 2013).

Rushdie, S. (1982) *Midnight's Children*, New York: Avon.

Sailaja, P. (2009) *Dialects of English: Indian English*, Edinburgh: Edinburgh University Press.

Sanders, B. (2005) *Youth Crime and Youth Culture in the Inner City*, New York: Routledge.

Sanga, I. (2011) 'Mzungu Kichaa and the Figuring of Identity in "Bongo Fleva" Music in Tanzania', *International Review of the Aesthetics and Sociology of Music* 42: 189–208.

Sanneh, K. (2010) 'Word: Jay-Z's "Decoded" and the Language of Hip-hop', *New Yorker*, 6 December. Available online at http://www.newyorker.com/arts/critics/atlarge/2010/12/06/101206crat_atlarge_sanneh (accessed 26 March 2013).

Saraceni, M. (2011) 'Reflections on the Rhetorics of the (Re-)Location of English', *Changing English* 18: 277–85.

Savelli, L. (2009) *Gangs across America and Their Symbols*, Flushing, NY: Looseleaf Law Publications.

Schneider, E.W. (2007) *Postcolonial English: Varieties around the World*, Cambridge: Cambridge University Press.

Scots Language Centre (2009) 'Scots within the Curriculum'. Available online at www.scotslanguage.com/articles/view/805 (accessed 5 June 2012).

Scott, M. (2008) 'Unsung Etymologies: Lexical and Onomastic Evidence for the Influence of Scots on English', in M. Mooijaart and M. van der Wal (eds) *Yesterday's Words: Contemporary, Current and Future Lexicography*, Newcastle: Cambridge Scholars Publishing.

Scottish Government (2006) 'Building the Curriculum 1 – the Contribution of Curriculum areas'. Available online at www.ltscotland.org.uk/Images/building_curriculum1_tcm4-383389.pdf (accessed 5 June 2012).

——(2012) 'Curriculum for Excellence'. Available online at www.educationscotland.gov.uk/thecurriculum/whatiscurriculumforexcellence/index.asp (accessed 5 June 2012).

Sears, C. (2012) 'Negotiating Identity in English-Medium Settings: Agency, Resistance and Appropriation among Speakers of Other Languages in an International School', *Journal of Research in International Education* 11: 117–36.

Selvon, S. (1956) *The Lonely Londoners*, London: Allan Wingate.

Sengupta, I.C. (1996) 'Indian English Supplement', in *The Oxford Advanced Learner's Dictionary of Current English*, Delhi: Oxford University Press.

Sex Pistols (1977) *God Save the Queen*, London: Virgin.

Share, B. (1967) *Slanguage – A Dictionary of Irish Slang and Colloquial English in Ireland*, Dublin: Gill & Macmillan.

Sharma, P. (2010) *Love, Life & A Beer Can! Should all be Served Chilled!!* New Delhi: Srishti.

Sherman, M. (2012) 'Opinion', *Jerusalem Post* (16 November), 21. Available online at www.jpost.com/Opinion/Columnists/Article.aspx?id=292100 (accessed 9 January 2013).

Signing Savvy (2013). Available online at www.signingsavvy.com (accessed 27 March 2013).

Simpson, J.A. and Weiner, E.S.C. (eds) (2008) *The Oxford English Dictionary Online*, Oxford: Oxford University Press. Available online at www.oed.com (accessed on various dates in 2012–13).

Singh, S. (1992) *Blueprint to Bluewater: The Indian Navy 1951–1965*, New Delhi: Lancer International.

Skinnyman (2004) 'Little Man', in *Council Estate of Mind*, London: Riddim Killa.

Slangordboka (2005–7) Oslo: Kunnskapsforlaget.

Smiley Culture (1984) *Cockney Translation*, London: Fashion Records.

Smith, J.C. (2010) *Encyclopedia of African-American Popular Culture*, Westport, CT: Greenwood.

Smith-Pearse, T.L.H. (2000) *The English Errors of Indian Students*, Chennai: Oxford University Press.

Sonnenfeld, B. (1997) *Men in Black*, Culver City, CA: Columbia Pictures.

Southland Times, Invercargill, New Zealand: Fairfax Media.

Språkrådet (2004) *Beiken-feiden 2004*. Available online at www.sprakradet.no/nb-NO/ Sprakhjelp/Raad/Norsk-for-engelsk/Importord/Beiken-feiden_2004 (accessed 5 April 2013)

Stanlaw, J. (2004) *Japanese English: Language and Culture Contact*, Hong Kong: Hong Kong University Press.

——(2010) *Wasei Eigo to Nihon-jin: Gengo, Bunka Sesshoku no Dainamizumu* [Japanese English and the Japanese People: The Dynamism of Language and Cultural Contact], Tokyo: Shinsensha.

Starkey, D. (2011a) Interview on *Newsnight*, first broadcast 12 August, London: BBC.

——(2011b) 'UK Riots: It's Not about Criminality and Cuts, It's about Culture, and This Is Only the Beginning', *The Telegraph*, 19 August. Available online at www.telegraph.co.uk/ news/uknews/law-and-order/8711621/UK-riots-Its-not-about-criminality-and-cuts-its-about-culture.-and-this-is-only-the-beginning.html (accessed 25 March 2013).

Stavsky, L., Mozeson, I.E. and Mozeson, D.R. (1995) *A2Z: The Book of Rap & Hip-Hop Slang*, New York: Boulevard.

Steel Panther (2009) 'The Shocker', in *Feel the Steel*, New York: Republic Records.

Sugarhill Gang (1979) *Rapper's Delight*, Englewood, NJ: Sugar Hill Records.

Sunday Star-Times, Wellington, New Zealand: Fairfax Media.

Swift, J.S. and Wallace, J. (2011) 'Using English as the Common Corporate Language in a German Multinational', *Journal of European Industrial Training* 35, 892–913.

Sydney Slang Dictionary (1882) Sydney: H.J. Franklin.

Taylor, J.R. (2012) *The Mental Corpus: How Language Is Represented in the Mind*, Oxford: Oxford University Press.

Tempest, P. (1950) *Lag's Lexicon*, London: Routledge & Kegan Paul.

Thorne, T. (2006) 'Slanguistics or Just Lemon Meringue?'. Available online at www.llas.ac. uk/resources/paper/2725 (accessed 12 February 2013).

——(forthcoming 2014) *Bloomsbury Dictionary of Contemporary Slang*, 4th edn, London, Bloomsbury.

Times of India (2001–3) [corpus data] New Delhi: The Times Group.

Times of India (2010) Mumbai: The Times Group.

Tippa Irie (1985) *Complain Neighbour*, London: Greensleeves Records.

Tobin, L. (2007) 'Crack Their Code: The Words Kids Don't Want You to Know', *The Guardian*, 20 March. Available online at www.guardian.co.uk/education/2007/mar/20/ students.educationguardian2 (accessed 22 March 2013).

Toop, D. (1984) *Rap Attack 3*, London: Serpent's Tail.

Toto, S. (2008) *Japan's Top 50 Blogs*. Available online at www.tokyotronic.com/2008/01/ japans-top-50-blogs.html (accessed 12 Feburary 2013).

Tozer, J. (2009) 'Convicts Use ye Olde Elizabethan Slang to Smuggle Drugs Past Guards into Prison', *Daily Mail*, 8 June. Available online at www.dailymail.co.uk/news/article-1191475/ Convicts-use-ye-olde-slang-fool-guards.html (accessed 27 March 2013).

Traveller's Rest. Available online at www.travellersrest.org/shelta.htm (accessed 1 August 2012).

Turner, G.W. (1987) *The Australian Concise Oxford Dictionary*, Melbourne: Oxford University Press.

Twitter. Available online at https://twitter.com (accessed 1 May 2013).

UNO, Språkkontakt og Ungdomsspråk i Norden – Talespråkskorpuset, Oslodelen [Language Contact and Teenage Language in Scandinavia – The Norwegian Corpus of Oslo Teenage Language], English Department, University of Bergen. Available online at www.uib.no/ uno (accessed 5 April 2013).

Urban Dictionary. Available online at www.urbandictionary.com (accessed on various dates 2011–13).

Urban Dictionary Blog. Available online at http://blog.urbandictionary.com (accessed 17 May 2013).

Vaux, J.H. (1812) *A New and Comprehensive Vocabulary of the Flash Language*, Newcastle, NSW. Available online at http://gutenberg.net.au/ebooks06/0600111.txt (accessed 27 March 2013).

Volume 10 (1994) *Hip-Hopera*, New York: RCA Records.

Wakefield, E.J. (1845) *Adventure in New Zealand I*, London: John Murray.

Walmsley, A. (2007) 'Digital Immigrants Lost in Translation', *Marketing*, 28 November. Available online, by subscription, at www.lexisnexis.com (accessed 22 March 2013).

Warner Drive (2005) 'The Shocker', in *Fully Loaded*. Palm Springs, CA: Rancho Relaxo Records.

Watson, M. and Macleod, M. (2010) *The Edinburgh Companion to the Gaelic Language*, Edinburgh: Edinburgh University Press.

Weldon, F. (2002) *Auto da Fay*, London: Flamingo.

Weller, A. (1981) *The Day of the Dog*, Sydney: Allen and Unwin.

Westbrook, A. (2002) *Hip Hoptionary*, New York: Harlem Moon.

Wikipedia. Available online at http://en.wikipedia.org (accessed on various dates in 2013).

Williams, J. (2003) *The Original Dancehall Dictionary*, Kingston: Yard Publications.

Williams, Z. (2006) 'Conservative to the Core', *The Guardian*, 14 April. Available online at www.guardian.co.uk/commentisfree/2006/apr/14/comment.gender (accessed 12 February 2013).

Williamson, K. (2012) 'Lexicography of Scots before 1700', in I. Macleod and J. Derrick McClure (eds) *Scotland in Definition: A History of Scottish Dictionaries*, Edinburgh: John Donald.

Wintour, P. (2010) 'Candidates to Watch as Labour Fills Seats in Last Week before Election', *The Guardian*, 8 March. Available online at www.guardian.co.uk/politics/wintour-and-watt/2010/mar/08/general-election-candidates (accessed 22 March 2013).

Yadurajan, K.S. (2001) *Current English: A Guide for the User of English in India*, New Delhi: Oxford University Press.

Yagoda, B. (2011–13) *Not One-Off Britishisms*. Available online at http://britishisms.wordpress.com (accessed 17 May 2013).

Yomekawa, A. (ed.) (2003) *Nihon Zoku-go Daijiten* [Unabridged Japanese Slang Dictionary], Tokyo: Tokyodō-shuppan.

Yoneyama, S. (2008) 'The Era of Bullying: Japan Under Neoliberalism', *Japan Focus: The Asia-Pacific Journal*, 31 December. Available online at www.japanfocus.org/-Shoko-YONEYAMA/3001 (accessed 25 May 2012).

Yule, H. and Burnell, A.C. (1886) *Hobson-Jobson: A Glossary of Anglo-Indian Colloquial Words and Phrases, and of Kindred Terms; Etymological, Historical, Geographical and Discursive*, London: John Murray.

——(1903) *Hobson-Jobson: A Glossary of Anglo-Indian Colloquial Words and Phrases, and of Kindred Terms; Etymological, Historical, Geographical and Discursive*, 2nd edn, London: John Murray.

INDEX

WORD INDEX